WE TESTIFY
WITH
OUR LIVES

WE TESTIFY
WITH
OUR LIVES

HOW RELIGION TRANSFORMED
RADICAL THOUGHT
FROM BLACK POWER TO
BLACK LIVES MATTER

TERRENCE L. JOHNSON

Columbia University Press   *New York*

Columbia University Press
Publishers Since 1893
New York   Chichester, West Sussex
cup.columbia.edu

Library of Congress Cataloging-in-Publication Data
Names: Johnson, Terrence L., author.
Title: We testify with our lives : religion transformed radical thought
from black power to Black Lives Matter / Terrence L. Johnson.
Other titles: Religion transformed radical thought from black power
to Black Lives Matter
Description: New York : Columbia University Press, [2021] |
Includes bibliographical references and index.
Identifiers: LCCN 2020056191 (print) | LCCN 2020056192 (ebook)
| ISBN 9780231200448 (hardback) | ISBN 9780231200455 (trade
paperback) | ISBN 9780231553629 (ebook)
Subjects: LCSH: Black power—United States. | African American
radicals. | African American intellectuals. | African Americans—
Intellectual life. | Radicalism—United States—Religious aspects—
Christianity. | Civil rights—Religious aspects. | Civil rights
movements—United States. | African Americans—
Politics and government.
Classification: LCC E185.615 .J628 2021 (print) | LCC E185.615
(ebook) | DDC 323.1196/073—dc23
LC record available at https://lccn.loc.gov/2020056191
LC ebook record available at https://lccn.loc.gov/2020056192

Columbia University Press books are printed on permanent and
durable acid-free paper.
Printed in the United States of America

Cover design: Lisa Hamm
Cover image: Michael A. Cummings,
James Baldwin . . . Born Into a Lie (2019)

CONTENTS

ACKNOWLEDGMENTS

I owe the publication of this book to the enduring love and support of my family, namely my wife, Jill, and my children, Zoe and Zarek. My mom, Velma, Emmitt, and Eric continue to support me in immeasurable ways. David, Abby, and Nico always provide the needed humor and smiles to recharge my tired thoughts. Support from extended family has been invaluable: Milton, Jimmy, Mary, Michael, Dolores (Bubbe), Nedra, Roberta, Doris, Paulette, Terrence, Cathy, Jeffrey, Ted, Barbara, and a host of cousins, nieces, and nephews. I am also indebted to several student researchers: Joshua Dostal, Samuel Appeal, Easten Law, Ray Kim, Micah Musser, Matthew Hamilton, Howard Tai, and Erum Haider. Several colleagues and friends provided invaluable feedback at different stages in the book's development: Lewis R. Gordon, Beverly Guy-Sheftall, Louis Massiah, E. Ethelbert Miller, Jacob Olupona, Janine Spinola Taylor, Dianne Stewart, Jonathan Fichter, and Jonathan Tran. I am grateful to Susannah Heschel and Vaughn Booker for their invitation to present a chapter from the book at Dartmouth College. John Carlson and Jason Bruner invited me to share a portion of this project at Arizona State University's Religious Studies Forum.

Ulrike Guthrie provided invaluable editorial assistance. I thank my friend Michael Cummings, whose quilt is the cover art for the book.

A special thank-you to Wendy Lochner, the staff at Columbia University Press, as well as to the readers who provided insightful comments during the blind review process.

I dedicate the book to the memory of family members who passed away while completing it: Mary Kate Johnson, G. Robert Gibson, Beatrice Carlisle, Michael Gibson, Stanley Paige Johnson, and Ruth Williams.

PROLOGUE

Those of us who stand outside the circle of this society's defini-
tion of acceptable women; those of us who have been forged in
the crucibles of difference—those of us who are poor, who are
lesbians, who are Black, who are older—know that survival
is not an academic skill. . . . It is learning how to take our
differences and make them strengths. For the master's tools
will never dismantle the master's house. *They may allow us*
temporarily to beat him at his own game, but they will never
enable us to bring about genuine change.

—Audre Lorde (1979)

I n nine short words, Audre Lorde transformed how Blacks
saw themselves nearly two decades after the birth of the
Black Power movement: "The master's tools will never dismantle the master's house." Still recovering from the assassina-
tions of Malcolm X and Martin Luther King Jr., and watching
in slow motion the decline of civil rights activism and the Black
Arts movement, Lorde offered a balm to a wounded people, a
public proclamation of what many already intuited or believed
in their bones: Blacks would never be accepted in white society

through mimesis, or through elaborate appropriation of language, dialect, culture, or ethos. This strategy of employing the master's tools had long been employed in Black political struggles to achieve citizenship and political rights but with minimal success. Racial uplift ideology, liberalism, and the Talented Tenth— to name a few of the dominant political traditions and tropes in African American political thought—likewise yielded few substantial benefits for the masses of African Americans in the post–civil rights era, said many Black Power activists.[1] Lorde and others intended to carve out a *counter* political strategy, one that was based on a path forged by the grammar of Black politics and designed to take seriously Blacks' own overlooked traditions.

Even as Black politicians and civic leaders rose to prominence in major cities like Cleveland, Atlanta, Los Angeles, and Washington, DC, the infrastructure of these cities was controlled largely by economic and political forces outside those communities.[2] In fact, Black political leaders bore the burden of trying to repair generations-old wealth and social disparities with inadequate economic and federal assistance and an opaque political vocabulary based on false premises of upward mobility. Ongoing legal battles over school busing and desegregation, housing discrimination, and employment bias only reinforced the difficulties.[3] The dogged resistance of both the federal government and far too many white citizens to treat Blacks as wholehearted citizens, and guarantee their equal protection under the law, almost always stymied Black people's belief in the utility of electoral politics.[4] They were exhausted and perplexed, battered and torn asunder, to borrow a phrase from W. E. B. Du Bois. Such injuries created deep despair for some. For others, the social conditions warranted a far more substantial political imagination than the rights-based and free-market platforms formulated by Black-elected officials. Both the despair and optimism created a context ripe for a political intervention to explore the varieties of radicalism simmering in the debris left behind in cities abandoned by state actors and the white middle class who had left for suburbia. Black women resurfaced in Black-led cities to restore areas forsaken as wastelands by elite power brokers. Rhonda Williams describes as unsung this invisible but constant presence of Black working-class women in Baltimore, who looked within their own communities and social networks to imagine and fight for safe and adequate housing in the inner city.[5] "Viewed as 'objects of charity' and policed by the state because they received government aid, poor black women mounted housing and social welfare campaigns. Joining generations of low-income, working-class activist women, these women mobilized in communities. Some drew on familial historical legacy, and others built on the knowledge gained from their community participation efforts. . . . But they also did something different: This new generation of activist women pushed for respect, a right to representation, and power as not only citizens, but as human beings deserving of basic rights."[6] The Baltimore women forced their elected officials to see Black constituencies as human beings in need of basic social services, rather than as social problems to be disciplined, incarcerated, or even killed.[7] Their efforts and political imagination embodied the backbone of Lorde's thesis: building new tools from the flesh of the abandoned and the blood of the slain.

Lorde's vulnerability and steadfast courage moved both her audience and subsequent readers of her speech. Her words beckoned them to revolt against perfunctory social integration and appropriation of liberal political ideals of equality and inclusion and capitalist values that promoted vast wealth inequality and stark individualism. Underscoring her criticism of Western individuality's entanglement within the women's movement was a reflective hermeneutic that demanded self-reflection within a radically new community. The "master"—in whatever iteration he might appear—was doomed to be reproduced within and among unsuspecting persons, and those who borrowed the master's tool would be effaced in some form. The present and future, Lorde exhorted, demanded a reckoning with the "master." Her audience, and by extension all Blacks, could not simply continue as before.

As scholars continue to confront Lorde's axiom, several insightful responses have surfaced in the last decade. Lewis and Jane Gordon raised a biting but remarkably constructive criticism. Enslaved Africans in the New World appropriated, rejected, and expanded the master and "his" vacuous tools time and time again. At times, "slaves have historically done something more provocative with such tools than attempt to dismantle the Big House. There are those who used those tools, developed additional ones, and built houses of their own on more or less generous soil."[8] They recommend transcending debilitating Western ideals through the strenuous work of imagining, cultivating, and building their *own* intellectual and cultural traditions, rather than focusing on the "master" and his tools. Religion is a primary case in point. Through hoodoo, Afro-Christianity, Islam, Black Judaism, and nontheistic expressions, enslaved Africans invented, reformulated, and envisioned religion through vastly different methods and approaches from the religious dogma handed to them by Christian missionaries and enslavers. Lorde was clearly aware, if only minimally through folklore, poetry, and literature, of the religious dynamism in the Black diaspora. And while her speech did not point to this religious heritage, the epistemic transgressions in her guiding principles echo the religious radicalism and the ethical commitments emerging from Black religion and subsequently informing the contours of Black politics.

Hers was an insightful way of building a political and social vision from *difference*. Rather than focus on representational politics or symbolic integration aimed at producing an unencumbered (but also nonexistent) sense of equality, a theory of difference signaled to Lorde a way toward political freedom *and* human fulfillment, a wholeness of a kind rarely articulated during the civil rights movement. Rather than appeal to equality and liberty from within the then burgeoning tradition of Anglo-American political liberalism, Lorde called for a radically different approach to anti-Black racism and women's political and economic subjugation. She yearned for a new theory of politics that established itself in humanism, a reconfiguration of categories and metaphors to help articulate the existential, political, and *spiritual* pain among far too many Blacks, women, gays, and lesbians. Similar to the Black women in Baltimore, and Du Bois's sociological worked aimed distinguishing Blacks from their social *problems*, Lorde's credo cradled a political imagination oriented in developing a humanistic politics, where difference, not tolerance, animated deliberations and ensuing change. For Lorde, a philosophy of difference created the conditions to articulate a holistic political framework.

Lorde understood that difference to be an analytic category to deconstruct and understand the ways an anti-Black society promotes equality, the common good, and solidarity without taking into account how race, class, and gender circumscribe the terms of liberty and equality. Difference, for Lorde, emerges within a multidisciplinary framework, one oriented in humanism, literature, gender, class, and race to deconstruct existing definitions of freedom, justice, and labor.

This theory of difference is an exhausting category to execute, for it assumes a dialogical model of deliberation based on a normative commitment: the transformation of bodies, civil society, politics, religion, and gender through ongoing interrogations of existing social and cultural norms. By introducing difference as an analytic category, Lorde's credo uncovered the political contradictions many elite Black male politicians tried to bypass: the guiding social principles of integration and equality, for instance, assumed justice and freedom translated into ideological sameness or familiarity in politics, religion, and culture. While Lorde did not fully articulate her expansive vision in her speech, the spirit of her proclamation reverberated in and outside academic classrooms, finding an especially welcoming home in unusual African American contexts such as Black churches, heteronormative classrooms at Historically Black Colleges and Universities, and grassroots political movements shepherded by Black women and men. The master's tool, as critically imagined by Jane and Lewis Gordon, landed in the hands of women, men, and gender nonconforming persons who carved out a new political ideology engaged in radical difference and social transformation.[9]

Not since the Black Power and Black Arts movements had African Americans witnessed a sweeping public rebuke of the nation's dominant political vocabulary of equality, integration, and assimilation. That vocabulary, Lorde suggested in her speech, ignored the physical, psychic, and structural violence toward nonwhites and women who attempted to cash in on the promises of equality and equal protection under the law. Her theory of difference altered the political climate, introducing into Black political thought a hermeneutical tool for building a political vision and strategy based on the political and existential suffering meted out to Blacks in a white supremacist society. Long before Seyla Benhabib's provocative account of *the encumbered self*, Lorde anticipated the weaknesses of a bifurcated political theory entrenched in and divided by a public/private and political/religious distinction.[10]

Lorde outlined a theory of difference in her 1979 speech at the "Second Sex Conference" in New York City, where she invoked her stinging political cry: "The master's tools will never dismantle the master's house." Her cry exposed the epistemic limits of liberal (white) feminism. For far too long, white middle-class feminists had failed to discuss differences of race, sexuality, and class.[11] They turned to liberal categories of equality and equality of opportunity to make sweeping claims about social justice without taking into account the degree to which race (in particular) foreclosed opportunities of equal access and equality. Lorde showed white feminists the degree to which racial and gender hierarchy deepened when they bracketed race within their political conceptions or embraced a color-blind or color-neutral approach to solving misogyny. White feminists who decried the sins of patriarchy were almost always silent, according to Lorde, on issues of race and anti-Black racism. She pushed them to speak out: "What does it mean when the tools of a racist patriarchy are used to reexamine the fruits of that same patriarchy? It means that only the most narrow parameters of change are possible and allowable."[12] The liberal white feminist agenda carved out space for white women to sit in positions of leadership and authority. But it did so without reconfiguring and reconstituting the route to and acceptable norms of governing and yielding political and economic power to others, specifically Blacks. "As white women ignore their built-in privilege of whiteness and define *woman* in terms of their own experience alone, then, women of Color become 'other,' the outsider whose experience and tradition is too 'alien' to comprehend."[13]

Lorde's rebuke exposed two critical points: first, Black elected politicians, Black nationalists, and liberal white feminists often described social injustice in ways that were too flimsy for the heavy lifting needed to grapple with the ontological implications

of race, class, and gender. In this, Lorde anticipated future debates
on identity and ontology. Contemporary scholars such as K.
Anthony Appiah and Victor Anderson remind us that in contemporary African American philosophy, race and gender are socially
construed categories that too often emerge from "heroic" accounts
of African American life. But because they are performed in such
a way as to mirror essentialist views of race and gender, they reify
the white/Black racial binary that both scholars eschew.

Second was Lorde's criticism of tepid political activism that
aimed to expand existing institutions and social structures rather
than transform political discourse and economic conditions
from the bottom up. The move was bold. The former focuses on
political inclusion as the primary objective of social and economic activism. The latter employs integration as a political
tool to dismantle and disrupt ordinary and uncritical practices
as evident in Ella Baker's leadership strategy and focus within
the Student Nonviolent Coordinating Committee (SNCC). The
civil rights agenda focused primarily on the former. It assumed
that inclusion was the key to securing equality and equal opportunity. The rights-based agenda also assumed that the right to
vote translated to or signified human dignity. In other words,
the civil rights platform imagined political participation as an
automatic expression of human dignity.[14] Lorde's critical analysis underscored the heft of her feminist and lesbian political
vision to rethink gender, sexuality, and class. Lorde "challenged
the women's movement to move beyond the notion that white
womanhood was the national pattern and paradigm into which
to incorporate the histories and lived experiences of women of
color in the United States and abroad."[15]

Many readers will understand why civil rights activists envisioned voting both as a sign and extension of human dignity.
As Lewis R. Gordon writes, the Negro problem, as W. E. B.

Du Bois articulated it, frames anti-Black racism as fundamentally the denial of humanity within Black bodies, a racism that manifests itself in and through law, discourse, traditions, and cultural habits.[16] For Lorde, and Black Power activists as well, locating one's human dignity or humanistic expression in the right to vote was insufficient. For what happens to one's human dignity when the state suppresses political rights or restricts political participation? For competing and overlapping reasons, Lorde and Black Power activists wanted to recast political expressions of human dignity from the ground up.

The post–civil rights agenda focused on dismantling the long link between politics and human dignity. Lorde's writings anticipate whether political liberalism could address the pressing problems facing Blacks in general and Black women in particular: their lack of political power, economic exploitation, and dehumanization. Lester C. Olson writes that Lorde's "speech highlighted the unexplored topic of domination and power and their role in sustaining difference as a form of radical otherness. [Indeed,] Lorde used an analogy between racism and sexism to shape insights about distinctive reformist and radical political commitments within feminism."[17] The distinction between "reformist" and "radical" politics is biting, a reminder of ongoing debates among Black writers and activists on political ideologies such as the politics of respectability, racial uplift, and Black radicalism. The tension is in Lorde's condemnation of white feminists. Lorde's prescient observations anticipated contemporary debates identifying the primary benefactors of the civil rights movement as white women. For as a result of the movement, white women's voices increasingly could be heard and felt in previously all-male spaces. Their growing influence during Lorde's lifetime was undeniable and obvious to her. But she asked them a poignant question: Did their representation translate into any meaningful structural, personal, or experiential *change* for non-white and working-class women?

Lorde articulated what few thinkers of her generation discussed publicly: *Now that we're here, at the master's table, what shall we do?* The latent question framing Lorde's speech is, in fact, a matter of deep ethical import and one entrenched in leftist tradition within Black political thought. Take, for example, Frantz Fanon's ethical exploration of the white/Black binary within colonialism. In *Black Skin, White Masks*, Fanon asserts, "Man is motion toward the world and toward his like. A movement of aggression, which leads to enslavement or to conquest; a movement of love, a gift of self, the ultimate state of what by common accord is called ethical orientation."[18] This ethical imperative is an extension of the dialectic between the affirmation one receives from the person one loves or admires. The "endorsement" one secures in this loving relationship, conversely, elicits an enduring longing for "recognition" and validation. Within the context of Fanon's writing, this ethical orientation is complicated by the tension between the colonizer and colonized, a relationship predetermined by white supremacist beliefs in white superiority and Black inferiority and inhumanity. He asks whether "true" love can exist between a white man and a Black woman in light of these historic and lived experiences of Blackness as subhuman and inadequate in relation to the "universal" and human white man. What fuels the encounter between them is a longing for mutual affirmation of their distinct social locations in the world. One is affirmed, directly or indirectly, through acknowledgments of his superiority, and the Black woman is affirmed by virtue of landing varying forms of validation from her white love.

A number of disconcerting issues emerge within Fanon's characterization that are far too complicated to unpack here. But the ethical orientation that binds the two is a compelling threshold for understanding the perennial problem of the white/Black binary since it emerged beginning in 1619. Consider the following two points: First, it describes the political and nonpolitical discourses that impede and subsequently undermine efforts to establish freedom and justice on grounds of equality and equal opportunity without exposing and deconstructing the social discourse based on the tension between "aggression" and "enslavement" and love and meaning-making. Second, Fanon's argument provides a way of dismantling the problem: the turn to ethics. The ethical orientation is a dialectic between aggression/enslavement /conquest and a movement of love/meaning-making.[19] The ethical concern raised helps to explain some of the inadequacies of early feminists and Black liberal thinkers: that the very epistemic tools they inherited and appropriated seemed to be impeding fundamental structural transformation for Blacks, women of color, and working-class women.

As Lorde exposed the limits of the liberal feminist politics and praxis of her time, she gave Black women, especially "poor," "lesbian," and "third-world" women, permission to embrace and reveal what had long been buried, swept into crevices, and forsaken. She replaced liberal individual autonomy with the category of interdependence, and specifically interdependency between women. In doing so, Lorde carved out the intellectual terrain from which women, and especially Black and Brown women, could discover, cultivate, invent, and imagine freedom within their theory of difference.

Interdependence drives Lorde's understanding that freedom emerges in and through an embodied consciousness that fuels individual, group, and social transformation. This line of thinking, Olson cleverly notes, is linked to Lorde's reliance on W. E. B. Du Bois's theory of double consciousness, a striving toward a "truer" self and social world. But in order to ignite a nuanced conversation on individual and group freedom within the context of social domination, Lorde appealed to a new, thicker political vocabulary as a way to move beyond the embarrassingly parochial political language of Black elected officials and white feminists.

As an example, Lorde took fear. Sharing with the audience her own battle with cancer, Lorde acknowledged that personal fear and silence could become political impediments. Fear can suffocate, she acknowledged. It can also protect—though not necessarily in an ultimately beneficial way. For though by being afraid and doing nothing one can protect oneself from the "censure," "contempt," "death," and "pain" that many women experience when they stand against patriarchal and heteronormative philosophies, such freedom from pain in any political struggle is momentary. Besides, politics and political engagement against oppressive power will always produce pain at both the personal and communal level. If we ignore this pain, the political struggle will fail to break itself from binary oppositions between public and private, good and bad. She says straightforwardly, "We all hurt in so many different ways, all the time, and pain will either change or end."[20] Given the goal, Lorde insisted that we resist the temptation to run away from fear and hide behind silence, and noted realistically and hopefully, "My silences had not protected me. Your silence will not protect you. But for every real word spoken, for every attempt I had ever made to speak those truths for which I am still seeking, I had made contact with other women while we examined the words to fit a world in which we all believed, bridging our differences."[21] She shows that fear as a political category is a powerful and liberative tool. By reconfiguring fear, by displacing it from the *self*, the realm of cognition and emotion, and by rehabilitating it into a political and spiritual source of consciousness, an extension of interdependence, fueling the enlargement of *difference* among and between women, by all this Lorde establishes an important point: rather than overcome difference, we should expose, embrace, and reckon with it for creative and transformative purposes.

Asking women, Black women in particular, to recast their difference into an accessible language is a daunting request given that Black women embody both the ire and pleasure of the modern Western world and are simultaneously the symbolic caretaker and the despised whore, as Saidiya Hartman reminds us.[22]

Yes, it is easy to understand why Black women would remain silent and bracket their psychic and physical pain. On the one hand, they risk scorn from Black men if they condemn intraracial sexism, homophobia, and domestic violence. On the other, Black women's already fragile relationship with white feminist organizations risks deeper fragmentation if they express their long-buried concerns of racism and classism within those white feminist organizations and political platforms. Without a doubt, Black women's identities were strained and wounded as they tried to straddle racial hierarchies, gender expectations, and muddied class lines prior to and during the civil rights era and Black Power movement.

Still, Lorde urged Black and Brown women to retrieve this ongoing strained and wounded reality and use it instead as a political resource to develop their group and interior "power." She was convinced that by turning inward and firmly embracing interdependence, Black women could gain a clearer sense of their unique roles in the transformation of gender, race, class, and sexuality. This move, Lorde believed, would create the conditions for discovering the beauty and truthfulness of their buried and despised traditions and cultural practices.[23]

This embodied consciousness of interdependence and difference is evident among Lorde's benefactors, most notably in

Alice Walker's *In Search of Our Mothers' Garden*, where Walker reclaims the familial context of the garden as reflecting the liberating space of Black women's interior and public epistemology. In an insightful account of Lorde's political vision, Cheryl Higashida, author of *Black Internationalist Feminism*, identifies the poet-warrior as a chief architect of Black internationalist feminists "of the postwar Left" who "contributed to and engaged critically with the renaissance of African American women's fiction" that fueled local interests in global politics.[24] The Combahee River Collective played a critical role in Lorde's formation as it affirmed a Black feminist response to Black Power and anticipated a theory of intersectionality. Lorde's theory of interdependence and difference seem to emerge from this collective of Black women scholars, activists, artists, and writers.

Nudged by Lorde, focusing on interdependence in the exploration of Black political freedom opens the necessary reflective space for us to explore social categories without fear or concern of the overarching gaze of patriarchy and of liberal approaches to justice, freedom, and liberation. "It is [about] learning how to stand alone, unpopular and sometimes reviled, and how to make common cause with those others identified as outside the structures in order to define and seek a world in which we can all flourish."[25]

This turn to interdependence is not individualistic or designed to offer comfort in the familiar or parochial sense of self or community. Rather, it is both a hermeneutical turn away from and a political act against an ideology of *otherness* as either foreign or familiar. Instead, interdependence compels Black women in particular to "scrutinize" the truthfulness of their language, tradition, and praxis as a way to avoid static and suffocating dictums of what should and should not be appropriate within a social movement, ethical practice, and political philosophy.

Lorde's theory of interdependence and difference sets the stage for what can be described as the ethical turn in politics. This extension of the political imaginary is a missing dimension in the literature on rights-based political philosophy and, by extension, the liberal reformist tradition in Black political thought at the end of the twentieth century and beginning of the twenty-first. By ethical, I mean a tradition distinct from Western norms of ethical duty, responsibility, or virtue. Certainly fragments of these traditions are evident in the ethical turn I am mapping out. Nonetheless, the ethical turn as I construe it surfaced when enslaved Africans rejected Christian slaveholders' pernicious justification of slavery and appropriated the Exodus narrative as a sign of their impending emancipation. From Negro spirituals and jazz to Black preaching, the ethical turn is steeped in deliberative reflection, reflective wholeness, and critical humanism. It is heuristic and constructive, a way of engaging politics and moral inquiry without systematizing a singular agenda, directive, or formula for political engagement. Ethics in this context involves the disruption, dismantling, and rebuilding of debilitating social and economic structures with the expressed desire to achieve human flourishing and dignity for all.

As far back as the nineteenth century, Black abolitionists and freedom activists foregrounded their emancipatory pursuits in terms of ethical responsibility, religious orientation, and humanistic strivings within the dominant political traditions in Black politics, namely racial solidarity, racial pride, the politics of respectability, and Black Power. The ethical turn, as hinted at in Du Bois's theory of double consciousness, assumes enslaved Africans transcended social death as they resisted epistemic annihilation through slave revolts, ancestral re-memory, and other forms of cultural production. That one's reflective starting point (rooted in white supremacy's domination of and subsequent violence against

Black and Brown bodies) can be the source from which one begins to build a transformative conception of freedom. In a Hunter College commencement address, Lorde reminded us that "facing the realities of our lives gives us motivation for action . . . For you are not powerless . . . [change can happen in] our day-to-day decisions, the way in which we testify with our lives to those things in which we say we believe, that empower us. Your power is relative, but it is real. And if you do not learn to use it, it will be used, against you, and me, and our children."[26]

Lorde's characterization of interior/individual/group power is the starting point for imagining and understanding the ethical turn manifested in the early iterations of the Black radical left after the civil rights movement. The revolutionary embrace of interdependence that Lorde develops in her speech is the struggle to live by the deeds of our words and the ongoing stumbling in our strivings to grasp the senselessness of a violent and dehumanizing world. The pursuit of ethics and the ethical turn is encumbered; it is wrapped in a tradition circumscribed by Black religious narratives and ideological aspirations encumbered by transnationalism, community empowerment, and economic emancipation.

The ethical turn—this ongoing effort to give flesh to freedom— has been an unaddressed aspiration latent in rituals largely ignored in discussions on Black politics, freedom, and justice. The main reason for this void is, I suggest, the absence of any sustained attention to Black religion's wide-ranging role in sustaining Black politics and political thought. African American interpretations of the Bible as a "talking book"[27] and claims that "God is a Negro"[28] within Afro-Christianity underscore and frame the rhetorical and epistemic terrain from which Black religions understand freedom, community, and justice. With this framework, Black religious radicalism sets the conditions for the emergence of organizations such as the Universal Negro

Improvement Association (1914) and the Nation of Islam (1930), both of which play a significant role in framing Black Power. Black religious radicalism serves as a cite through which African Americans re-imagined their freedom; the reflective turn away from biblical justifications of African enslavement and beliefs in Black inferiority symbolizes ordinary expressions of the ethical turn in Black political thought.[29]

The insertion of the ethical compels us *and condemns us* to imagine political actors as more than rights-bearing citizens, but as persons seeking human flourishing, dignity, freedom, and a deep sense of belonging even as they remain bound by oppressive public laws, cultural norms, and systemic structural barriers. The Black Power movement, for example, embraced *Blackness* as political weapon designed to ignite a major social revolution. Through this radical shift, activists cultivate the grounds for the emergence of Black feminists, Womanists, and Black liberation theologians to gain a platform in the Black radical tradition. Lorde is a prime example of the ethical turn. She framed her criticism of the master's tools to imagine a new humanism through sustained political engagement. In fact, the title of this book, *We Testify with Our Lives*, is taken directly from Lorde, who invoked the words to admonish us to bear witness to human flourishing and dignity *through our actions*. "Change, personal, and political, does not come about in a day, nor a year. But it is our day-to-day decisions, the way in which we testify with our lives to those things in which we say we believe, that empower us."[30] For a people without land and economic independence, for a people marked by a history of exile, their most potent political resource is the testimony of their resistance, perseverance, and death in struggle. This is the flesh of the ethical turn.

Some fifty years after Black Power and during the climax of Black Lives Matter, the post-Obama era in the United States faces a world increasingly torn by nationalism, white supremacy, xenophobia, and religious bigotry. How do we respond when the legislative and executive branches of government condone through legislation, silence, and lies the destruction of Blacks, Muslims, and immigrants from Central and South America and Africa? *We Testify with Our Lives* explores how Black Power and its ethical turn can give us new insights into the search for freedom, ethical action, social justice, and democracy in our many efforts to embolden human flourishing and build democratic possibilities for all.

1

POLITICS OF HEALING

"Are you sure, sweetheart, that you want to be well?" Velma Henry turned stiffly on the stool, the gown ties tight across her back, the knots hard. So taut for so long, she could not swivel. Neck, back, hip joints dry, stiff. Face frozen. She could not glower, suck her teeth, roll her eyes, do any of the Velma-things by way of answering Minnie Ransom . . . [who was] the fabled healer of the district. . . . "I like to caution folks, that's all," said Minnie, interrupting her own humming to sigh and say it, the song somehow buzzing right on. "No sense us wasting each other's time, sweetheart." The song running its own course up under the words, up under Velma's hospital gown, notes pressing against her skin and Velma steeling herself against intrusion. "A lot of weight when you're well. Now, you just hold that thought."

Toni Cade Bambara, *The Salt Eaters*[1]

T he *Salt Eaters*, Toni Cade Bambara's first published novel, takes place in the fictional southern town of Claybourne a few years after the civil rights era and Black Power movement. Published in 1980, the novel centers on Velma's relationship with the community healer and her encounters with the ancestors. Through a series of flashbacks during her healing session, the reader stumbles, sometimes forcibly, upon the narratives, twists, and subplots buried within Velma's life. Of central concern in the novel is a community's loss of innocence and its effort to piece together a fragmented identity, one in which flesh and spirit are alien to each other at the reflective, epistemic realm but coexist in the interior soul and material soul-life. "Part of the pleasure of the novel," John Edgar Wideman asserts in a *New York Times* book review, "derives from these dislocations and affronts (are we really supposed to believe the conversations between people and spirits?), the sudden juxtaposition of the real and unreal, the imaginary and the actual. . . . [The novel] questions and finally erodes the basis upon which such distinctions customarily depend."[2]

The past and living present, pent up inside Velma, a computer expert, could not find its way outside her tormented body. The endless debates in smoke-filled rooms over women's role in public protests, the energy devoted to community organizing, and the scars left behind from fractured romantic relationships had nearly destroyed her. Velma turned everywhere for solace, searching for a place to release the burden of the past and present.[3] The narrator muses:

> She had been listening for years to the starchy explanations from the quacks who called themselves guidance counselors, social workers, analysts, therapists, whose views had more to do with their own habits . . . than anything rooted in the natural, the real. [Folks] might have faith in fools whose faith resided in a science that only filled people's lives with useless structures, senseless clutter, but she knew better. They needed some way, she knew, to be in the world, to move about, to explain things, to make up things to go on living blind. . . . And in time Velma would find her way back to the roots of life.[4]

Finding her way back home, recovering an unknown past, and manipulating a frightful present reality together foster Velma's suicidal tendencies. Torn asunder by her husband's infidelity, left bewildered by Black male opposition to women's political agency, alienated from a community divided over earlier tropes of racial solidarity, Velma yearns for a new sense of belonging. Death was the route to a new beginning, she surmised, a place of belonging where the tension between the past and present, political and psychic, and the sacred and secular, would not drown her political hope, cultural longings, or religious strivings.

The Salt Eaters is as lyrical as it is poetic and precise in capturing both the psychic and physical wounds of a people, those disfigured, persecuted, and killed in the 1960s during their pursuit for freedom, justice, and equity. Hers is a novel unlike any other on the movement. Bambara takes the reader down the twists and turns of strife born from within to narrate a people's heterogeneous consciousness. She peers into unexplored crevices, where African cultural and religious practices are as equally rehearsed and reinvented as Marxism and anti-colonialism are appropriated and reconfigured to comprehend anti-Blackness and gender bias in a self-described struggle for Black liberation. There, Bambara unearths and breathes life into the "cultural workers," woman and men invested in healing a wounded people for purposes far beyond securing voting rights, landing a corporate board seat, or attaining admission into a prestigious college or university.

In this, her only published novel,[5] Bambara characterizes "healing" as a fundamental and necessary component of achieving individual and collective freedom, as necessary as exercising the rights, duties, and obligations prescribed by a people's traditions and cultures. The premise is compelling, if not confounding: the political prescription to freedom involves acknowledging and creating the conditions for healing from the dehumanizing effects of structural anti-Blackness, sexism, and classism. In a jarring question, "Do you want to be well?" Bambara rewrites the conditions for both defining Black radicalism and executing Black politics following the demise of the American civil rights moment. By placing Velma Henry at the center of Black Power's political discourse, Bambara claims the centrality of the Black body, particularly the Black woman's body, as a primary site in and through which freedom is discovered and disclosed in Afro-Modern thought. Negative and positive freedom are secondary, though without any hesitation necessary for rights-bearing citizens. Bambara, however, is concerned with burdens that subjects carry as they attempt to exercise their duties, rights, and obligations. Shifting away from the masculinist discourse of obtaining "Black Power" to achieving "wellness," Bambara assumes two things: political struggles should be equally as focused on the body and wellness as they are on racial and gender oppression and political rights, and existence and survival philosophies are necessary pretexts to securing liberation.[6]

Bambara is known primarily for her short stories as well as her groundbreaking 1970 publication of *The Black Woman,* a volume of original writings by Black women aimed at countering widespread accounts of anti-Blackness based largely on patriarchal views of Black men within the post–civil rights movement. Bambara plays a crucial role in collecting the archives needed to establish Black feminist and Womanist traditions. Beverly Guy-Sheftall, a chief architect of Black feminist studies and the founding director of Spelman College's Women's Research and Resource Center, describes Bambara's anthology as monumental to the field. "Hegemonic black nationalist discourse, characterized by both masculinist and heterosexist frameworks, has been particularly influential within activist-intellectual communities and has stifled the development of more egalitarian models of black models of black empowerment which are free from ideological traps of sexism and homophobia."[7] Bambara's anthology, as well as her literary writings and filmmaking, inserted gender and sexuality into existing debates on Pan-Africanism, Black Power, Black nationalism, and Black spirituality and religion cohesively and without dogmatic appeals to provide a nuanced and complex understanding of Black life. Her editor and friend Toni Morrison called Bambara "outrageously brilliant,"[8] one whose brilliance opened each character's raw humanity to us all. Whether a "whore" or healer, Bambara's characters offered insight into what it meant to live in tension with our dogged circumstances without pity or condescension. "Although her insights are multiple, her textures layered and her narrative trajectory implacable, nothing distracts from the sheer satisfaction her story-telling provides."[9]

Bambara introduces a novel argument in *The Salt Eaters* to support her re(interpretation) of Black radicalism: political activism does not begin or end with a political strategy or hermeneutical lens to eradicate racial oppression. Rather, the intersectionality of gender, race, and class is the presumptive starting and end point for exploring domination. This legitimates the "authority" of the "Black subject," and she, in turn, carves out the question to guide Black politics. Instead of asking for Black Power, the central question in the novel asks and builds the case for a politics of healing. Eleanor Traylor claims that the narrator's call for healing is directed at Velma Henry as well as to the reader. "We must believe that she is healed and that believing demands of us the plunge that Velma takes. It is a demand of this narrator for that plunge that captures my heart and requires my whole head."[10] This is one of the most distinguishing features of the novel—the dismantling of the binary between the reader and text, religion and politics, culture and rights, through a singular question. W. E. B. Du Bois employed a similar move in *The Souls of Black Folk* in 1903 when he introduced an enduring question of the twentieth century: "How does it feel to be a problem?" The question is the backdrop to racial uplift ideology and Black nationalism during the early part of the twentieth century.[11]

Bambara transforms Du Bois's descriptive question into a constructive one, shifting the epistemic concern away from racial oppression and its analogue, the white normative gaze as the primary concerns of the disinherited, to the Black subject to understand when and how she will respond to the social world. Bambara's turn away from traditional Afro-Christian tropes aligns with Black women's writings during the post–civil rights era. Trudier Harris notes that Black women writers "turned their attention to other ways of knowing, other kinds of spirituality, other ways of being in the world."[12]

HEALING AND EMBODIMENT IN AFRO-MODERN THOUGHT

More than three decades after Bambara's novel, political theorist Shatema Threadcraft makes a similar argument in her profound criticism of Black liberal political philosophers like Tommie Shelby and Charles Mills, both of whom tweak and extend Rawlsian political liberalism to address racial oppression. What Threadcraft characterizes as their "contractual model of justice," she notes, fails to address gender, specifically the performance and construction of women's "reproductive" abilities and "caretaking capacities." She comments, "Neither can we assume, for example, that affording blacks' greater control over their political and material environments will afford greater protection for black bodily health and bodily integrity, and we must guard against this."[13]

Threadcraft's argument is noteworthy. Afro-Modern thought's masculinist vision of justice is primarily material and fundamentally garnered through acquisition.[14] This vision is inadequate. She notes that it only reveals half the story.

> Any theory of corrective racial justice inspired by Rawls, whose theory of justice focuses on establishing fairness in man's efforts to control his political and then his material environment, must include at a minimum explicit additional provisions designed to establish justice within the black intimate sphere . . . that black intimate capacities have been profoundly diminished under racial domination in ways that theories of corrective racial justice must explicitly address.[15]

Threadcraft exposes and chips away at the gender norms and biases of Black liberal political theory with the assistance of Martha Nussbaum's capabilities approach. Threadcraft is most interested in correcting previous thinkers' inattention to Black women's "embodied existence" as it relates to their health and physical and emotional concerns.[16]

To build her argument, she recovers two important points from Nussbaum. First, she embraces Nussbaum's emphasis on the person or social actor both as a "political and social animal" in search of the good within context of the social world.[17] The point moves beyond, and in tension with, Rawls's primary insistence on protecting one's right to control and exercise political rights within one's social environment, without regard to physical capabilities or emotional concerns. Second, Threadcraft retrieves Nussbaum's conception of human dignity to underscore the limits of a social-contract model of justice. The subject within the contractarian theory is defined as purely rational and distinct from her "animality." The capabilities approach, as quoted by Threadcraft, envisions the "rational as simply one aspect of the animal, and, at that, not the only one that is pertinent to a notion of truly human functioning."[18] According to Threadcraft, the capabilities approach offers two correctives to existing liberal theories. First, it offers a viable strategy for determining the holistic needs of Black women and their children, notably in the areas of health care, caretaking, and emotional concerns.[19] Second, Nussbaum's theory considers the social constraints of gender binaries, especially those, according to Threadcraft, placed upon "feminine embodiment." This would include sexual harassment and rape.[20]

Threadcraft's criticism is valuable, but I don't think it goes far enough. Her reliance on a corrective racial liberalism, even as extended through the capabilities approach, overlooks two dire points. First, the Du Boisian Negro problem is never directly raised when Threadcraft outlines the reasons for her turn to Nussbaum. Second, human dignity still appears to be construed through the preexisting binary of politics versus religion and male versus female. Gender as a social construct produces certain needs. But what about the ways in which the social world constructs gender and leads to a prescribed performance of gender? In either case a new framework is needed to explore gender and "intimate justice."

Building on Threadcraft's valuable criticism, I turn back to *The Salt Eaters*, where Bambara carves out an imaginative space to explore Black politics and political thought, moving away from theories of justice to philosophies of freedom. Through Minnie the priestess, Bambara demonstrates how Black Power fails to take into account the existential question emerging from the violence and trauma of racial terror: "Do you want to be well?" Instead, political activism in Black Power begins and ends with the masculinist question haunting and influencing its conception of Black life: Do you want *Black Power*? Without taking

into account existing forms of power among Black working-
class resistance against poor labor conditions in places such as
Mississippi, as noted by Robin D. G. Kelley, or Black women's
political organizing and economic success in supporting Black
schools and colleges, Carmichael's relevant cry cast a veil over
Black women's wealth of institutional and community power.[21]

Placing Bambara's novel within Black political thought, specifically Afro-Modernism, shifts the conversation away from
examining racist theories, policies, strategies, and categories to
portray and understand accurately anti-Black racism to imagining, embracing, and pursuing transformation vis-à-vis healing
a wounded self and broken community. The aim here is not to
eradicate the political for the safety and security of contempla-
tive navel-gazing but to expand the political to include holistic
accounts of humanistic strivings. Political theorists rarely give
any attention to the psychosocial dimensions of oppression,
and yet many of our nation's literary giants such as Morrison,
Wright, and Baldwin build their narratives on characters who
are seeking to become whole as they struggle against oppression,
violence, and domination. Maybe this explains the pushback by
some Black feminists against Ralph Ellison's trope of invisibility
in his acclaimed novel, *Invisible Man*. Through Bambara's literary imagination, invisibility assumes that the white gaze is normative and formative in the construction of Black consciousness.
The trope delegitimizes counter-publics, minimizes the weight
and veracity of life within the Du Boisian veil, and disregards
the creative genius within one's interiority and immediate epistemic traditions. On the one hand, Bambara does not completely
reject invisibility as a dehumanizing and operative trope in Black
life; on the other hand, her inward turn to the counter-publics in
Black life suggests implicit limits of invisibility's universal applicability among the disinherited and dispossessed.

Bambara's literary intervention of political healing is considerably subversive. It sets the stage, following Du Bois's question of *how does it feel to be a problem*, for the "recognition"[22] of the Black radical tradition within Afro-Modern thought. Bambara's healing session unravels the mental toil of anti-Blackness and misogyny on countless Black women. "These legacies are rooted in slavery and cultivated by generations of black Americans for the purpose of survival. Minnie's question, then, extends beyond Velma's current state to a *desire* to be well in an uncertain future that is every day impacted by patriarchal and racist institutions; wellness requires continuous and purposeful action."[23] By recognizing the speaking-thinking-feeling "subaltern,"[24] Bambara legitimizes the multilayered consciousness of Black women in the form of a question: "Do you want to be well?"

The invention extends as far back as nineteenth-century Black radicalism. The late historian and philosopher Cedric Robinson notes that the Black radical tradition did not begin by coalescing around "a critique of Western [philosophy] but from a rejection of European slavery and a revulsion of racism in it totality."[25] Making sense of the problem and fighting it happens during the varying stages of the revolt and rejection of racial dominance. Like Bambara, Robinson points to the most important function of political struggle—that of surviving the dehumanizing encounter with white supremacy. Within this context, religion emerges as an essential part of the political imaginary. As Robinson notes, when slaves could not rebel, "the people prepared themselves through *obeah*, voodoo, Islam, and Black Christianity. Through these they induced charismatic expectations, socializing and hardening themselves and their young with beliefs, myths, and messianic visions that would allow them, someday, to attempt the impossible."[26]

RELIGION AND REVOLT

What is striking about Bambara's characterization of the post–
Black Power movement is the degree to which "religion," "revolutionary ethics," and Black folk religion[27] and spirituality are
central to recovering the fragments of Velma's identity, and
imagining and constructing, in the broader sense, new beginnings for a community left stung by war and social upheaval. As
Courtney Thorsson aptly describes it, Bambara builds a nation
"on the pages of the novel through polyvocality, simultaneous
temporality, shifts in point of view, and various modes of knowledge,"[28] primary of which is Black religion and its esoteric practices. Their practitioners show up in all kinds of complicated ways,
mostly formed and fashioned by Black women. For instance, they
are healers, conjurers, and diviners. The women discuss tarot card
readings, astrology, and magic with ease, and without blinking
an eye can shift the conversation to political organizing, gender
discrimination, and police brutality as if they are all compatible,
possibly even complementary. Beyond linking folk traditions to
revolutionary politics, Bambara narrates Velma's healing session
through indigenous folk culture and traditions.

The Salt Eaters opens with Velma Henry sitting at the feet
of a spiritual healer after a botched suicide attempt. Minnie,
the Priestess, healer, keeper of tales, wisdom-giver, and conjurer, manipulates the present moment through the Black folk
speech act of humming. The strange but familiar sound rattles
Velma. Similar to the spirituals bellowing forth from the tiny
Black church W. E. B. Du Bois stumbled upon at the turn of
the twentieth century, Minnie Ranson's rhythmic and repetitive
humming summons the ancestors, the millions gone. Sitting
face-to-face with "her own habits of illusion," Velma finds

herself gasping under the weight of broken promises, unborn dreams, and tattered relationships. The veteran Black Power activist is haunted by a past that will not die or surrender itself to love, reconciliation, or death. "A grown woman won't mess around in mud puddles too long before she releases . . . [quips the Priestess.] Release, sweetheart. Let it go. Let the healing power flow."[29] Velma wants to claim an unsubstantiated self and soul. But she can't.

Torn asunder by displacement and subjugation, all she knows is struggle, the constant weaving together of scraps: *marching in Selma, voter registration drives, and boycotts against segregated businesses.* Making do with brokenness. The mundane, all- too familiar political struggles converge within Velma's psyche as an extension of her desire to find warmth from another's touch, security in another's body you can claim as yours, or the fulfill- ment from another's gaze and recognition of your humanity: these all translate into the abnormal and grotesque when experi- enced in and through Black bodies. The healer, Minnie Ransom, exposes what too many of us refuse to consider: the extent to which white supremacy, state-condoned violence against Blacks, and self-doubt bind us to a false sense of consciousness that is divided by a Du Boisian double and triple consciousness.

Velma's healing session symbolizes the literary tradition of rememory,[30] a way of crawling back to history to examine and explore the various fragments of one's individual and group exis- tence. Whether she finds what she's looking for is uncertain. But in her search, Velma suspends, albeit temporarily, knowl- edge of the self and gives embodied existence to a set of esoteric practices. And it is in the liminal space between knowing and unknowing that new beginnings are possible for Velma—where ethics is linked to, but ultimately separated from, an omniscient God, where Spirit is distinguished from religion, and where humans pursue justice and freedom in the perennial struggle of becoming the salt of the earth.

Eroded by years of political, psychological, and psychic unrest, the narrator implicitly points to how the character's consciousness seeks to obtain and embody what Du Bois called a "truer" self, or soul-life. But this longing cannot be obtained through the normal Du Boisian framework. Instead, Black women and Black feminist movements of the late 1960s orchestrated a fundamental epistemic shift in Black political thought, "a turning away from the larger society and a turning toward each other. Our art, protest, dialogue no longer spring from the impulse to entertain, or to indulge or enlighten the conscience of the enemy; white people, whiteness, or racism; men, maleness, or chauvinism: America or imperialism."[31]

Through her literary analysis, Blacks are found to be neither *the* problem nor the embodiment of social death. Rather, by turning inward, excavating through the ruins of religion, art, folklore, etc., Bambara discovered fragmentary pieces of what sustained and fueled Black life through the middle passage to the end of Black Power. Turning to a "truer self" might be illustrative of what Kimberly Benston terms "unnaming," the process by which the formerly enslaved search for meaning and freedom. This "simultaneous unnaming and naming—affirming at once autonomy and identification in relation to the past"—underscores the enduring efforts to remember, reinvent, and reimagine a past in tension with the dehumanization under which they live. The "undoing" of slavery's "misnaming" of the enslaved, strangely enough, unfolds into a creative engagement with tradition, texts, and oral histories, producing a life otherwise unseen outside the Du Boisian veil.

Bambara's extension of the Du Boisian question pushes against Orlando Patterson's strident position that enslavement constituted the annihilation of a Black past, inaugurating into flesh the social death of a people.[32] This position assumes the complete eradication of imagination, the discursive tool to create, construct, and perform Blackness in and outside the context of "home." Regardless of white supremacy's violent stronghold on Black life, time and time again enslaved Africans in the New World invented new epistemic possibilities.

One of the most creative and ongoing traditions involves African American biblical hermeneutics and Black literary traditions. Soon after enslaved Africans were introduced to the Bible in the late seventeenth century, they constructed a new way of "reading" scripture. Instead of leaning on church doctrine or the slaveholder's interpretation of scripture, they transformed the Bible into a talking book, as Henry Louis Gates Jr. and Allen Callahan have ably documented. They inserted themselves into the Exodus narrative and retrieved its account of liberation and freedom as the justification for their own quest for emancipation. Bambara references the eclectic uses of religion in the 1930s by Father Divine, who embraced new models of celibacy and love to reorder or disrupt gender norms, as embodying glimpses of what liberation could mean for Blacks.[33] We see glimpses of this in *The Salt Eaters*.

As Velma wrestles with the wounds from social and psychic upheaval, she recovers what historian Yvonne Chireau reformulates as "vernacular religion"—hoodoo, root working, and esoteric magic practices—to shed light on the entangled narratives through which humans find what I call complex forms of "sacred subjectivity" within noninstitutionalized religion and religious practices. Indeed, through conjure and divination, human hands learn how to cultivate a sense of the sacred, aesthetic, and ethical. Sacred subjectivity exposes both the epistemic limits and strengths of our double and triple consciousness. It, too, illumines new ways of "knowing," reflecting back and pointing to a new humanism.

To this end, religion is a resource for what Charles Long calls "a crawling back through one's history,"[34] a way of reimagining a past and reconstructing the present. By returning to the past, Velma suspends, albeit temporarily, knowledge of the self and surrenders to a counter-religious knowledge, that of conjure and divination. And it is in the liminal space between knowing and unknowing where new beginnings are possible for Velma, where beauty sits in the presence of God, and the material is transformed into the immaterial. The literary scholar Gay Wilentz calls the movement within the healing session as a journey toward "recovering" the missing parts of ourselves. "The movement toward health is linked to a turning inward and outward, to recovering lost parts of ourselves, to the ritual of transformation, not only for individuals but for the earth itself. When Bambara calls for an "ecology of the self," she is both returning to the source of health as part of a balance among self, community, and the earth, and expanding notions of political activism and spiritual growth as part of a healing act."[35] Healing both as recovery and transformation characterizes the unachieved political momentum Bambara's characters experienced during the radical sixties. Black Power, absent of the generative dimension of healing, left its activists inadequately prepared to address their political and psychic trauma. This is the backdrop, I believe, to establishing what Frantz Fanon calls a new humanism in a postcolonial world. Maybe vernacular religion can be the starting point for imagining humanism, of thinking in, outside, between, and above colonialism, the white/Black binary, and the lingering divide between the civilized and the barbarian. The quest for a new humanism is embedded in a call to assert ethics and to employ *the ethical turn*. This kind of reflection *and* active engagement with our community, God and gods, assumes that our starting point, our competing and overlapping subjectivities, may contain the resources for building what we have yet to imagine.

Like a committed archeologist (as Eleanor Traylor calls Bambara), the writer and documentarian uncovers the epistemic sources for undoing the political conundrum. What does it look like? It involves a "free society made up of whole individuals." What she means here is a social world where subjects are neither simply rational nor animalistic but a combination of both and more. The goods sought after by subjects extend far beyond rights and obligations and reach into the "health or disease within the self and the community."[36] In her abrupt shift away from searching for answers to the "Negro problem," she does not bracket or reject Du Bois's underlying argument; instead, the author looks behind the veil, discovering that the real *problem* is within Western society's belief in the African's innate inferiority and Western Christianity's binary between evil and good, saint and devil. All of this establishes a hierarchical worldview where *White* dominates over *Black*. Du Bois grappled with Western domination in terms of how it affected life within and beyond the veil. Bambara creates the conditions in her novel to explore Du Bois's question alongside its analogue: "How does it feel to live in a world divided by artificial and brutal categories of race, gender, and religion?" For all intents and purposes, the "problem" is in fact not the Negro's creation and thereby not her concern, as the reader discovers in *The Salt Eaters*. Rather, the subject's "soul-life," as Du Bois characterized it, is the first-order concern. With this realization, the journey toward emancipation starts with undoing, unnaming, and rebuilding oneself and the group. She explains:

> The genocidal bloodbath of centuries and centuries of witch hunts
> sheds some light on the history of the hysterical attitude white

men have regarding their women. Unfortunately, it tainted the relationships of men and women in Africa and in exile. Just as the notions of Heaven and Hell, the elect and the damned, reinforced elitism. And the notion of sainthood through martyrdom, submission, and the embrace of death moved us all farther and farther from our once harmonious relationship with the self and nature.[37]

The dehumanization, Bambara explains, is not isolated to violence or barbarism; it is imbued in the banal categories, symbols, and significations we take for granted, as in patriotism versus protest, a distinction too often invoked to distinguish "good" from "bad" cultural expressions of civil disobedience. Black sit-ins at segregated restaurants and public spaces in the 1960s, for instance, were characterized by many as "protests," of complaining about a good they did not have a legal right to possess. In contrast, white parents who used their bodies to block Black children from integration in public schools, in places like Little Rock, Arkansas, were too often characterized as citizens exercising their democratic rights.[38] Blacks often responded to white backlash by re-appropriating founding texts such as the U.S. Constitution to affirm their own cry for inclusion and equity. The narrator's healing sessions beckon us to heed the guiding principles through alternative means of undoing the political imaginary through healing.

BUILDING POLITICAL NARRATIVES

Bambara's political vision encapsulates the comprehensive and competing worldviews of Black life, including religion, the arts, music, and esotericism, to help underscore the psychosocial dimensions of Black existence within the New World. Influenced by Frantz Fanon's multilayered vision of freedom and revolution in *A Dying Colonialism*, Bambara moves away from decoding the "problem" of Blackness and gender in her groundbreaking anthology, *The Black Woman*,[39] to an emancipatory interpretation of *Blackness* as embodying some of the tools needed from emancipation. To be sure, Bambara's anthology is a response to the masculinist nature of Black Power, Black male patriarchy, and Black Power's attempt to silence and control Black women's voices. In "On the Issue of Role's," Bambara's challenges the useless of traditional gender binary roles by exploring new conceptions of the "family." She argues that family is "an extended kinship of cellmates and neighbors linked in the business of actualizing a vision of a liberated society." To this end, "revolution begins with the self, [and] in the self" within extended kinships, where individuals may discover themselves anew in their quest for freedom and "autonomy."[40] I don't think this is a paternalistic vision or essentialist construction of race as her novel, short stories, and essays all to varying degrees acknowledge both the limits and performative aspects of identity. By placing the "cultural workers" at the center of Black politics, Bambara is unsettling the normative framework even as she leaves unsettled the opaque question of what revolution looks like for emancipated women, men, children, and trans communities.

At issue here is something akin to the struggles Black musicians, artists, and literary critics faced as they deconstructed the metaphysics of whiteness during the Black Arts movement following Black Power. Fear of reinventing old forms of anti-Blackness and archaic gender roles loomed large for brothers and sisters seeking new worlds of existence. Kimberly Benston puts it this way: "The danger it courts is that of dismantling one metaphysical/ideological system by erecting another, thus recapitulating the political structure underlying textualist-idealist aesthetics."[41] But Bambara strives to avoid the dilemma by

constructing *Blackness* in and through mediums previously subdued and silenced by white Christian missionaries and slaveholders: divination, ancestral remembrance, tarot card readings,
and indigenous healing rituals and practices. The liminal nature
of esoteric traditions and Africana religious practices guards
against static implementation of rituals—even as the rituals
themselves are rooted in scripture and generations of exegeti-
cal debates. Bambara illuminates these traditions not for facile
imitation but to shed light on the humanistic possibilities within
an anti-Black world.

The political and aesthetic possibilities of Black religion Toni
Morrison perfected in *Beloved*, where the narrator painstakingly peers into the interior life of a mother's resistance and a
"dead" daughter's resilience, paints the most engaging literary
account of enslavement. However, seven years before *Beloved*'s
publication, *The Salt Eaters* had already transformed the literary benchmarks for deconstructing Black life by appealing
to religion to shift "Blackness" from the margins to the center
of disciplinary concerns. Through onerous accounts of post-
traumatic experiences following the demise of the Student Nonviolent Coordinating Committee and Black Power, readers find
themselves seeing from within scarred bodies tired from years
of political struggle. Strange as it may seem, it is a view from
nowhere and simultaneously a view entangled in the thick terrain of social upheaval, personal anxiety, group uncertainty, and
self-loathing. From this unwavering position, Bambara relies
on the "cultural workers" both to name and characterize the
debris left behind in a community when the movement seems
to implode and then scale back in size and stature. Such individuals are the interpreters of what is happening in a community,
bearing the responsibility of performing and producing what
Lucius Outlaw in his early work called "cultural hermeneutics."

They are the Minnie Ransoms of the world, ordinary women and men who occupy outsized roles during ordinary and extreme times. Cultural workers are unique only insofar as they symbolize the ongoing creativity that is *always* present, regardless of the external opposition, violence, and suppression. They imagine, create, and perform freedom for those too sick, immobilized, or afraid to do so for themselves.

Besides the shattered dreams of immediate political and economic equality, racial solidarity, and just treatment between women and men, the decade following Black Power exposed a principle far more debilitating and difficult to curtail: anti-Blackness as a social ontology reproduced and sustained through social and cultural rituals. Functioning as an ontological erasure of spirit, belief, faith, and hope, it demands a peculiar, inventive response from those circumscribed by its piercing sword. Resistance is foundational. Perseverance is fundamental. Foresight is essential. Above all else is the capacity to heal oneself and one's community during the revolution and from the daily assaults of living under siege. Like *Beloved*'s Sethe, anti-Blackness may demand the blood of one's child. Or, similar to Richard Wright in *Black Boy*, it may manifest itself in arson. The price of freedom varies, but it nonetheless must be reckoned with prior to substantively exercising liberty, equality, and rights. As Bambara notes in a reflection on Frantz Fanon's *A Dying Colonialism*, "revolution begins with the self, in the self."[42] Of course, many of Bambara's characters will exercise their constitutional rights without ever healing from the effects of anti-Black racism or achieving freedom. For many of them, the "weight" of being free or "whole" is too burdensome, a load bearing ethical consequences that are never met. At issue is whether or not Bambara is advocating an individualism at the expense of community. Derek Alwes, in "The Burden of Liberty: Choice in Toni

Morrison's *Jazz* and Toni Cade Bambara's *The Salt Eaters*," suggests that for Bambara the ethical choice "always involves subordinating individual freedom."[43] But the healing session is an indication that neither individualism nor communitarianism is the desired goal; rather, the dialogical exchange between the self and community aims to create the contextual conditions for a whole person to emerge as an extension of the community's wisdom traditions. Alwes duly notes that "self-construction" translates politically as the burden of becoming well, as political consciousness for Bambara's characters is deeply communal, spiritual, and contingent upon the individual's ongoing engagement with the community and its traditions. In other words, the self is always a messy conglomeration of visible and hidden memories of our past and unfolding present.

LITERATURE AS POLITICS

Bambara's unique literary position achieves three critical goals that are noteworthy for expanding Black political visions. First, she develops an "ideological and epistemological theory" of freedom, a categorization I borrow from Benston's *Performing Blackness*, which underscores the quest for humanism and humanistic strivings over and against individualistic liberal conceptions of rights and equality. Second, Bambara provides a pathway beyond an idealized ontological Blackness popularized by masculinist theories of Black Power. As a cultural nationalist who believes in the primacy and privileging of "Black" and "African" traditions, she did not compromise on the necessity for a cultural nationalism that was also anti-sexist and anti-heterosexual. Third, the healing ceremony advances nonessentialist conceptions of race and gender. By this I mean the performative dimension of gender and *Blackness* expands the conceptual space to imagine what Benston calls an "open-ended signifying"[44] of what freedom encapsulates and what humanistic freedom might resemble. That is to say that healing as a ritual practice opens the possibility for dismantling social constructions of race and gender in ways that are reductionist or duplicitous in other discursive exercises within Black political thought. But the engagement between the healer and the wounded person reifies categories like race, gender, and ancestral rememory to disrupt the banality of those categories in an effort to transgress them. Incorporating a politics of healing into strategies of political emancipation may appear to be counterintuitive to the primitive eye, but the narrator masterfully demonstrates how human passion and sorrow are entangled in the political imaginary. Indeed, healing and indigenous spiritual practices "are genuine powers that represent the most reliable source of cultural unity, and consequently, political power."[45] The veracity of the healing session sits in its privileging of the individual, both as an extension of community and as a singular individual with independent goals and aspirations. Unlike in "public" debates, when arguments might conceal underlining moral commitments and cultural motivations, the healing session exposes what is often concealed in other settings. For this reason, the guiding principles of the healing session is designed to disclose rather than to defend one's beliefs or positionality.

The Salt Eaters provides three important points for broadening our understanding of Black religion in general and African American ethics in particular. First, that vernacular religions, hoodoo, magic, and healing and harming traditions are not incompatible with institutionalized religion. Instead, they shed light on the complex forms of sacred subjectivity, where human hands shape the immaterial into flesh. Second, that Black Christian theologies of liberation allow one to understand how persons survive tragic histories, but they do not provide a pathway for transgressing the tragic motif is noteworthy. Put differently, ontological Blackness, as Victor Anderson says so eloquently, locks Blacks into a heroic narrative that gives little, if any, attention to the grotesque and mundane. Minnie and Velma offer an answer to the problem raised by Anderson. The healing sessions bear witness to the narrative of ontological Blackness and struggle to detangle it. Lastly, that healing involves some form of psychic death. As one returns to the past, as Velma does, one releases and actively discards aspects of one's past that are suffocating and self-denying.

The healing sessions remind me of the ethical struggle Frantz Fanon, a key ancestral figure for Bambara, invokes in his work. A case in point: *The Damned of the Earth*, the translation Lewis R. Gordon assigns to what is commonly translated as *The Wretched of the Earth*, is one of Fanon's most important works, if not the most visible text among social activists and intellectuals. Written at age thirty-five and in a matter of ten weeks, the book grapples with the cultural and political implications of colonialism and offers a vision for imagining human existence in tension with Black subjugation. In his interpretation of the text, Gordon focuses on the misreading among scholars and activists of Fanon's call for revolutionary violence. Gordon is clear: any disruption to the social conditions in colonialism and apartheid, for instance, demands an individual and collective struggle that is violent by virtue of its disruption to the social order. This kind of revolutionary violence creates the conditions for embodying freedom and giving birth to the ethics I invoked earlier. According to Gordon, "although one's liberty, or absence of constraints could be handed over by another, it is the struggle for liberation that actually engenders one's freedom."[46] Indeed, the struggle for freedom is the substance of ethics, and dare I say also the *saltiness* of Black Power.

FREEDOM IN ANOTHER NAME

The novel centers around the community infirmary, where doctors, conjurers, and the ancestors tend to the "sick and shut-in," to borrow a phrase from Black religious communities used to denote the incapacitated condition of its members and friends. Inside the infirmary, the narrator guides the reader down a winding road pursued by a community of friends and observers on a quest to heal someone. The ritual symbolizes two key factors for embodying wholeness, the narrator's metaphor for freedom: First, healing one's psychic or physiological wounds cannot be achieved in isolation, tucked away in a retreat center or psych ward within a hospital. The community in its broadest sense is interwoven into the ritual practice. Second, the ceremony is filled with cantankerous onlookers, community members who challenge Minnie Ransom's techniques and question whether the individual can be healed. Such a characterization of the ritual demystifies the contours of healing as a sacred ritual set apart from ordinary and routine vicissitudes found in any community.

In both instances, healing is a prerequisite for imagining the delineations of freedom, both as idealized and epistemological. The distinction is necessary for imagining freedom without any boundaries. Idealized freedom, for instance, is seemingly straightforward, construed in terms of good and bad actions in the world. But as the narrator unfolds her plot, the reader soon discovers its limits. In a conversation between Minnie Ransom and Old Wife, her guardian ancestor, they disagree over Minnie Ransom's healing techniques and preparedness for healing.

In the long and sometimes sprawling exchange in which the priestess is justifying past practices, the Old Wife is seemingly criticizing Minnie Ransom's minimalist prayer life and eye for men. The back and forth banter assumes that the healer's behavior and practices are impeding her supernatural gifts. Minnie Ransom's retort is noteworthy. "When you gonna learn, you ole stick in the mud, that 'good' ain't got nothing to do with it? They packed me off to seminary thinking helping and healing and nosing around was about being good. It was only that I was . . . available."[47] Here, the priestess reminds her guardian that the primary impediment to healing is one's body, and specifically the openness of one's body to serve as a vessel through which the sick may heal themselves. The healer's sexuality and implied minimalist prayer life, interestingly enough, have nothing to do with one's vocation. In Western Christianity, popular and often misguided interpretations of the clergy assume that priests and priestesses are "ordained" based on their good behavior and elect status conferred upon them by the divine and ecclesiastical authority. The narrator pushes back against this perspective. Minnie Ransom is aided by twelve community members known as "The Master's Mind." In doing so, she opens up the priesthood to everyone, especially those who make themselves available to what the narrator often calls the Source.

Freedom in its varying forms sits at the center of the healing session. What seems to characterize epistemological freedom is far more ambiguous to comprehend, as it surfaces within the novel in unexpected places. Like the time when Minnie Ransom's family found her "on her knees eating dirt," which embodies for the narrator epistemological freedom: finding one's way back to nature, both the literal and metaphorical roots of tradition and rituals.

After Minnie Ransom left Bible college to chase her fantasies in New York City, she returned home to her southern roots. Frazzled and disoriented from the slow deterioration of her aspirations and from the expectations placed upon her, Minnie Ransom is left numb and silenced from ancestral callings.

The "sight of [a] full-grown, educated, well-groomed, well-raised" daughter romping in the dirt like an animal or rodent "was too much to bear."[48] All of this happened after her visitation by the spirits, specifically Karen Wilder, who had been a seer and prophet in the community before her death. As Minnie's guardian ancestor, she surfaces to help the priestess find peace and assurance in her gift. Known as Old Wife, Wilder leads her to the site of the infirmary. "And there, squatting in the dirt at the top of the bluff, still listening, Minnie was told to clear the path that led up to the cliffs, set the trees, fix the rainbow, erect a fountain and build the chapel in The Mind. And going there—the cooling dark, the candles, the altar—she saw the gift and knew, for at least that instant, where the telling came from."[49] As the narrator reveals, epistemological freedom arises from and remains entrenched in an ongoing dialogical exchange in community, both real, imagined, and constructed. It is not an event one achieves or embodies wholeheartedly; rather, epistemological freedom is the movement toward listening in and through the entire body: ears, limbs, and heart, and becoming the vessel of the source of one's ancestral lineage.

THE INFIRMARY AND SPEAKER'S CORNER

The infirmary is not simply a secularized church or temple. It represents an example of an organic resource that academics bracket and dismiss as otherworldly or irrational. The narrator centers the novel around this place of healing, worship, and communal gatherings, as if it were an extension of the lived counter-publics she traversed during her years as a writer in Harlem. Any street corner in Uptown could be transformed at moment's notice by anyone with a bullhorn and a fiery message.

Known as Speaker's Corner, it was a place where men and women of all statures, ranging from Malcolm X to the unknown but rhetorically sophisticated church lady dressed in white, stood to gather the lost sheep. Here, three things happened: competing religious and political ideologies found a home in the counter-public; the sound of Blackspeak reinforced or legitimated Black rhetoric and idioms; and political visions were created based on the rules internal to the community. The Speaker's Corner was the life source of Harlem. "I don't think a community is viable without a Speaker's Corner. If we can't hear Black people speak, we become captive to the media, and we disacknowledge Black-speak."[50] "So the Speaker's Corner made it easy to raise critical questions, to be concerned about what's happening locally and internationally. It shaped the political perceptions of at least three generations."[51] The novel is a literary extension of the Speaker's Corner, one that takes place in an infirmary, the Southwest Community Infirmary. Indeed, the infirmary operates as a counter-public sphere. It is a place where "workers, dropouts, students, housewives, ex-cons, vets, church folk, professionals, and an alarming number of change agents" found refuge and the opportunity to pursue the performing arts, martial arts, and educational coursework.[52]

It is difficult to name its counterpart in African American culture, where anyone in possession of zeal and courage could land a public platform. The Speaker's Corner is a symbol of the unacknowledged tolerance of perspectives and life stories that were entertained and sometimes embraced in counter-public spaces, even when the arguments bellowing from their Black souls were murky, unintelligible, or outlandish. But protecting the so-called outlandish allowed both the well and wounded to find comfort in the politics of healing that surfaced at the Speaker's Corner. This venue also enhanced the existing overlap between religion and politics in a community already familiar with religion's role in shaping politics and vice versa.

Competing religious and political views shaped the delineation of freedom within Bambara's literary vision. The views ranged from the women from the "Sanctified Church, and they might talk about the research they were doing on the Colored People's Conventions of the Reconstruction era" to the Rastas and members of the Socialist party.[53] Religion was fluid, not a fixed doctrine but a set of guiding principles to be applied to varying contexts and social problems. Religion informed politics, but it was not necessarily political or always retrieved to justify a political position. Rather, the spirit of religion seemed always to occupy a constant and shifting conceptual space within one's religious subjectivity and among the narrator's host of political actors, even if religion happened to negate a political belief or strategy. To this end, religion is dynamic both in Bambara's literary imagination and Black counter-publics. As a sustaining tradition and set of beliefs, Black religion materializes in the novel and in the ruins of slavery's ongoing reincarnation as a stunning repudiation of white supremacy and cultural beliefs in Black inferiority.

The Speaker's Corner is noteworthy for the "Blackspeak" emerging from it. This was a kind of training ground for maintaining and developing the oral tradition of call and response, a space for one to speak as well as to learn how to carve out space for unfamiliar, competing points of view. "[T] he Speaker's Corner made it easy to raise critical questions, to be concerned about what's happening locally and internationally."[54] It was also a nation within a community sealed off by the Du Boisian veil. Inscribed within Blackspeak sat a politics of healing, a therapeutic project to heal a wounded people and a space to confront and tackle what Bambara calls the three forms of alienation faced by Blacks: alienation from an "African past,"

"U.S. economic and political power," and the "self as wholly participatory in history."[55] This might explain why Africa surfaced within the imaginary of enslaved Africans as a sacred symbol both in Afro-religion and Black politics. Charles Long made this argument in his groundbreaking *Significations*. Bambara's retrieval of religion and Africa anticipates Long's work by normalizing conjure, divination, and ancestral memory in Afro-Religions religions and Black politics.

A little more than fifty years after the emergence of Black Power, during which mostly Black women and children used their bodies as a political and *theological* weapon to fight against white supremacy and legalized racial oppression, I believe it is fitting to return to *The Salt Eaters* as a starting point for reflecting on our current plight as a nation. While many leading political theorists, public intellectuals, and religious leaders are asking why so many white working-class Americans are disgruntled with (for instance) the media and our government, and are struggling to comprehend why evangelicals overwhelmingly supported the Trump presidency, Toni Cade Bambara shifts the conversation away from liberal political philosophy—that is, away from questions concerning political rights, equal access, and religious liberty—to a conversation about ethics as a therapeutic and theohumanist democratic form of embodiment and political agency. When the healer asks, "Do you want to be healed?" she is illuminating the extent to which both bodies and institutional practices, to some extent, depend upon varying forms of subjugation and discriminatory acts and beliefs to maintain their life force.

Framed within the context of African American interpretations of the Gospel of Matthew, the question is also translated into a call for *political action*: "*You are the salt of the earth; but if salt has lost its taste, how can its saltiness be restored? It is no longer good for* *anything, but it's thrown out and trampled underfoot."*[56] The narrator of this gospel is building a narrative shortly after Jesus's death in an effort to remember his best teachings and to provide meaning to his disciples, many of whom feel alienated and dejected.

Today, many of us are still grappling with how to organize, find meaning, and understand a political context in which racial hatred, bigotry, xenophobia, and sexism have become normalized and legitimated by our elected officials in ways not experienced since my late grandmother was a sharecropper in Alabama.

I write this today weary and burdened by a heavy heart. To be frank, I do not have any hope in our institutions. I do not trust our leaders. And sadly, my faith is waning in the two places where Blacks and others could once find refuge: religious institutions and higher education. Yet our ancestors beckon me—beckon us—to return to our history, what we have cultivated as sacred, to find our strength, power, and human dignity. Toni Cade Bambara directs our attention to Black Power, and it is within this movement, I believe, that we can find the resources to address the political concerns that our current liberal philosophy cannot address.

For Black Power was the fleshing manifestation of ethics and the ethical turn within African American moral traditions. As I construe it, the ethical turn is the ongoing recentering of Black subjectivity as central, necessary, and foundational in any humanistic endeavor to imagine, interpret, and invent existential and epistemic legitimacy. To combat both the political and moral justifications for oppression, Black Power turned to "revolutionary ethics" to establish the philosophical justifications for Black economic empowerment, group consciousness, and self-reliance.

Raising the question of whether or not we want to be healed compels us as a people and a nation to consider three important points about race and anti-Black racism: First, anti-Black racism is a comprehensive political and theological tool designed to reinforce black inferiority through acts of violence and discipline. This allows us, then, to justify police shootings against unarmed Black "thugs" and to normalize Black-on-Black violence as reflective of an inherent immorality. Second, political liberals assume that equality and equal access will eliminate racial bigotry. This belief ignores the degree to which culture, cultural inheritance, and economic structures create unprecedented obstacles to achieving equality. Third, by framing Black history as a narrative of Black resistance and ingenuity—a classic tale of a people rising from slavery to freedom—we fail to account for the psychic and physical wounds of racial hatred upon the Body—both of the colonized and the colonizer. As we can see, healing serves as a discursive category, a kind of critical lens through which we actively engage our past, future, and present. To this end, healing serves as a category in and through which I am imagining African American ethics and the ethical turn within the Black Power movement.

I am not attempting to ignore Black Power's strict political and economic agenda; instead, I want to emphasize how the ethical turn steers the movement's political and economic vision of humanistic nationalism. And *The Salt Eaters* captures the movement's ethical imagination unlike any writer in Bambara's generation.

The novel's characterization of healing helps show what I mean by ethics and the ethical turn. The healing session is a prime example of ethics as a therapeutic and theo-humanistic expression in two fundamental ways: First, it creates the conditions through which the divine and divinities are revealed. In this space, the priestess takes on a peculiar role: both an otherworldly mediator and a this-worldly therapist, very similar to Du Bois's characterization of the Negro preacher. Minnie's healing session, however, is not so unfamiliar in that Minnie follows a predictable, somewhat routine script. Indeed, the narrator is quick to remind the reader of the session's normalcy. "Over the years it had become routine: [Minnie] simply placed her left hand on the patient's spine and her right on the navel, then clearing the channels, putting herself aside, she became available to a healing force no one had yet, to her satisfaction, captured in name."[57]

Here, healing involves a guide, a sacred healer of sorts. Minnie, in this instance, is the link between these divided and overlapping worlds. The priestess manipulates the material world, and in this act of conjuring, she not only opens the way for Velma but gains affirmation of her priestly gifts.

> And there, squatting in the dirt at the top of the bluff, still listening, Minnie was told to clear the path that led up to the cliffs, set the trees, fix the rainbow, erect a fountain and build the chapel in The Mind. And going there—the cooling dark, the candles, the altar—she saw the gift, and knew, for at least that instant, where the telling came from.[58]

We see the degree to which the Priest and believer stand on similar ground, and yet they require different things from each other. Without Minnie, Velma struggles to understand the source of her ailment. Minnie stands in need of Velma to confirm the divination and presence of the gods. In fact, the divine knowledge Minnie imagines and constructs emerges only in the exchange with the sick. To be sure, Minnie is not the divine source of Velma's healing or the motivating factor behind Velma's longing to return to her living past; instead, the Priestess manipulates the material world enough so that Velma might feel slightly at ease as she surrenders to the other world and communes with her ancestors. As we can imagine, there's a kind of unspoken mutual agreement between Minnie and Velma, a communion of sorts.

Second, ethical expression within the healing session emerges during the temporary suspension of Velma's awareness of the present. The suspension or bracketing of an immediate narrative ever so slightly opens the door through which Velma enters in pursuit of the past, where events are contested and scrutinized. When she comes face-to-face with the past, she recoils, and turns her head to find comfort in an unknowing.

> Velma groaned, sore and sodden, coming in from the muddy planks, stumbling, her feet entangled in sheets, reeling toward the sound of tambourines and joy, reeling and rocking on the stool, the mud going white linoleum underfoot, the tent canvas, the bedroom walls yellow latex paint, and the sting of disinfectant overpowering, making her squint.[59]

Past experiences and familiar faces emerge during her recovery of the past as she sits on the stool next to Minnie. As her mind wanders, she tries to control what she imagines and sees. Eventually, she loses and slips further into a past too overwhelming at times to comprehend. Velma eventually returns to the present, where she finds something new:

> Minnie Ranson staring. Her hands sliding off the shoulders of silk. The patient turning smoothly on the stool, head thrown back about to shout, to laugh, to sing. No need of Minnie's hands now. That is clear. Velma's glow aglow and two yards wide of clear and unstreaked white and yellow. Her eyes scanning the air surrounding Minnie, then examining her own hands, fingers stretched and radiant. No need of Minnie's hands now so the healer withdraws them, drops them in her lap just as Velma, rising on steady legs, throws off the shawl that drops down on the stool [like] a burst cocoon.[60]

In some respects, Velma is struggling to imagine the impossible—that is, to see beyond the horizons of the tormented historical moment. Impossible, as Minnie asserts, because "sometimes a person held on to sickness with a fiercesomeness that took twenty hard-praying folk to loosen. So used to being unwhole and unwell, one forgot what it was to talk upright and see clearly, breath easily, think better than was taught, be better than one was programmed to believe."[61] Velma seems to have forgotten how to be whole, or to breathe or to imagine because of the tragic sense of life that dogged her. Have we forgotten what it means to be well? What it feels like to be healthy?

The healing session, however, offers a glimpse of something different, an altered form of our raced and gendered identities. In this ambiguous state of existence, where the ancestors and the Divine are invoked, innocence emerges in tension and coexisting with the tragic, sacred, and mundane. In the engagement between Velma and the spirit world, for example, the self as one knows it dies. She feels her soul and can see and taste a soul-life, an imaginative framework for thinking and feeling in tension with the *raced* and gendered body.

This disruption of ontological Blackness, a reimagining of body-spirit-mind, is the emergence of the ethical. Not ethics as in a set of predetermined and static rules or duties but ethics as disruption, dismantling, and rebuilding in an effort to expand, deepen, and complicate our sense of what it means to be human and to be political in a liberal democracy.

The novel does not subscribe to a normative sense of liberation as necessarily emanating from God; rather, the freedom that Velma and others yearn to embody emerges in the practice of recovering, dismembering, reconfiguring, and reconciling oneself to a place between this-worldly and otherworldly imaginations. This process of becoming is an ethical and sacred act of attempting to become whole again in a society bent on keeping us torn asunder.

When new movements surface, such as Black Lives Matter, gay marriage, trans community rights, Palestinian requests for statehood, or Occupy Wall Street, readers may find themselves returning to the familiar and rejecting the calls of the disinherited. But they should stay there. Like Velma, they must be open to what is unfamiliar, foreign, and possibly even distorted—in order to become the salt of the earth.

Bambara calls upon her readers to open their hearts to the spirit of justice, and then to open their mouths to join in protest with the poor, weak, homeless, elderly, and abandoned. They—we—cannot grow weary because of increasing violence or the threat of empire striking back. Scripture tells us that the mountains may sink in the sea, and the earth may tremble, but those who believe in justice and freedom cannot use turmoil as an excuse for giving up or for ignoring the very real problems we see.

Moving forward in *We Testify with Our Lives*, I retell the widely known narrative of Black Power in and through ethical turns invented in struggle, aiming to sketch out alternative paths toward securing the freedom dreams of the ancestors and the hope borne by their children. In the words of the Negro spiritual, *I opened my mouth to the Lord, and I won't turn back. I will go! I shall go! To see what the end is going to be!*

2

AWAKENING TO BLACK
POWER CONSCIOUSNESS

Purtiest singin' ever I heard / 'Way ovah on de hill / De angels shout
an' I shout too / Singin' wid a sword in ma han'
Purtiest shoutin' ever I heard / 'Way ovah on de hill / De angels sing
an' I sing too / Shoutin' wid a sword in ma han'
Purtiest preachin ever I heard / 'Way ovah on de hill / De angels
preach an' I preach too / Preachin' wid a sword in ma han'
Purtiest prayin' ever I heard / 'Way ovah on de hill / De angels pray
an' I pray too / Prayin' wid a sword in ma han'
Purtiest mournin' ever I feard / 'Way ovah on de hill / De angels
mourn an' I mourn too / Mournin' wid a sword in ma han'[1]

When Stokely Carmichael cried out "Black Power"
in 1966, his words cut through the crowd like the
sword in the Negro spiritual "Singin' wid a sword
in ma han.'" In thus preaching liberation to a captive audience
anxious to revolt against the status quo, Carmichael joined a
litany of Black activists who waxed rhetorical to articulate latent
desires and aspirations that others in the audience could not or
refused to express. Speaking as the heir[2] to the late Malcolm
X's fiery and visionary message of self-love, self-help, and self-
determination, no one was spared Carmichael's penetrating

retort—"We want Black Power!"—as he condemned the politics of accommodation that encouraged civil rights leaders to rebuff the growing political momentum among young and college-age activists such as Carmichael.

Surrounded by armed white police officers on public school grounds in Greenwood, Mississippi, Carmichael's impromptu speech at the March Against Fear[3] poured a balm on the open wounds of those injured by years of protest against a formidable adversary. Finally, a shining new prince had surfaced ready to articulate in the boldest terms the pain and aspirations of the people. A young Howard University graduate standing tall and unarmed between hundreds of activists and armed state troopers prepared to kill, maim, and subdue the crowd, Carmichael symbolized the power that the people wanted to see in the flesh.

The two groups glared at each other until Carmichael's booming voice diverted their attention. "This is the twenty-seventh time I have been arrested—I ain't going to jail no more, I ain't going to jail no more,"[4] he bellowed, the new chairman of the Student Nonviolent Coordinating Committee (SNCC).[5] He had already been arrested earlier that very day for his role in organizing the march. He wasn't about to be arrested again. The boldness of his words galvanized the marchers. Revitalized, they waved their hands and raised their voices in support. His next words first stunned and then energized his enthusiastic supporters: "We want Black Power!"

The words momentarily stopped and silenced everyone in earshot. Again, Carmichael shouted "Black Power." Some gasped at the phrase. But then, as he began to intone "Black Power" in a cadence like a Black preacher, the younger members of the audience began clapping their hands and shouting back "Black Power!"[6]

The rhetorical refrain had been nearly a year in the planning, and it symbolized SNCC's expanding political ideology of promoting Black-controlled institutions—banks, co-ops, and political parties—and purging whites from its leadership ranks.[7] At SNCC's June 10 meeting, Carmichael had devised a plan to use the march as a testing ground for the slogan "Black power for Black people,"[8] according to the historian Claybourne Carson. "Carmichael's use of [the] black power slogan immediately became the central controversy of the march."[9]

This chapter tells the story about how Carmichael, Ella Baker, and a group of college-age African Americans changed the course of Black political thought and the modes of political civil disobedience. By designing a political strategy aimed at (first) "self-emancipation,"[10] (second) cultivating a cultural conscious-ness, and (third) ending "caste systems among Blacks and their allies,[11] SNCC and its leftist members compelled the civil rights establishment's most prominent leader, Dr. Martin Luther King Jr., to reconsider liberalism[12] and the voting-rights platform as the primary and essential political tools to end racial domination.

Unlike any other political tropes in Black politics since W. E. B. Du Bois's double consciousness and the color line, SNCC's Black Power movement, handled through rhetorical force and shrewd organizing, symbolized an ideology of global proportions. On the one hand, Black Power's far reach had everything to do with its internationalist agenda of coalition-building among colonized people in and around Third World nations. On the other hand, the outsized response to Black Power, by far more pernicious than favorable, reflected the threat it posed to dehumanizing politics domestically and to colonial-ism abroad. The position I offer here stands slightly at odds with Peniel Joseph's powerful narrations of Black Power's significance in America's political imaginary. While Joseph sees Black Power as "reimagining the range of America's democratic rhetoric and practice," which "ushered in" Barack Obama's presidency in 2008,[13] I envision Black Power's enduring legacy as reinvoking a human rights agenda based on the Black internationalism popular during the Cold War.[14] Black Power, then, reifies *Blackness* not to assert domestic self-interests but to pivot toward a global political vision based on shared and overlapping experiences of anti-Blackness and colonialism. What SNCC members in the late 1960s called "humanistic nationalism" symbolized the group's deepening commitment to transnational politics.

SNCC's ongoing political developments must be characterized within the context of Black feminist criticisms of Black Power's masculinist framing, especially as it manifested in maintaining traditional gender roles within Black political organizations and prevented Black women from public-facing with masses during public protests. Hazel Carby argues that "while contemporary black male intellectuals claim to challenge the hegemony of a racialized social formation, most fail to challenge the hegemony of their own assumptions about black masculinity and accept the consensus of a dominant society that conceives of African American society in terms of a perennial 'crisis' " [that] compromised Black women and their specific political visions.[15] This is true. But in some instances, like Carmichael's public cry, Black masculinity is detangled and transformed into a form of public mourning.

Eric Garner's gasping cry in 2014, "I can't breathe," captured the cruel and heinous criminality of police offers who only envision Black and Brown bodies as pure brutes. What became a national cry for systemic police reform, Garner's "I can't breathe" also denoted an expression of grief and grievance with long-term ethical implications for society. The theologian Ashon Crawley rightly notes that cry "charges us to do something, to perform, to produce otherwise than what we have. We are charged to end, to produce abolition against, the episteme that produced for us

current iterations of categorical designations of racial hierarchies, class stratifications, gender binaries, mind-body splits."[16]

Carmichael's cry is different but emerges from a similar existential trajectory; both denote responses to structural forces that
deny the humanity of Blacks. For Eric Garner, the cry was a literal response to modern-day lynching; Carmichael's cry, on the
other hand, emerged as a form of non-violent resistance against
armed and violent segregationists. Both invoke the cry to trigger
structural and existential transformation. From this public cry,
Crawley notes, "an ethical charge" surfaces for those who choose
to hear the rumblings from the underside. In both instances, two
important moves happen. Black masculinity, as characterized by
Carby, is dismantled, transforming pain, grievance, and rage into
a form of public mourning. Surrounded by armed white police-
men and their dogs, Carmichael leads the nonviolent marchers
in a litany of harms against his public protests. Both his words
and body are transformed by the gutter cry to express grief and
grievance toward the apartheid state led mostly by "good" white
Christian men and women.

What does this mean for a political theorist? At the bare minimum, the tension among racial uplift ideology, Black nationalism, social contract theory, and communitarianism do not offer
adequate tools for exploring social dehumanization and how it
affects political culture, gender roles, class structures, and economic opportunities. By this I mean that classical political categories for differentiating Black political thought, until Black
Power, have failed to capture the comprehensive nature of political and economic injustice. Anti-Blackness is not an aspect of
social discrimination; rather, it is the foundational cornerstone
of the nation's political economy. Taking seriously the aesthetic
dimensions of public protests, i.e., the public cry, is one site of
entry into the problem of Blackness.

By way of Black preaching and storytelling, to name a few, the public cry serves two political purposes. First, it denotes the varying articulations of human pain, joy, and suffering within Black life, from the sorrow songs and the blues to hip hop. The expressions mature through the dialogical nature of Black music's organic relationship to the listener. Within this deliberative framework, political protests from behind the veil are not designed to cling to what is familiar for the sake of winning the debate or political race; rather, the engagement between the protestor and politician seeks to interrogate existing norms, beliefs, and ideologies with the goal of producing transformational political results. Second, the public cry lifts the veil on the multiple methods of responding to oppression and domination. Noteworthy examples include Fannie Lou Hamer's infamous retort, "I'm sick and tired of being sick and tired," and the Nation of Islam's theological doctrine that the white man is the devil. While the public cry might be absurd to the untrained ear in Black music and preaching, it is astonishingly effective in figuratively and literally seizing public spaces and institutions through its potent vocalization of suffering and pain. In doing so, the public cry unsettles, disrupts, and unnerves those with in ear's range. Subsequent transformation is possible.

To understand more fully the political and social implications of SNCC and Black Power within Black life, I explore two critical debates that happened during the late 1960s: the disagreement between King and Carmichael regarding Black Power, and SNCC's internal debates over whites and their leadership roles within the organization. Before diving into the polemics between Black Power and the civil rights movement's liberalism, it is important to sketch out SNCC's history and political ideology when it formed at Shaw University under the guidance of the veteran political strategist and activist Ella Baker.

SNCC's RADICAL ORIGINS

Since SNCC's inception in 1960, Ella Baker and the founders regarded themselves as subjects belonging to political struggles in and beyond U.S. borders. The organizers "initially identified with anti-colonial activity in Africa as a source of moral and political inspiration for their own movement for social and political change in the United States."[17] As the symbolic relationship fortified through organizational links and SNCC members' travel to Africa and elsewhere in the African diaspora, it morphed into pointedly leftist politics including Pan-Africanism and socialism.[18]

Ella Baker played a critical role in the organization's vision and structure. A beloved New York labor advocate and student of global social movements, Baker charged the students with establishing and maintaining an "emancipatory" vision for themselves and the people they were organizing. In fact, Baker designed the structure of the founding meeting to encourage a sustained conversation rather than a series of workshops facilitated by "experts." According to the noted historian Barbara Ransby, "Baker urged those in attendance to give southern students, who were disproportionately black and less politically experienced, the time and space to meet separately, setting the stage for them to be the principal framers of whatever organization might emerge."[19] It was Baker's visionary leadership model that established the terrain for a nonhierarchical and anti-sexist organizational structure. To her credit, she did not spoon-feed the two hundred or so young and vibrant conference participants. Instead, Baker structured the retreat so that on-the-ground organizers maintained a visible and active role in the two-day conference.[20] Another important point to note is Baker's insistence that the organization remain independent, out of harm's way from established civil rights groups. "In Baker's view, the students who convened at Raleigh needed to be encouraged to take the lead because they were at the forefront of the struggle and represented the greatest hope for a renewed militant, democratic mass movement, not simply because they were young."[21] The conference concluded with the forming of SNCC.

The organization's first two years, writes Ransby, focused on sit-ins and participation in the Freedom Rides, which bused mostly northern college students to the South to integrate interstate travel. The strategy was taxing and far more lethal than imagined. No one could have predicted the level of violence by white vigilantes against the nonviolent group.[22] The external violence, and the lack of support from the federal government to secure their safety, created internal strife and threatened the group's longevity in terms of its unabashed commitment to nonviolence. After fierce debates among key organizers such as Diane Nash and Bob Moses, according to Ransby, SNCC members abandoned the high-profile protests and directed their attention to "empowering" people in local communities to solve their problems ("direct action") and to promote voter registration and education.[23]

Between 1962 and 1966, three internal debates and concerns steered SNCC's strategic objectives and laid the groundwork for Black Power and Stokely Carmichael's subsequent national and international rise to prominence. First, humanistic nationalism emerged as a conceptual category to frame the concerns and long-term objectives of SNCC's radical arm and engagement with Third World politics; second, meeting notes and personal letters of SNCC members suggest that they debated freedom more frequently than they grappled with liberation, suggesting that the SNCC was interested primarily in providing the resources for people to survive and possibly flourish within otherwise pernicious living and working conditions; freedom, then, involved an ongoing striving toward an unachievable ideal; third, as the organization's leaders promoted voter registration and education in rural communities, such as Alabama and Mississippi, they grew increasingly aware of the absence of any material political or economic power among African Americans.

Stanley Wise, a member of SNCC's central committee, characterized the moment as the biblical battle between David and Goliath. "I believe," Wise says, "that SNCC is now in the process of building among a power-less people . . . a community which is surrounded by nothing but power [that] maintains it by brute force."[24] He and others identified the missing elements of their strategy as well as the civil rights agenda—the economic, political, and social power to lift and transform mountains of poverty and underfunded public schools. So was the predicament of a "power-less people," as characterized by Wise and others, who sat in the Atlanta office debating the political agenda of a "power-less people." While SNCC's archives contain extensive letters, speeches, and reading lists on Black nationalism, socialism, and Marxism—clearly indicating the depths to which members scoured resources for answers to 'Negro problems'—SNCC leaders were not prepared for the ensuing public battle themselves and traditional civil rights organizations following Carmichael's 1966 Black Power speech in Mississippi.

Carmichael's public assault against the civil rights movement exposed the limits of the movement's singular philosophical agenda of legal political equality. He notes, "What we discovered was that apparently no one in the movement had taken the time to seriously analyze the unexamined assumptions underlying the concept of integration or its practical feasibility as a strategy."[25] The "unexamined assumptions" of integration and voting rights depended largely upon an unexplored *public conscience*: the benevolence of whites. For the movement's liberal political philosophy could only work if white liberals were convinced that such rights benefited their own moral, economic, and political interests. In the absence of Black power—political *and* economic—voting rights, integration, and equal access were evanescent, meaning unsafe, insecure, changeable, volatile, and unpredictable political ideals dependent on moral suasion and white goodwill. Political structures might expand, but without political and economic Black power, the long-term political protection of African Americans would be at the whim and mercy of the state (and non-state) actors. How would such a "power-less people" function in such a terrifying and liberal American democracy?

BLACK POWER, 1966–1967

Carmichael's answer was unequivocal: self-determination and independence from white philanthropy through Black economic and political power. When Carmichael bellowed "Black Power," his rejection of the civil rights agenda was a discursive performance, the "naming"[26] of a new movement within the consciousness of African Americans. In what can be characterized as an epistemic insurrection, Carmichael transgressed predetermined political boundaries prescribed by race and gender. He demanded power, not from whites or the federal government, but from his own people, African Americans. And while the media at the time focused on the rhetorical refrain of Black Power as a symbol of anti-whiteness, Carmichael's refrain actually meant something else.

The insertion of Blackness, as a modifier of power, initiates within the consciousness the "unnaming" and "naming" of a mischaracterized people. Immediately, *Blackness* is both real and unreal. Let me explain: In the crudest sense, the call for Black Power began an overdue conversation on self-love and what it would look like to embrace Blackness not as equal to anything else but as accepted on its own terms and conditions. Keep in mind that Carmichael's initial retort in Greenwood, Mississippi, was not comparative. He did not say he wanted to possess power like it was embodied and executed among whites, Jews, or the Irish. His cry for Black Power was linked to his own power-lessness, which is why he followed the refrain ("We want Black Power!") with his anguish over being arrested. How can he ever measure up as man, as a human, if he is detained whenever he asserts his "inalienable" rights? At a structural level, the symbol of *Black Power* made visible the invisibility of literal Blackness in spaces of power and influence while at the same time illuminating the shortcomings and failures of race as a legitimate signifier of intelligence, capabilities, and morality.

Subsequently, Carmichael's explosive Black Power speech in October 1966 to a mostly white audience at the University of California, Berkeley introduced in more detail the principles and foundations of the refrain he had chanted months earlier in Mississippi: that securing voting rights without economic and political power would fail to achieve full-scale freedom. In fact, he "condemned" the nation for its racist stance against African Americans: "It seems to me the institutions that function in this country are clearly racist and that they're built upon racism. And the question then is, how can black people inside of this country move? And then how can white people who say they're not a part of those institutions begin to move?"[27]

Three important factors frame Black Power. First, freedom is the aim of Black Power. Freedom is not given by the state or non-state actors but is pursued in the political, economic, and cultural strivings of the people. "A man is born free. You may enslave a man after he is born free. And that is in fact what this country does . . . so that the only act that white people can do is to stop denying black people their freedom."[28]

Second, voting rights legislation, and for that matter all legislation designed to end legal segregation, is far more meaningful to white Americans than it is to African Americans. At the
pragmatic level, voting-rights legislation is obviously the necessary step to guarantee the constitutional rights afforded to all
citizens. But Carmichael implies that without a belief in the
humanity of African Americans, legislation will remain ineffective, limited, precarious, and easily vetoed. In other words, it
is increasingly difficult to enslave or deny the rights to fellow
human beings, especially when they do not pose an imminent
threat to you. "I maintain that every civil rights bill in this country was passed for white people, not for black people. . . . So
some boys had to write a bill to tell the white man, 'he's a human
being; don't stop him from voting.'"[29]

Third, power is described as the tool or resource that can
"legitimate" the actions of a people based on internal dynamics,
traditions, and customs cultivated by the group. Contrary to popular opinion at the time, Carmichael in the early iteration of the
movement did not construe power in terms of asserting aggression
toward whites or the government. Instead, he maintained that
power is best executed by the group itself if it wants to overcome
oppression. There's a subtext to power as well. It is designed to
embolden political subjects, according to Carmichael, to engage
critically the nation's use of power domestically and internationally. In other words, Carmichael is extending the duties and
obligations of citizenship. Uncritical acceptance of legalized and
social segregation, for instance, undermines the guiding doctrines
of democracy and restricts the aims of freedom and liberty. "We
[in the SNCC] are raising questions about this country. I do not
want to be a part of the American pie. The American pie means
raping South Africa, beating Vietnam, beating South America,
raping the Philippines, raping every country you've been in. . . .
The question is, how do we raise those questions? How do

we raise them as activists?"[30] The rhetorical moves Carmichael made have political potency: he appropriates *Blackness* to dismantle naive assumptions regarding American liberal values and how they are lived out both domestically and abroad.

Through national and international press attention, Carmichael's speech shamed the nation by revealing both the contradictions of and limits to a constitutional democracy that birthed and bred slavery, Jim Crow, and Black economic exploitation. The speech revealed to the world that a nation that took pride in its moral and political exceptionalism had failed to provide the economic and political infrastructure needed for a large portion of its population—Blacks—to accumulate and execute their group power. The voting-rights agenda, in Carmichael's eyes, was insufficient, and merely a pragmatic response to white supremacy that did not address the structural, legal, economic, and political impediments that both fueled and reinforced the moral problem of Blackness: the unchallenged and allegedly universally agreed upon *belief in Black inferiority*.

Instead of relying on the moral goodwill of the nation and benevolence of white lawmakers (as the early King was doing), Carmichael was attempting to reconfigure the political aims and aspirations that Blacks themselves were seeking. In a rhetorical sense, Black Power was designed both to inspire a disinherited people and to destroy white supremacist beliefs in Black inferiority. But at the time no one, not even Carmichael, anticipated the long-term political and cultural implications of Black Power.

KING TACKLES BLACK POWER

When Martin Luther King Jr., received word of Carmichael's unprecedented speech, his heart sank. He felt betrayed by his protégé. Carmichael seemed to be undermining King's approach to garnering group political power through exercising their voting rights. King was not bothered so much by either the tone or the rhetoric of Black Power. He understood the source of the frustration, which "was born from the wombs of despair and disappointment." To King, "Black Power is a cry of pain."[31] So instead of directly criticizing the burgeoning political movement that Carmichael was now leading, he focused on its usefulness for improving the economic and social conditions of Blacks. King feared that the use of Black Power as a rhetorical device and political strategy would sabotage the civil rights movement's efforts to secure meaningful legislation for Blacks and that it would alienate moderate whites.

Indeed, Carmichael's cry triggered widespread debates, dividing old friends and bringing to an abrupt halt the last vestiges of unity between the left and right wings of the desegregation movement."[32] Granted, Black Power was not a new concept, as historian Manning Marable reminds us. But this time Black Power captivated the entire country, casting a cloud of uncertainty over the declining civil rights agenda.[33]

The debate between King and Carmichael revealed more vividly than ever the expanding schism between religion and politics, respectability politics and Black radicalism, the Black church and "secular" politics, and racial solidarity and humanism. This disagreement between the two leading men in Black politics had far more consequential effects on Black religion and politics than many have previously acknowledged. It represented the first sign within the white media of the erosion both of the Black church and the messianic leader in the figure of King. The emergence of Black Power underscored the growing disdain among SNCC members and its allies for the civil rights movement's unwavering reliance on the politics of respectability and racial uplift. This erosion, which for years had been evident in Black churches and examined in Black-owned newspapers, was primarily ideological but nonetheless substantial in upending traditional liberal approaches to justice and freedom.

The debate between King and Carmichael was a fight for the direction of Black politics and Black political philosophy. These two men stood at the crossroads of a political movement struggling to produce enduring material results. Once dominated by Christian symbols, beliefs in nonviolence, racial uplift ideology, and the politics of respectability, the core principles of the civil rights agenda faced increasing interrogation amidst SNCC's growing anxiety over the Vietnam War and its relationship to the persistence of anti-Black racism in the United States. To be sure, this was a fight between two driven men, a fight propelled by masculinity to determine the scope and direction of the movement. It, too, was a fight over how to rebuild the conditions for democracy within an empire conflicted over its hegemony and its treatment of its allegedly bastard children. King characterized this point aptly: it was a debate between (Black) national consciousness and the (moral) conscience of a nation and its people.

In the days and weeks that followed the Meredith march, King increasingly voiced his skepticism of Black Power publicly. His primary concern stemmed from Black Power's political viability. In *Where Do We Go from Here: Chaos or Community*, King describes his firsthand encounters with the impatience of young activists. He believes they are justified in their beliefs but thinks their actions nonetheless undermined the broader political agenda of equality. According to King, the "gulf between the laws and their enforcement is one of the basic reasons why Black Power advocates express contempt for the legislative process"[34] In his eyes, Black Power activists possessed neither the interest nor the endurance to build a meaningful piece of political legislation or a political platform. They wanted to disrupt the status quo without having determined a comprehensive agenda on how to repair and build upon the existing political and economic infrastructure.

King challenged the political efficacy and moral veracity of a movement based largely on a rhetorical weapon. Moreover, he feared Black Power would destroy any and all political relationships with white powerbrokers in philanthropy and politics alike, relationships he had been at pains to foster. More importantly, King seemed to suggest that Black Power undermined the core philosophical values of creating and sustaining a Beloved Community.[35] He did so by asking three key questions: first, whether the rhetorical force of Black Power had any programmatic political value; second, whether Black Power would create existential as well as economic freedom; and third, whether Black Power's emphasis on consciousness diminished his call for a collective moral conscience.

In his essay, King highlighted the growing tensions between the young activists and established civil rights leaders. He recalled overhearing Black Power activists debate the wisdom of nonviolence in a social context like Mississippi, where beating and killing Blacks were cultural pastimes. They wondered aloud why "white liberals" were marching alongside them, "invading" their political movement. King seemed surprised by what he heard: "I guess I should have not been surprised. I should have known that in an atmosphere where false promises are daily realities, where deferred dreams are nightly facts, where acts of unpunished violence toward Negroes are a way of life, nonviolence would eventually be seriously questioned."[36]

King acknowledged the existential need for Black Power. He understood that it emerged from a "cry of disappointment" and was born from the "wounds of despair."[37] But he feared that bitterness born of despair would lead to political and moral blindness, a frame of thinking that would make it impossible to build allies across racial lines because such bitterness would foreclose those political relationships. And without those allies, without those political relationships, without an expansive coalition—King feared from his experience—no political program or progress would be achievable.

Though King applauded the "positive" elements of Black Power for building economic and political strength among Blacks, he was not sure those goals could be obtained because of the "problem of power": the "confrontation between the forces demanding change and the forces of power dedicated to preserving the status quo."[38] He seemed to imply here that the acquisition of economic and political power without a fundamental *tweaking* of power would reinforce and reinscribe the very same hegemony that Black Power was attempting to dismantle and transform. The rhetorical move, King admonished, ought to include a discussion of the relationship between power and love. He argued that the two concepts are linked and dependent on each other. As he noted, "power without love is reckless and abusive and . . . love without power is sentimental and anemic. Power at its best is love implementing the demands of justice. Justice at its best is love correcting everything that stands against love."[39]

King agreed with Black Power's criticisms. Power is "unequally distributed" in the nation, which fueled the civil rights movement's effort to achieve its political goals through "love and moral suasion devoid of power." Carmichael's focus on power, especially expressed in the form of acquisition and redistribution, simply mirrored the abusive use of power that King believed was operative within the current political framework of white racists.[40] "It is precisely this collision of immoral power with powerless morality which constitutes the major crisis of our times."[41] Here, King was attempting to build a philosophical framework for resisting the incorporation of imperial tendencies into the movement by offering new vocabularies for developing "creative and positive power" for the sake of expanding the landscape of democracy.

Finally, on a more conciliatory note, King agreed that Black Power was a "psychological call to manhood."[42] That is, Black Power was a public pronouncement of the human dignity inscribed within all Black bodies and a denouncement of slavery's attempt to link political and social "depravity"[43] to the biological inferiority of Blacks. "The whole dirty business of slavery was based on the premise that the Negro was a thing to be used, not a person to be respected."[44] Having once been deemed inferior, however, one must eventually declare oneself not so—and do it fiercely. King believed a call to a "new sense of manhood" is a necessary step in creating "racial pride" and "an audacious appreciation" of Black "heritage."[45]

Still, King wrote, Black Power's growing rejection of interracial solidarity was doomed to failure. "Since we are Americans the solution to our problem will not come through seeking to build a separate black nation within a nation, but by finding that creative minority of the concerned from the oftentimes apathetic majority, and together moving toward that colorless power that we all need for security and justice."[46] This quotation is telling. The creative nonwhite will open the door for a new kind of power, said King, one that is not dominated or controlled by force but by love. King recognized the strategic move invoked by Black Power, which seemed to distinguish between bad and good uses of power. The former, according to Black Power proponents, is based on individualism, acquisition, and domination; the latter espouses concern for all, social cooperation, and deliberate forms of engagement with power based on moral conscience.

The moral conscience that King invoked drove his criticisms of power and "retaliatory violence."[47] At issue for King was Black Power's attack of integration and nonviolence. Violence against white racist attacks might appeal to the ego, King suggested, but it did not address the conditions in which evil or racism emerged.

Responding to Black Power's use of rhetorical violence against colonialism, King offered a biting response to Carmichael:

> Humanity is waiting for something other than blind imitation of the past. If we want truly to advance a step further, if we want to turn over a new leaf and really set a new man afoot, we must begin to turn mankind away from the long and desolate night of violence. . . . A dark, desperate, confused, and sin-sick world waits for this new kind of man [and woman] and this new kind of power.[48]

While King criticized SNCC's turn to Frantz Fanon because of what King believed was the psychiatrist's advocacy of violence, King in fact sounds very much like Fanon. King's emphasis on a "new humanity" is very much in line with Fanon's impeccable political and psychosocial analysis in *The Wretched of the Earth*.

In a strange, possibly prophetic sense, King's criticisms of Black Power actually illuminated its subversive political strategy: its attempt to dismantle and disfigure Black "manhood," establish radical transnational solidarity, and expose the shortcomings of liberal democracy." All of this symbolized for King the fragments of a fledgling political agenda—but not an actionable, practical, or effective one.

King's problems with Fanon stem in large part from his liberal political imagination. In his article "In Pursuit of a Just Society," Robert Michael Franklin has written one of the best accounts of King's role within the political liberal tradition. As Franklin notes there, King merged "Black Christian activism and non-religious, liberal egalitarianism" to build his conception of a just society.[49] While deeply rooted in liberalism's penchant for individual rights, King was also weaned on communist criticisms of capitalism and society. These therefore informed his political imagination, but remained largely muted in his early writings and sermons. According to Franklin, "the crux of [King's] position would seem to suggest that any adequate theory of justice (or social policy) must protect the equal liberty of all citizens and provide a decent living standard for the most oppressed members of the community."[50] This underlying theory of justice underscores King's political thought throughout his early writings and sermons.

IMAGINING REVOLUTION
FROM INSIDE THE VEIL

What was Black Power's response to King's liberalism? Placing an emphasis on building a stronger Black political entity in order to achieve economic and cultural ends for self-sufficiency. During the 1967–1968 phase of Black Power, SNCC and Carmichael bandied about terms such as "revolutionary ethics" and "culture" to underscore the political agenda of Black empowerment. The shift was not only ideological but reflective of an ethical turn in Black political thought. SNCC was grappling with both political and existential questions: "Who am I?" "What shall I do?"[51] Such questions guided SNCC's internal debate and its developing radical political vision, one informed by two competing but overlapping political concerns facing Black political thought. On the one hand, meaning and application of power, humanism, and freedom consumed their debates; on the other hand, their primary weapon against oppression was Black social protest. Without adequate economic or political force, nonviolent civil disobedience seemed to be the only viable option for achieving their goal.

Black Power, however, was far more than a protest against racial and economic domination. SNCC's radical arm sought to deepen Black politics by building a political strategy in conversation with the long-standing but ignored tradition of Black internationalism. In their eyes, what Ella Baker, Frantz Fanon, and Malcolm X characterized as anti-Black racism was a violation of human rights, a fundamental crisis of what it means to be human within a capitalist system oriented in race and gender oppression.

By linking together long-standing political traditions, Black internationalism, and human rights activism, the members themselves probed existential questions otherwise overlooked by liberalism, questions of what and who we ought to be. The move here underscores SNCC's turning away from liberalism's desire to achieve equality and human dignity through political and voting rights alone to a radical, reflective understanding of—and striving toward—a freedom constituted by what some members called "humanistic nationalism." The category was never defined within the group's meetings; however, it served as a signifier for a culturally informed commitment to human rights activism.

HUMANISTIC NATIONALISM

Humanistic nationalism represented an Afrocentric response to anti-Black racism both domestically and internationally. It appears to be the link between SNCC's emphasis on transnational rights and interest in promoting cultural specificity. Whether or not the group could pursue humanistic nationalism was a contentious debate within SNCC. Some of its members questioned the appropriateness of humanistic nationalism for African Americans. Is it possible, the members H. Rap Brown and Ethel Minor asked, to pursue a nationalist appeal to Black Power while cultivating a universal call for humanistic activism? Other members imagined African American political struggles as possessing the moral philosophical fortitude to establish a humanistic agenda based on SNCC's communitarian idealism. Wise interrupted the discussion to expose the inconsistencies within this debate: How could SNCC justify building a political platform based on humanistic principles while simultaneously promoting a separatist agenda of excluding whites from the organization? "It seems to me that if we are going to have to start articulating the humanistic nationalist idea," he said, the group must grapple with the ways Black Power seems to restrict the group's interest in global human rights.

This was not the first time members had debated the merits of Black Power. Writing to James Forman on October 11, 1966, Joyce Ladner, then a doctoral student and SNCC member, expressed her concerns about Black Power and asked whether Carmichael had sufficiently defined the term. "What kind of definition do you think he will be able to give black power to keep it moderate enough and yet radical enough to keep the camps together?"[52] The ongoing quest among Blacks to develop political philosophies that serve the dual purposes of justifying one's full humanity while simultaneously fighting for political freedom are motifs within Black political thought. Wise and Ladner exposed a political conundrum rarely examined in the political literature on Black Power or within Black Power Studies: that of the role of humanism and humanistic nationalism within SNCC in particular and Black political thought in general, both of which emphasize Black cultural expression through self-love, self-determination, and economic and political independence.

As far as one can tell, SNCC's "humanistic nationalism" did not transfer into a fully-fledged strategic vision in the same way as its successful voting registration and education promotions unfolded in the South. The reason for this has everything to do with the timing of Carmichael's Black Power speech in Greenwood, Mississippi, after which SNCC members struggled to express its profound implications. As mentioned earlier, the radical arm of SNCC was steadily gaining popularity within and in terms of control of the organization. But the otherwise meticulous and strategic leaders were now forced to respond publicly to what previously had been only an internal debate.

Members grappled with a number of options as they attempted to solidify the conceptual framework of humanistic nationalism. Among them, SNCC leader H. Rap Brown called for "revolutionary ethics," a radical approach to combat political subjugation and the existential concerns often ignored in mainline Black liberal politics. Although Brown never developed this category, the category illustrates SNCC's shift away from liberalism, racial uplift ideology, and accommodationist philosophies to human rights activism.[53] The most available and politically expedient vocabulary in twentieth-century liberalism, both within Anglo-American political liberalism and African American liberalism, lacked the necessary categories or conceptual schemes to comprehend the totalities of anti-Black racism. But that did not stop them. They began imagining politics and political struggles in terms of transnational coalitions, a moving beyond primary nationalist interests (i.e., civil rights) to a broad transformative movement based on *humanistic* nationalisms. In fact, it was through a sense of humanistic nationalism and a loosely defined understanding of human rights that the left-leaning SNCC members advanced their transnational support for ending colonialism in Africa and apartheid in South Africa. With this new and developing ideology, humanistic nationalism framed, albeit mostly rhetorical, SNCC's pursuit to join alliances with Black and Brown bodies to end white supremacy throughout what they called the Third World.

Both King and Carmichael struggled to develop meaningful and substantive political strategies to understand and respond to the enduring hatred of Black peoples that translated into immeasurable legal, social, and economic barriers. The early and mid-career King pursued a pragmatic approach, one shaped by moral suasion, political efficacy, and faith in reason's ability through legislation to guide society into the full promises of democracy. Carmichael, on the other hand, retrieved Black Power both to expose the political and economic constraints of a racialized liberalism that minimized the rights available to Black citizens and drastically reduced the use of moral suasion as a political weapon.

The debate between King and Carmichael must be read alongside both Black radical politics and the Black church as a counter-public sphere. Both traditions push against the civil rights emphasis on the reformist politics of elite civil rights leaders by demanding widespread economic and political power for Blacks and their communities. On the one hand, the power imagined within the Black radical tradition would not only allow Blacks access to historically segregated institutions and publics but would also empower them with the epistemic, economic, and political resources to help dismantle and transform those very same contexts.

The tension between the leaders underscores the radical shift in politics and political vision beginning in the mid-1960s. The young, mostly urban college students and activists of SNCC were rejecting liberalism in favor of a radical political vision of Black Power, one that unabashedly condemned America as an imperial nation drowning as a result of its excesses of material- ism and racial hatred.

Like countless other sit-ins and marches, the Meredith March for Peace symbolized the embodied reaction to what remained an internal tension within the civil rights movement: the desire for rights and the need to exert self-determination. Working through this tension seems to be a fundamental cornerstone of the movement. Indeed, SNCC's first chair, Marion Barry, described the organization in 1960 as a group "seeking a com- munity in which man can realize the full meaning of self, which demands open relationships with others."[54] In sum, civil rights protests reinforced human dignity through civil disobedience. This was all about employing the politics of respectability as a tool both to expose the contradictions of American democratic ideas and to shame the self-described elitist, privileged, city on the hill. This approach established constitutional democracy and moral beliefs as being linked and central to making real the nations' liberal ideals.

By lifting the veil on the internal political squabbling in Black life, one glimpses the multidimensional nature of Black politi- cal thought occurring in the 1960s. After attempting to restore human dignity in and through acts historically confined to whites, thinkers like King and Carmichael came to realize that a singular approach to liberty and freedom would not address the constant but shifting moral problem of Blackness. Black Power exposed the weaknesses of the rights-based approach to achiev- ing human dignity.

A deep and unrelenting desire to *heal* Blacks from years of unprovoked and routine physical and psychic violence against them by whites in large part drove their fight to end legal seg-regation, racist housing laws, and exploitative labor practices, to name a few. Maybe this explains why the politics of respectabil-ity was at the forefront of the desegregation movement in the late 1950s and early 1960s, and even possibly why countless Black women and men from all socioeconomic backgrounds adored Malcolm X[55] while rejecting the Nation of Islam.

The tension between political rights and self-determination/economic independence was rarely discussed outside the veil of protection of Black churches or social groups. Outside Black communities, when King addressed (white) political or civic groups, he generally focused on rights and equality separate from Black self-determination. Carmichael sensed that there was an inconsistency in King's (early) pragmatic political rhet-oric. For Carmichael, King's strategy concentrated too heavily on appealing to the benevolence of liberal whites at the expense of creating a holistic vision of freedom and justice based on the tension between rights and (Black) *self-determination*. Carmi-chael ushered in his strategy like a thief in the night, armed with a sword aimed at mending old wounds and carving out new political imaginaries.

3

MARTIN LUTHER KING JR.'S
RELIGIOUS RADICALISM

On April 4, 1967, at the famed Riverside Church in New York City before a mostly Anglo-American audience of three thousand clergy from mainline Christian denominations and Jewish groups, Rev. Martin Luther King Jr. urged his ministerial colleagues to break their silence and to join their voices with his in condemning the U.S. government for its "perverse" participation in the Vietnam War and in calling for a swift end to the "tragic war." How could they protest racial discrimination at home while turning a blind eye to the injustices in Vietnam was the question King pondered in one of his most compelling critiques of American imperialism, "Beyond Vietnam: A Time to Break Silence."

The war grew even murkier as King examined the war's destruction among poor and Black communities in the United States At the expense of innocent Black and poor lives—the same persons denied equality and equal access at home—the nation had drafted the disenfranchised to fight a war historians would call senseless and unjustified in subsequent years. Needless to say, King grew

increasingly compelled to see the war as an enemy of the poor at home. Perhaps the more tragic recognition of reality took place when it became clear to me that the war was doing far more than devastating the hope of the poor at home. It was sending their sons and their brothers and their husbands to fight and to die in extraordinarily high proportions relative to the rest of the population.[1]

Theirs were rights that no one, including the federal government, needed to protect and sustain. But they found themselves under siege as the nation scrambled for able bodies to send to Vietnam. The disinherited and dispossessed found themselves in a foreign land, killing and destroying instead of liberating the people—and being killed. The time was now to speak in unison and to denounce unequivocally the nation and war, "beyond the prophesying of smooth patriotism to the high grounds of a firm dissent based upon the mandates of conscience and the reading of history."[2]

King joined the growing chorus of protest against his homeland, and for perhaps the first time in a public address one could hear more clearly Black Power's influence on King's political imagination. At the forefront of King's speech was a strategically necessary rebuke of empire and violence. When asked by agitated African Americans how he could condemn violent protests for social justice in America while remaining silent on the nation's violence in Vietnam, King said, "Their question hit home, and I knew that I could never raise my voice against the violence of the oppressed in the ghettos without having first spoken clearly to the greatest purveyor of violence in the world today—my own government."[3] In response, and with a clarity otherwise not witnessed before, King broke ties with political liberalism and Anglo-Christianity and articulated a wide-reaching and substantive anti-imperialist critique of the United States based on its ongoing negation of and violence against Blacks.

Anticipating some criticism from naysayers who believed a Black preacher and civil rights leader should focus much more narrowly on the "race problem," King appealed to the Black political struggle as a necessary framework for understanding his overt turn to human rights advocacy and transnational politics. According to King, the Black struggle to end *U.S.* segregation and racial exploitation symbolized a broad quest to end *all* human degradation and subjugation throughout the world. "We were convinced that we could not limit our vision to certain rights for black people, but instead affirmed the conviction that America would never be free or saved from itself until the descendants of its slaves were loosed completely from the shackles they still wear."[4] It was true: the nation could never make real its democratic aspirations as long as "it destroys the deepest hopes of men the world over." One sure way to eradicate all hope was to support a political culture and foreign policy agenda based on racial hierarchy, violence, subjugation, and alienation.

King's speech revealed the steady deterioration of the rights-based political philosophy that had long dominated his civil rights strategy to secure voting rights and abolish segregation. While many scholars and journalists have since hailed the speech as an extension of King's nonviolent philosophy, they have done so without contextualizing his address within the conceptual scheme of Black Power. "Beyond Vietnam" reflected King's growing reliance on the ideas of Black Power and its anti-imperialist and anti-war political rhetoric to highlight the contradictions and limits of American democracy.

Whether King intended it or not, the speech linked the prophetic leader to a tidal wave of criticisms of American foreign policy. But unlike other critics of the Vietnam War, King specifically linked the nation's foreign policy agenda to its racist and discriminatory laws against Blacks, as well as the violent force employed to maintain the nation's racial hierarchy. American foreign policy, then, was part and parcel of the same logic it used to build and sustain racial domination through legal codes and cultural norms.

King's political move was stunning and bold. It marked his deliberate turn away from his Christianity-centered politics of nonviolence and liberalism to a political vision informed by the Black radical tradition, most notably Black Power. As noted by the historian Nikhil Singh, King's speech "opened a bridge between past and future black radicalisms and their more expansive dreams of freedom."[5] Singh indicates that King's political shift is neither "quixotic or aberrational" but solidly rooted within the Black radical tradition in Black political thought and loosely shaping Afro-Christianity and mainline Black churches. I agree with Singh but want to extend his argument a bit more.

Also informing the radicalism emerging in King's later sermons and speeches extends back to Afro-Christianity and its inventive tradition in biblical hermeneutics. Specifically, the slave's understanding of the Bible as a "talking book"[6] fundamentally alters the encounter between the slave and Christianity. When the slave inserts herself into the "text" and "talks" back to it, she redefines her subjectivity, slavery, and Black suffering as necessary epistemic sources for understanding the human condition. The interpretive move is substantial. It initiates within Black religion, Afro-Christianity, and the Black church in particular a dialogical understanding of how African Americans should engage scripture. It is an encounter between a knowing-feeling subject and the Bible (the canonical text used by slaveholders and slave traders to justify African enslavement). The significance of the slave's interpretive invention cannot be understated. At a minimum, it assumes the scripture is alive and serves as a resource for understanding and interpreting the world at hand. Notwithstanding the dynamism of the talking-book tradition, two fundamental guiding points underscore the tradition's enduring hermeneutics: First, the reader is never locked into or confined to a singular reading of any passage for the duration of one's religious orientation; social circumstances and ongoing ecclesiastical debates and concerns will animate and inform hermeneutics and its application. Second, the reader inserts herself and community into the text both to discover and confirm God's promise to emancipate, protect and heal God's children. This is the backdrop that informs King's theological and political vision. The lessons we can learn from King are towering, and they are many. But I want to focus here on only two: First, readers can appeal to human suffering as a hermeneutical tool to expand both the limits and possibilities of retrieving scripture to comprehend and promote human flourishing in contexts of inexplicable oppression, and second, scripture can be used for life-inventive purposes, in ways that inform, repudiate, and enhance concrete political activism. I begin by looking at the conditions that encouraged King's radicalism. I then turn back to biblical hermeneutics as it is expressed in Black preaching traditions to contextualize King's theological background. Finally, I explore King's speech in more detail before turning to his understanding and use of Black suffering and the link he makes to human rights activism.

KING'S EXPANDING RADICALISM

Why did King make this move at this juncture in his life? I believe there were at least two reasons: First, Black Power fundamentally changed the landscape for both conceptualizing and executing Black politics in the United States and the Caribbean. Stokely Carmichael's Black Power speech and the growing radicalism of SNCC established an unprecedented rift between liberal integrationists and left-leaning Black activists. The rift forced Blacks to confront not only political disenfranchisement but also the psychosocial and violent dimensions of racism—specifically, the normative beliefs in Black intellectual, aesthetic, and moral inferiority. Black Power emerged as a political vision to secure legal rights and protections under the law as well as to establish a benchmark for understanding freedom as political, moral, and existential. How best to grapple with these themes vis-à-vis public policy and cultural norms grew increasingly contentious during the heyday of Black Power. Second, as King's nonviolent civil rights agenda garnered him international fame, he became increasingly comfortable in his role as a global leader of peace and nonviolence. Indeed, the winner of the Nobel Peace Prize in 1964 for his nonviolent campaign against racism increasingly imagined his leadership "beyond the calling of race or nation or creed is this vocation of sonship and brotherhood." As he said on April 4, it is "because I believe that the Father is deeply concerned especially for his suffering and helpless and outcast children [that] I come tonight to speak for them."[7] King anticipated the global magnitude of the movement long before its climax in the 1960s. To be sure, by the late 1950s King had found himself on the world stage, beginning with his trip to visit Gandhi in India and as a member of a U.S. delegation to Kwame Nkrumah's presidential inauguration in Ghana. Though King's Riverside Church address was not his first time engaging in global politics, to that point it was nonetheless his most famous public articulation of his widening political imagination, and it established a framework for his plunge into class, poverty, and race within the Poor People's Campaign.

King's increasing radicalism surfaced wholeheartedly in his Riverside speech. Thomas Jackson, in *From Civil Rights to Human*

Rights: Martin Luther King, Jr., and the Struggle for Economic Justice, persuasively argues King's radicalism is evident, albeit minimally, in his 1963 "I Have a Dream" speech and more blatant in 1965 when King's dream crumbles before his eyes. "That dream shattered when whites murdered voting rights workers in Alabama, when police battled blacks in Los Angeles, when he met jobless and 'hopeless' blacks on desperate Chicago streets, and when he saw hunger and poverty in rural Mississippi and Appalachia."[8] Fragments of his radicalism can be found in his early speeches, as far back as 1956 in an address to Alpha Phi Alpha fraternity in Buffalo, New York,[9] where he invoked his vision of the beloved community. This radical vision, which Susannah Heschel described as a moral vision woven together "by a bond rooted in a commitment to a moral demand that stands apart from the laws of the state,"[10] oriented his political activism and informed his theological commitments. In fact, his moral commitment and dogged commitment to divine justice and the Beloved Community" softened his heart to SNCC's radical arm and increasingly turned him toward Black Power.

SNCC's influence on King's political shifts is significant. A student of history and regular consumer of politics on the ground, King would have been aware of SNCC's growing radicalism. The historian Nikhil Singh acknowledges that while King was influenced by Black Power advocates, Black Power activists "had difficulty formulating coherent theoretical or programmatic approaches to transforming society."[11] This might explain why King initially held Black Power at arm's length. However, Singh seems to minimize SNCC's influence on King and its sustained protest against war in general and the Vietnam War in particular.[12] In 1966, a year before King's address, SNCC issued a public statement regarding the nation's foreign policy and its stance on Vietnam. It expressed its "right" and "responsibility" to express an opinion on foreign affairs and policy decisions made by the federal government. The organization also expressed its opposition to the nation's involvement in Vietnam for two fundamental reasons: First, it accused the nation of holding unstated clandestine reasons for its interest in the freedom of the Vietnamese people, claiming the nation neither ensured nor protected the rights of Blacks in the United States and therefore could not ensure freedom for the people in Vietnam. SNCC identified one of its members, an enlisted navy man named Samuel "Sammy" Young Jr., as a prime example of the ignored onslaught on Black life. Young was murdered in Alabama for attempting to desegregate a whites-only restroom. "The murder of Samuel Young in Tuskegee, Alabama, is no different than the murder of peasants in Vietnam, for both Young and the Vietnamese sought, and are seeking, to secure the rights guaranteed them by law. In each case the United States government bears a great part of the responsibility for these deaths."[13] Second, SNCC accused the nation of violating international law by entering into the Vietnam War. King was well aware of SNCC's expanding political strategy and probably struggled to embrace all aspects of its international platform without losing white allies. But, like the Hebrew prophets, King stood at the crossroads: condemn power or appeal to white liberals through negotiation and consensus-building. He chose the former.[14] Michael Eric Dyson notes that King's political and theological shift stemmed from his expanding "understanding of the psychology of race." Dyson writes, "Only when one believes that bigotry flows from an unconverted heart does one work to transform an opponent's soul. But when one believes, as King did, that racial sentiments are shaped by deeply entrenched ways of life, one's moral obligation is to challenge the practices that preserve racism. King was dissatisfied with the important but limited gains that his earlier work had won."[15]

BLACK PREACHING AND THE POLITICS
OF BIBLICAL HERMENEUTICS

King's radicalism was fueled by two unsuspecting Afro-Christian traditions: Black preaching and African American biblical hermeneutics. In both traditions, political action is linked to affirming the human ontology of Blacks through sacred texts in an effort to grapple with three fundamental and overlapping concerns: divine justifications for slavery, Black inferiority, and landlessness. As many scholars have already noted, the African slave trade of the mid-Atlantic stood out from other periods of human trafficking and exchange because of its basis in beliefs in the African's innate inferiority and nonhumanness. Christianity played a fundamental role in cementing these beliefs into the "afterlives" of slavery. The sociologist Orlando Patterson, in exploring the unique nature of the African slave trade, notes, "In the U.S. South there developed the last and most perfectly articulated slave culture since the fall of the Roman Empire. The religion that had begun in and was fashioned by the Roman slave order was to play the identical role eighteen hundred years later in the slave system that was to be Rome's closet cultural counterpart in the modern world."[16] If Africans were not human (as many Christians and scientists surmised), then the process of justifying their enslavement and maintaining their subhuman social standing would be easier to maintain among nonslaveholders who might otherwise object to slavery.

The Black preacher has long been known as the intermediary between the enslaver and enslaved and the private/public sectors and their Black constituencies.[17] This has been especially true of Black preachers from mainline denominations such as the African Methodist Episcopal Church and historic churches such King's Ebenezer Baptist and Harlem's Abyssinian Baptist. By nature of their proximity to power, Black preachers are often lauded by white liberals and governmental organizations for community leadership, whether the honor is deserved or not. The messy relationship between institutional power and local churches reinforces both the stature of Black preachers and the importance of linking together religion and politics within the counter-public tradition of the Black church. The latter point is crucial to understanding the political implications of Black preaching.

The speech-act or "speakerly" tradition of Black preaching strengthens, develops, and even expands shared visions of emancipation and liberation in scripture. Essentially the sermon is a dialogue or call and response between the preacher and congregation. In the shared performance and ritual Black preaching, participants embrace the long-standing truthfulness of scripture, even as the preacher pushes against and extends the interpretive boundaries of the narrative at hand. By doing so, "the Black preaching tradition . . . sets the stage for imagining and implementing shifting and expanding views of truth and authority within the Black church in particular and Black religion in general," as New Testament scholar Brad Braxton noted in a recent interview with the author of *We Testify*.

I locate Black preaching within the "speakerly" tradition, what Henry Louis Gates Jr. calls the dialogical engagement between the text and speaker, the "oral and written voices" in a given text.[18] The interpretive move establishes a highly poetic and improvisational encounter, "namely a profoundly lyrical, densely metaphorical, quasi-musical, privileged black oral tradition on the one hand, and a received but not yet fully appropriated standard English literary tradition on the other."[19] There's a performative element in the textual encounter, one that assumes prior knowledge of the accepted readings of the text, on one hand, and a cultural acceptance of hermeneutic improvisation on the other.

Within the context of this speakerly preaching tradition, ongoing and expanding interpretations of narratives in scripture create the conditions for developing transformative interpretations of sacred texts.

Alongside the speakerly tradition emerged a radical vision of the text itself. During slavery, many enslaved Africans made the Bible their own "talking book." They didn't approach the Bible to seek answers, according to the New Testament scholar Allen Callahan, but rather to "provoke . . . the development of a critical sensibility, a penchant for interrogating themselves and others. The Bible has been their license for calling things into question."[20] Thus, retrieving scripture to engage questions related to suffering, ontology, and existence transpired routinely among Black preachers during and after African slavery. Within the dialogical and performative traditions in Black preaching materialized two fundamental assumptions regarding the norms and expectations of hermeneutics: religious dogma and doctrine are living and ongoing, not sealed off from the world like dead scripture, but always to be taken up and engaged anew.

King's widening political philosophy was fundamentally cultivated and nurtured by such Black preaching. Informed by the Protestant Black church's call-and-response culture, Black preaching to King and his contemporaries was a conversation between many different actors: preacher and God, preacher and text, and preacher and congregation. The context would always shift, but the purpose of Black preaching as a dialogue between God, the preacher, and the congregation remained constant. Without a robust tradition of justifying scriptural interpretation with church doctrine—rules determined by a general body of clergy or lay people—Black preaching relied primarily on the affirmation of the congregation through call and response to determine the veracity of the claims asserted in the sermon at hand.

This type of exchange established an unprecedented understanding of hermeneutics, tradition, and authority by removing them from the supposed divine knowledge of the priest or confines of the ecclesiastical body and placing them in the hands of the people. In other words, the people—clergy and ordinary laypeople alike—could co-determine the theological appropriateness of scripture and its uses as they saw fit. This meant that the members within a congregation did not need to seek denominational approval for scriptural interpretation. The New Testament scholar Vincent Wimbush notes three significant interpretive moves among the African slaves and their interpretations of the Christian bible that underscore radical traditions of interpretation in Black religions: First, African slaves discovered when they opened scripture a "language-world,"[21] narratives, signs, and symbols through which African Americans discovered new vocabularies to articulate their historically contingent circumstances. Second, the biblical interpretations that emerged echoed theological beliefs and cultural concerns bandied about in prior communities. Third, scriptural interpretation stemmed from universally rehearsed and renarrated theological themes found in "sermons, songs, testimonies, and public addresses."[22]

James Weldon Johnson's *God's Trombones* is a fine example of hermeneutic invention in Black literary and preaching traditions. The collection of sermonic poems spans the thematic scope of the Bible, opening with "The Creation" and closing with "The Judgment Day." The eight chapters are written within what the theologian Theophus Smith calls the African American "folk preaching tradition, with its rich appropriation of biblical narrative and symbolism," which was inspired by another Black preacher Johnson heard in Kansas. When this preacher realized he was losing his audience, as Smith recounts, he closed his Bible, stepped in front of the pulpit, and spontaneously performed the talking-book tradition through preaching:

> And God stepped out on space,
> And he looked around and said:
> I'm lonely—
> I'll make me a world.
> And far as the eye of God could see
> Darkness covered everything,
> Blacker than a hundred midnights
> Down in a cypress swamp.[23]

Johnson renarrated the account to offer a richly construed texture of Black preaching and its deliberative uses of improvisation. As the narrator notes, God unfolds creation through an elaborate performance, as if God creates by molding the sun "into a shining ball" and flings "it against the darkness [,] spangling the night with the moon and stars."[24] Described with splendor and strength, God here signifies the performative style African Americans would expect from a talking-book tradition, where characters affirm and push the existing textual boundaries. The historian Gregory Carr suggests that Johnson's monumental work is designed to underscore the layered nuances of Black worship as well as grapple with existing debates regarding the nature of God in relationship to the social conditions facing African Americans. "The poems' rich language illustrates many contextual themes present within the traditional black church worship experience, humanizes the often-caricatured black preacher,"[25] and grapples with the political tensions in narratives of the Negro problem. With this extraordinary backdrop, the talking-book tradition more broadly and Black preaching in particular cultivated a nuanced and radical understanding of the Divine and sacred texts: both can be directly engaged through prayer, lament, or ecstatic worship regardless of one's standing in the community.[26]

African American biblical hermeneutics cultivated a subversive disposition toward texts, institutions, authority, power, and culture. This explains why, for instance, Black churches dating back to the early twentieth century opened their doors to non-Christian leaders including Marcus Garvey, Malcolm X, Stokely Carmichael, and Angela Davis, and continue to do so to this day—think political candidates, for instance. So, it should not be unusual or unexpected that King carried this tradition with him to Riverside Church, where he rebuked America and the liberal philosophy he desperately admired.

The dialogical nature of African American biblical hermeneutics feeds into King's political philosophy. When King exposed the weaknesses of the civil rights agenda in the Riverside address, he was in fact acting as a good Black preacher: interrogating the "text" at hand—in this case the Vietnam War—based on a reflective and dialogical engagement with his primary interlocutors—scripture, civil rights activists, Black power leaders, and pacifists.

KING AND THE GRAMMAR OF BLACK SUFFERING

By all accounts, Black preaching and African American biblical hermeneutics are exemplar case studies for examining the ongoing efforts among Blacks to reform heretofore racist American practices through the radical inclusion of *Blackness*, including a grammar of suffering within their political vocabulary. If liberalism could address the burden of ontological and sociological claims of anti-Black racism and the grammar of suffering, its ideals would eventually manifest themselves into the building blocks for establishing a truly just society. Before diving into the content of the Riverside address, it is critical to sketch out the theological canvas that nurtured King's vision, particularly the one articulated in that speech.

His increasingly defiant position was undergirded by his understanding of Black dehumanization. One way to characterize the dehumanizing experiences of *Blackness*, of *Black existence*, is to retrieve what the literary scholar Frank Wilderson calls a "grammar of suffering."[27] The provocative category draws "our attention not to how space and time are used by enfranchised and violently powerful interests, but to the violence that underwrites the modern world's capacity to think, act, and exist spatially and temporally."[28] Wilderson rejects a "up-from-slavery interpretive motif," which explores racial dominance and oppression with the assumption that slavery ended in 1865. Slavery extended itself into a discourse that was produced and informed by the "exploitation and alienation" experienced by African Americans in a world divided and dominated by racial and gender hierarchies. Indeed, Blacks come to know the world and themselves through exploitation and alienation. Embedded in the political, economic, and cultural fabric of modernity is the assumption of the inferiority of Africans, Blacks, and Blackness, which ushers in the grammar of suffering. Wilderson traces this grammar back to slavery and sees its ugly face in contemporary cinema in the United States. With this backdrop, Wilderson ponders when the social world distinguished between "Slaveness" and "Blackness" and created the cultural codes to transform "Blackness" into a signifier for beauty, intelligence, and perseverance. "How, when, where did such a split occur?"[29]

Another way to characterize the grammar of Black suffering is through the violence and negation of freedom. King's understanding of Black suffering assumes the inherent worth and humanness of the "Black." Whether or not "Slaveness" or "Blackness" are distinct and viable categories has been answered in Afro-Christianity and the tradition of the talking book. As King suggests in his Riverside address, Black suffering is the hermeneutical lens appropriated to dissect and diagnose the problem of American imperialism both at home and abroad. Through the lens of Black suffering, King's political vision encapsulated the "tragic recognition" that his own country was the greatest "purveyor of violence in the world today."[30] In his address, King reframed anti-Black racism as a form of violence that violates human dignity, and by extension human rights. The shift King made here is an indication of King's increasing radicalism and singular rejection of a voting-rights platform. His radicalism was increasingly existential—grappling with the social conditions that impede fundamental freedoms. It is constructive, a way of engaging politics through disruption, dismantling, and rebuilding frameworks in order to achieve human dignity, thus giving flesh to democracy.

King's grammar of Black suffering is redemptive and makes an appeal to hope through its interpretive hermeneutical shift. This theological commitment to hope in the midst of ongoing assaults against African Americans near the end of King's life weakened his attractiveness to Black Power activists. As implied in Carmichael's speeches and writings, without substantial power and military force, hope in the face of evil exposes its deep inadequacy for eradicating Black suffering and oppression. Hope was not needed, Carmichael insisted. Instead, the people needed to exert their political will, capture and cultivate power, and execute a political agenda based on the collective interests of the community.[31]

KING AND THE RIVERSIDE SPEECH

When King delivered his now famous address at Riverside Church, the traditional civil rights agenda was already on the decline, losing traction among the young and growing leftist Black communities. Appealing to the moral conscience of the nation and the exceptional nature of this American democracy no longer garnered the same public support it had a few years earlier. The shift away from rights was evident years earlier in the speeches of Malcolm X, a major resource to which SNCC members turned to criticize the civil rights agenda. "As the aspiration of the Black American struggle changed from 'integration' achievements to material and humanistic values, Malcolm X, the spokesman of grass roots millions, began to organize the new ideas of the masses into a concise [and] workable program, but defined the urgent need for change in direction as well."[32]

Young college students, activists, and artists were revolting against elite politicians who were focused on making pragmatic political and economic gains in the United States without criticizing and addressing U.S. imperialism and domestic tyranny. Unlike the authors Anna Julia Cooper and Paul Robeson, who protested against colonialism and advocated a transnational political agenda in the liberation of Blacks throughout the African diaspora, the domestic platform of the civil rights movement, initiated by figures such as the politician A. Phillip Randolph, made a conscious effort to restrict the political aspirations of the movement. Carmichael and scores of other activists were determined to change the course of Randolph's political agenda.

As noted earlier, King anticipated the swift changes in the movement long before anyone took notice. His final speeches and writings after the Meredith March illustrate his shifting political and moral vision. A critical point is worth noting: King came to agree with Carmichael's call to acquire power in the broadest sense of the term. In a 1967 *New York Times* essay entitled "Black Power Defined," King admitted that the movement lacked the resources and intent to change the structural powers and cultural beliefs that fueled anti-Black racism. "We must frankly acknowledge that in past years our creativity and imagination were not employed in learning how to develop power. We found a method in nonviolent protest that worked. . . . Although our actions were bold and crowned with successes, they were substantially impoverished and spontaneous."[33]

The Riverside address is a compelling mix of confessionalism and public resistance against what he called the "greatest purveyor of violence in the world today—my own government." Addressing his fellow "Americans," King explains why the antiwar movement has captured the attention of his "moral vision." Why is he against the war? First, because it's an "enemy of the poor." The nation sent its poor brothers and Black stepchildren to war-stricken lands to "die in extraordinarily high proportions relative to the rest of the population." And second, because these poor brothers and so-called Black stepchildren fought for liberties for persons overseas that they themselves had never tasted in their own homeland. This criticism evolved from King's developing view of anti-Black racism as an extension of colonialism—that is, a human rights violation. Though King's papers suggest that he recognized early in his public life the limits of liberalism, he was nonetheless torn and conflicted. On the one hand, the political expediency of voting rights and integration appealed to King; on the other hand, his longstanding global humanitarian vision resonated with Black Power's move toward economic power and international human rights activism. Blacks, he said, should not "limit our vision to certain rights for black people, but instead affirm the conviction that America would never be free or saved from itself until the descendants of its slaves were loosed completely from the shackles they still wore." For, he continued, the nation can never be saved as long as "it destroys the deepest hopes of men the world over."

Following years of internal debates and political struggle, his address seems to be the culmination of the maturing voice of a prophetic leader willing to suffer the consequences for criticizing his nation and its dominant political philosophy based on rights and equality. Raising his voice in moral protest against the U.S. empire, King now joins in solidarity with Black Power's criticism of American colonialism.

Indeed, in this address King linked racism to American imperialism in ways unimaginable prior to the formation of SNCC and Carmichael's call for Black Power. And he linked the nation's foreign policy to a deeper problem that was tied to its treatment of Blacks. This move created the context for him to redefine anti-Black racism as a violation against human rights, an approach invoked by the late Malcolm X a few years earlier. King explained his position this way:

> This is I believe to be the privilege and burden of all of us who deem ourselves bound by allegiances and loyalties which are broader and deeper than nationalism and which go beyond our nation's self-defined goals and positions. We are called to speak for the weak, for the voiceless, for victims of our nation and for those it calls enemy, for no document from human hands can make these humans any less our brothers [and sisters and siblings].

King challenges his own love affair with American democracy and his desire to get the nation to fulfill its democratic promise. He publicly critiques them in a way that threatens his livelihood, in so doing joining an international movement against his native land.

Third, King reminded the audience of the difficulty of invoking nonviolence as a political strategy in a nation bent on using violent tactics to control dissident Black and Brown voices. "Their question hit home, and I knew that I could never raise my voice against the violence of the oppressed in the ghettos without having first spoken clearly to the greatest purveyor of violence in the world today—my own government."

King used the speech to create an ethics of disclosure, one that breaks the silence we often hold; its incorporation is both an invitation to join in an ethical struggle as well as a moral burden. Why? Because it asks us to make three important moves: First, the ethics of disclosure compels us to commit to allegiances that are "broader and deeper than nationalism and which go beyond our nation's self-defined goals and positions." This is a dangerous position to take, as it calls into question the veracity of political tribalism and solidarity. Second, we are called to "speak for the weak, for the voiceless, for the victims of our nation and for those it calls 'enemy,' for no document from human hands can make these humans any less our brothers." Third, there's a responsibility to gender justice. The people most devastated by the war are women and children. King explicitly highlights this gender injustice. As the United States continued in the war, King emphasizes that the Vietnamese "know they must move on or be destroyed by our bombs. So they go, primarily women and children and the aged. They watch as we poison their water, as we kill a million acres of their crops. . . . They see the children selling their sisters to our soldiers, soliciting for their mothers."[34]

In his address, King went far beyond the ordinary religious call for nonviolent resistance and moral leadership. The pragmatically driven political activist shifted away from the civil rights movement's focus on rights and equity to a political philosophy that examined and exposed the various uses of negative liberty within American liberalism—those political actors and institutions responsible for impeding justice and democracy for all. His address is a blueprint for moving forward as a nation, a political vision that casts aside nationalism, race, and "creed" in favor of a transnational global community based on shared principles of humanism and human rights.

King's speech was an act of truth-telling. It broke the code of silence of state-sanctioned violence against people of color. The political rhetoric was a significant shift away from what the historian Peniel Joseph characterizes as the "*heroic period* of modern civil rights struggles in both public memory and historical scholarship" where it employed human bodies and moral suasion to pursue liberty and justice.[35] Henceforth King embarked upon a more militant stance against the country from which he hailed for its potential to fulfill the liberal aims of equality and justice. The militancy is draped in the tradition of Black internationalism, in which humanism and humanistic appeals of rights *and* freedom overshadow tribal interests and nationalism. This rupture from the strict political liberalism that defined much of King's early public theological vision of American democracy created the conditions for King's latent militancy to give birth to or reflect an ethical turn in his political vision. This was a far cry from his early retrieval of ethics as a duty to abstract ideals; instead, his address testified to ethics as embodied and reflected a disruption of the political norms governing American liberal philosophy. This form of truth-telling enabled King to raise critical and difficult questions regarding both the limits and possibilities of America and its narrative of exceptionalism that fueled a kind of unfettered belief among Blacks of the possibilities of justice in America.

Third, his philosophy of nonviolence is challenged by America's increasing violence both domestically and abroad. "Their question hit home, and I knew that I could never raise my voice against the violence of the oppressed in the ghettos "without" acknowledging the ongoing violent attacks against African Americans by whites and state actors such as white police officers." But he remains unwaveringly nonviolent, as his theological commitments and public calling, he says, "take me beyond national allegiances."

The political shift King invoked here was remarkable in two important ways. First, this public condemnation of American race relations and foreign policy showed his support of Black Power's turn away from domestic politics to Black internationalism, or global politics. In fact, months before Carmichael's 1966 Black Power speech, King and Carmichael spent many hours debating the strengths and limitations of (re)invoking a Black internationalist agenda in the civil rights political platform during a time when segregation continued to impair voting rights.[36] Prior to King's Riverside address, he stood firmly against any political effort that would divert attention away from the domestic racial crisis.

Second, King's speech follows the late Malcolm X's efforts to frame anti-Black racism as a human rights violation that the United Nations needed to address. Black Power was increasingly weighing on King's theological vision of America as the promised land awaiting the rights-bearing children of Jim Crow. What were already rifts in his liberal model of justice seemed to crumble under the weight of expanding resistance against and violence toward nonviolent reform in the nation. Torn asunder on the one hand by liberalism's demand for political expediency and social cooperation and on the other by the Black radical left's demand for economic and political power for *all* people of color in colonialism or apartheid, King's riveting speech is his best-faith effort to piece together the tragic nature of Black life into a coherent political philosophy.

While I do not suggest that King wholeheartedly rejected the American jeremiad, I do think that his tepid acceptance of Black Power's criticism of American imperialism diminishes the jeremiad model within his increasingly internationalist vision of justice, freedom, and democracy—an internationalist vision I explore more fully with reference to Israel in chapter 6.

King was widely criticized for his address. An April 7 *New York Times* editorial condemned him for asserting that America's violent treatment of Blacks set the stage and politically justified America's war in Vietnam: "This is a fusing of two public problems that are distinct and separate," opined the editorial. "By drawing them together, Dr. King has done a disservice to both. The moral issues in Vietnam are less clear-cut than he suggests." The editorial invokes a thin conception of liberalism to support its argument: that race is socially constructed, a local matter that is easily solved by expanding equal rights to all, whereas human rights is universal and unabashedly apolitical in its moral vision of peoplehood. Hence, human rights as a political strategy muddies the domestic racial problem because it infers that anti-Black racism can't be solved by achieving rights alone. Instead, structural economic, social, and moral matters must also be interrogated.[37]

To be sure, King's address is a cautionary tale about what happens when you push the boundaries of political liberalism. Empire always strikes back, and the steady fragmentation—and some say decline—of the civil rights agenda never recovered after the movement's shift to human rights activism. Maybe this is the price of claiming and striving toward human dignity— that the radical imagination we invoke may cost us our worldly possessions—even our life.

Nonetheless, his speech offered a corrective to the nation's problem of moral egalitarianism by disentangling human rights and dignity from political justice. As Charles Mills aptly notes in "Dark Ontologies: Blacks, Jews and White Supremacy," political liberalism is firmly committed to imagining a world of "abstract individuals equally deserving of respect and characterized by freedom, equality and independence."[38] In a political system held together by white racial privilege, Black inferiority, and a complete emphasis on the male gender, human dignity and respect can only be embodied within those who are perceived to be white males, or those who knowingly and actively choose whiteness as a political ideology. Without political or economic power, according to the Jamaican activist Marcus Garvey, African Americans as a group cannot obtain respect or human dignity. Individual Blacks can become the exception through education and wealth, but the group will remain locked in a subordinate moral and social class known as a "dark ontology." By reimagining human dignity and respect beyond the category of rights, King dismantles, at least rhetorically, the racial contract and normative bias against nonwhites within the nation's dominant political philosophy, that is, political liberalism.

Two additional themes in his talk are worth noting: power and American imperialism. King does not imagine power abstractly. He recognizes and speaks about how power has been abused and mishandled both domestically and abroad, and especially when addressing Black and Brown bodies. His emphasis on power consequently is not aimed at Black and Brown bodies squeezing into an American dream; instead, it is designed to expand political and social opportunities for all, especially those in foreign lands such as Palestine and South Africa. This shift away from the familiar, domestic racial politics, to unfamiliar and sometimes unseen lands, is noteworthy. This concern to address "self-care," freedom, and human dignity reflects the ethical turn.

King's radicalism was animated by the violent conditions under which Blacks struggled to obtain freedom and justice. These conditions were a reminder that the struggle for rights could not be disentangled from the quest to achieve some sense of humanity and human dignity. To this end, politics and political action would always mean something more than securing rights or economic or political power. What was political also tackled the question, as Lewis R. Gordon asserts in *Existentia Africana*, of who and what I ought to be, and this question embodied ethics and the ethical dilemmas facing Black politics. The question of political affiliation or political ideology would inevitably return to the problem of existence and whether or not it would be affirmed and supported by the ever-changing or evolving notion of Blackness and the Black community, what some call identity politics.

When King compelled the nation to hear the "enemy's point of view, to hear his questions, to know his assessment of ourselves," he was invoking an ethical turn. By urging those in power both to hear the other and to "see the basic weaknesses of our own condition," King challenged the reason-driven claims of deliberation that adjudicate quibbles based on agreeable reasons without ever establishing the conceptual space for self-criticism. As a way of reconfiguring power and power relations, King's deliberative model is compelling.

King attempted to reconcile this tension between traditional civil rights politics and the Black Power movement by disentangling human dignity from political justice. In other words, voting rights and citizenship were no longer the primary benchmarks for denoting human dignity. By reimagining human dignity beyond the category of rights, he exposes, at least rhetorically, the limits of a political philosophy that is framed by an abstract model of equal opportunity without any regard for the *truths* of our lived and competing histories.

THE AFTERMATH OF BREAKING SILENCES

In the midst of the turmoil created by his Riverside address, King's moral vision and faith deepened, even as the foundation of his Christian identity began to change. He now saw himself as a disciple rather than a prophet. He tried to give flesh to John 14:12 "I tell you the truth, anyone who believes in me will do the same works I have done, and even greater works, because I am going to be with the Father." His messages grew increasingly radical, and attempted, consciously or otherwise, to give flesh to the Quaker belief that God is within all of us. He was less a voice proclaiming God's judgment against the nation and more a witness to God's power awaiting those who were willing to return to God. And for him this return to God is clearly political and pragmatic. Unlike St. Augustine's interior ascent to God, King's return is one that led him into the trenches, and his message transgresses national, racial, and religious boundaries. "Indeed, his last few years of public ministry were consumed by his passionate struggles for global peace and justice. Moreover, his last book concludes with this reflection on 'the World House,' his vision of the whole of humanity living as a single family in one house, the world."[39] Returning to God, for King at least, involved opening oneself up to discovering God in new places, even as his very own theological foundations were under attack.

King's radicalism appealed to humanism, and subsequently incorporated three important moves: first, what I call the *disclosure of the familiar*. By turning a critical eye to what is politically or socially familiar, moral agents gain insight into the latent and emerging cultural norms and assumptions governing their political views and theological commitments. This insight compels one to consider allegiances that are "broader and deeper than nationalism and which go beyond our nation's self-defined goals and positions." This is a dangerous, albeit necessary, position to take, especially for historically marginalized groups. For they are most dependent on the magnanimity of those they may insult.

Second, the disclosure of the familiar fosters *testimonies of lament*—public articulations of how the weak, marginalized, and disposed fare in our liberal society. In a theological sense characterized by King, it is a calling to "speak for the weak, for the voiceless, for the victims of our nation and for those it calls 'enemy,' for no document from human hands can make these humans any less our brothers." Testimonies of lament make an interesting intervention in public deliberations and what we call deliberative democracy: the articulation of sorrow as a necessary political expression or vocabulary.

Third, the disclosure emerges from a *moral conscience*, one informed by history and circumscribed in tradition and culture. Within this framework, moral conscience is neither based on cultural relativism nor a historical perspective; instead, moral conscience is the signification of the ongoing interrogation of the moral wisdom and moral inquiry of one's inherited culture as well as the overarching political ethos of the broader society.

INTERROGATING THE POLITICS OF RESPECTABILITY AND RACIAL UPLIFT

King's radicalism answers the moral, religious, and political concerns left unaddressed within the strict categories of Black liberalism and Black Power. These concerns surface in the quest to achieve human dignity. Many writers, including Frederick Douglass and Maria Stewart, suggest that full participation within American political life is one way to achieve human dignity. This is true. But what such writers ignore is the degree to which linking human dignity to the state might impede Black freedom, especially given the inconsistency of America's legal history in protecting Blacks from political, social, and economic violence. Earlier traditions, such as the politics of respectability and racial uplift, create the conditions for imagining and inserting the ethical turn as they emphasize human dignity both in and outside the parameters of the state.

Evelyn Brooks Higginbotham appeals to the category to describe the twentieth-century "religious-political" message of Black women educators, philanthropists, and civil leaders within the Black Baptist church. In conversation with racial uplift theory, these women resisted normative views of Black women as "hapless," lazy, and ignorant by establishing a tradition of reform within Black communities. Largely achieved by establishing schools and social agencies, these women employed a "discursive effort of self-representation, of re-figuring themselves individually and collectively. That effort of self-representation was an immense one, stretching well beyond the limited context of their relationship with Black Baptist men and white Baptists."[40] Black women's resistance "to the social structures and symbolic representation of white supremacy may be characterized as the 'politics of respectability' " which embodied a deep political dimension.[41] It was political to the extent that it supported political protest such as "petitions, boycotts and verbal appeals to justice" as it empathized "manners and morals." Keep in mind a critical point: the politics of respectability "assume a fluid and shifting position."[42] The politics of respectability is a dynamic tradition, one that expands and reimagines itself as new social circumstances emerge.

At issue for many contemporary Black feminists and Womanists is the tradition's reliance on "manners and morals," a reflection of its reliance on racist and sexist Victorian ideals of gender, race, and sexuality. I note the criticism. I also disagree with Higginbotham on one point: she argues that the "assimilationist leanings" of these Black women compelled Blacks to embrace the "dominant society's norms of manners and morals." But I wonder if what Higginbotham and her critics decry as acceptance is a mere performance of Victorian "womanhood" and does not equate to a wholehearted acceptance of Victorian ideals at the expense of *Blackness* in all of its many manifestations. In a strict interpretive sense, the embodied Victorian aesthetics, cultural norms, and social values symbolize to the contemporary reader a subtle symbol of Black self-hatred. To be sure, the colorism that emerged from this tradition within many social organizations, which privileged light-skinned over dark-skinned Blacks, is a strong historical reason for rejecting any political efforts to reclaim the politics of respectability in the twenty-first century. But if one reads the politics of respectability through the lens of the counter-public and the talking book tradition, then a radical vision of "Black genius" emerges from the tradition. The Victorian ideals under attack today are some of the very same traditions that informed and shaped activists such as Fannie Lou Hamer, Aretha Franklin, and Coretta Scott King. Adorning themselves in Victorian or middle-class dress and invoking certain respectable speech acts did not always lead to a displacement of Blackness. Instead, it was an ethical turn, an acknowledgment of empire, a way of performing respectability for all kinds of reasons, including safety, convenience, etc. But especially within the counter-public of the Black church, these women consistently transgressed the boundaries of respectability through intentional and subconscious acts of resistance. For Fannie Lou Hamer, she appropriated middle-class attire without impeding the epistemic value of the Negro spirituals and Black preaching. By invoking "This Little Light of Mine" during social protests, Hamer transformed how Black bodies are deployed in the public. Such transformed public bodies are almost always a vehicle through which song invokes the religious character of protest, a way of inserting one's subjectivity or humanness within the public sphere. Likewise, the Black Baptist church that nurtured Aretha Franklin's fledgling voice was not a space of Black radicalism. Her father preached traditional messages of racial self-help and uplift. However, those messages did not destroy her soul. Somehow the ideals of middle-class America were performed but without preventing her radical subjectivity from surfacing.

What disrupts the force of the politics of respectability is the dogged pursuit of subjectivity, of humanness, in an effort to pick up the pieces of one's fragmented life. This striving toward wholeness is deeply political for it symbolizes the routine and constant ways in which Black life resists and rejects attempts to annihilate Black bodies by demonizing the flesh and destroying their interiority. King, like the Black women Higginbotham explores, performed Victorian sensibilities for all kinds of reasons, but this did not prevent him or them from reassembling Blackness for the sake of rewriting the norms of what it means to be human. Dyson persuasively shows King's role in the movement is unique, in part, due to his critical appropriation of Black suffering as a tool for detangling static moral sensibilities and normative (anti-Black) commitments. "He was above all [the movement's] most popular—then its most misunderstood, and finally, its most prophetic—symbol, a man whose willingness to burn bridges in order to bring justice is nearly unparalleled in American history."[43] King compelled the nation to see itself not as an isolated nation of individuals but as participants in a "world-wide fellowship that lifts neighborly concern beyond one's tribe, race, class and nation [to] a call for all-embracing and unconditional love for all men."[44]

4

MALCOLM X AND THE SPIRIT OF
HUMANISTIC ACTIVISM

On April 3, 1964, in the midst of a contentious debate on the desegregation of Cleveland's public schools, the Cleveland chapter of the Congress of Racial Equality invited Malcolm X, one of the nation's most popular activist-intellectuals, to address a public symposium on education alongside Louis E. Lomax, the accomplished journalist and author. Speaking nearly a month after his resignation from the Nation of Islam following his censure by the Honorable Elijah Muhammad for controversial statements regarding the assassination of U.S. President John F. Kennedy, the thirty-eight-year-old Malcolm X stood behind the pulpit of Cory Methodist Church, the largest Black congregation in Cleveland, and articulated the political philosophy of his newly formed organization, the Muslim Mosque, Inc.[1] This ecumenical organization was designed to promote what the former national spokesperson for the Nation of Islam called a "new" civil rights agenda. "The entire civil-rights struggle needs a new interpretation, a broader interpretation,"[2] he had said.

Malcolm X maintained that giving Blacks the psychic, political, and economic tools for individual and group liberation, as Muslim Mosque sought to do, was a far more substantive goal

than what could be achieved by the pragmatic and thin political agenda of the traditional civil rights movement. He thought
the latter focused primarily on securing voting rights and
securing integration. Over time, his criticism of the civil rights
agenda had weakened. In an unusual shift in political perspective, though Malcolm X acknowledged in his address the need
for constitutionally protected rights for all citizens, he implied
that securing those political rights at the expense of acquiring
individual and group power was a grave mistake. Referring to
legislative roadblocks impeding the passing of federal civil rights
legislation, Malcolm X criticized the established Negro leadership for its naive belief in American goodwill:

> I'm not anti-Democrat, I'm not anti-Republican. I'm not anti-
> anything. I'm just questioning their sincerity, and some of the
> strategy that they've been using on our people by promising them
> promises that they don't intend to keep. . . . That's why, in 1964, it's
> time now for you and me to become more politically mature and
> realize what the ballot is for; what we're supposed to get when we
> cast a ballot; and that if we don't cast a ballot, it's going to end up
> in a situation where we're going to have to cast a bullet. It's either
> the ballot or the bullet.[3]

In an effort to draw attention to his underlying new political
agenda, here Malcolm X made a hyperbolic distinction between
the ballot and the bullet. Though overblown, the distinction
helpfully exposed the civil rights movement's lack of a theory
of freedom and power. Indeed, nearly three decades before the
political theorist Iris Marion Young exposed the failure of dis-
tributive justice to account for social and cultural phenomena
in shaping political agency in her *Justice and the Politics of Difference*, Malcolm X identified white supremacy as the primary

source of Black political and economic immobility and the reason for American democracy's inherent "hypocrisy" and imminent demise. To a large extent, Malcolm X emphasized, the right to vote had not translated into significant political and economic milestones for Blacks, especially the poor from urban areas. "All [the Democrats did] when they got to Washington was [to] give a few big Negroes big jobs. . . . That's camouflage, that's trickery, that's treachery, window-dressing."[4]

In his effort to illustrate such reliance on a narrowly construed rights-based agenda, Malcolm X admonished Blacks to seize their existing power, both social and financial, in order to establish economic, political, and psychological independence without seeking white validation or relying on white benevolence. Though his call for Black independence was not novel, the direction of his vision—toward a human rights political agenda—was noteworthy. "Civil rights means you're asking Uncle Sam to treat you right. Human rights are something you are born with. Human rights are your God-given rights."[5] Identifying anti-Black racism as a violation of human rights was a clever move. It also aligned Black political struggle in the United States with movements across the globe designed to end imperialism and racial injustice.

In what would become one of his most popular speeches, "The Ballot or the Bullet," Malcolm X outlined the general framework for interpreting his political and religious commitments following his 1964 departure from the Nation of Islam. This speech is one of Malcolm X's more comprehensive accounts of Black nationalism, which emphasized the traditional tenets of Black nationalist rhetoric: economic empowerment, self-help, and individual piety. "The political philosophy of Black nationalism means that the Black man should control the politics and the politicians in his own community; no more. The Black man in the Black community has to be reeducated into the science of politics so he will know what politics is supposed to bring him in return."[6] The science of politics was designed to complicate the traditional boundaries of American racial political discussions by incorporating human rights and ethics into debates on justice and democracy. Malcolm X's bold articulation and reframing of Black nationalism was a significant move. According to political scientist Frederick C. Harris, the speech represented Malcolm X's vision of an "independent Black politics [that] would shape perspectives on Black political life for decades."[7] Harris astutely links Malcolm X to a broader Black radical tradition within African American political thought, dating back to Martin Delany, W. E. B. Du Bois, and Ida B. Wells. I suggest that Malcolm X was far more invested in reconstituting democracy as a global concept and practice than in establishing an independent Black political movement circumscribed by American domestic politics.

Malcolm X's religious thought and political imagination underscore a radical politico-ethical tradition that speaks to a fundamental but neglected aspect of American democracy—namely, the idea that democracy cannot flourish without a radical (individual and collective) ethics. The necessity of such an ethics beckons us to consider the limits of moral agency and the degree to which, if at all, political actors can exercise and embody liberty, rights, and freedom within a white supremacist context. For Malcolm X, American democracy is unrealizable unless it can give an account of human finitude, or more specifically address the extent to which the *moral problem of Blackness* hinders the nation at the political and cultural level from imagining Blacks as "human" and therefore deserving of rights and freedom.[8] Interested in more than building another male-centered, Black independent movement, Malcolm X yearned, at least implicitly, to establish a political tradition in and through which Black bodies could heal and define themselves outside white supremacist constructions of Blackness, not only in the United States. In the absence of political, economic, and military power, securing political rights for African Americans would depend on white benevolence. Instead, Malcolm X pleaded with African Americans to define their political movement as a human rights struggle.

The effort to embody and execute such human freedom among a disenfranchised people raises two questions Lewis R. Gordon invokes in his humanistic philosophy, one existential- ist and one ethical: "Who am I?" and "What ought I to do?" Malcolm X's response was that the "ought" question should be understood from the perspective of the "victims" of American democracy: African Americans. Through this hermeneutical lens, standing from behind the veil of Blackness, Malcolm X not only introduced to the world the ignored concerns of the Black working class. He also generated in his late-career speeches an epistemic template by which a radical vision of human rights activism and ethics might be established.[9]

Malcolm X's agenda illumines a broader political narrative within Black Power—that of humanistic activism. Humanism in this context is a subjectivist turn, a move away from solidarity based on broadly conceived norms of community, liberalism, and liberal democracy. Three subtexts are woven into this humanism: first, the heretical subject as transgressing racial binaries and cul- tural borders; second, the conjurer or communal conjurer empha- sizing community or communal power over and against solidarity; and finally, the subversive priest, one who is committed to tradi- tion and at the same time always questioning norms and values.

These three (political) roles grew from two important aspects of the Black religion: the Bible as a talking book, and the preacher as conjurer, mediator, and healer. As a symbol, the Black church—and by extension its practices and models—was everywhere, including in politics, even when the people did not articulate or express a belief in Jesus or Christianity. Rhetorically,

Carmichael, Angela Davis, and others took on the rhetorical style of the Black preacher. Black preaching exhortation and the hermeneutical approach to scripture represent what Anthony Pinn calls the "non-written text(s)" that shape Black discourse and religious symbolism. This move reflects a kind of "humanistic corrective to theories of salvation, to a perspective on ethics highlighting Harriet Tubman, Henry David Thoreau, and Frederick Douglass, and concludes with a strategy for ritualizing ordinary life that anticipates current humanist community and secular 'church' activities."[10]

These nonwritten texts found a home in Black politics and political thought, making it difficult to find space within Anglo-American liberal philosophy and liberalism. Such politics framed equal opportunity and equal access in humanistic or existential terms tied to human dignity and human flourishing. This created a deep and shifting spirituality in Black Power, one with Afro-Christian roots but built upon Black faith in resistance and struggle as necessary prerequisites for human freedom. This political spirituality is built on three thinkers—Frantz Fanon, Ella Baker, and Malcolm X—to whom we turn in sequence.

FANON

Frantz Fanon's imprint on twentieth-century political philosophy and his role in shaping Black radical traditions throughout the African diaspora in the 1960s and 1970s is undeniable. Black activists and intellectuals found refuge in his writings, where Blackness was made visible, was embodied, and was cultivated into an epistemic resource for mapping revolutionary responses to anti-Black racism, colonialism, gender, and sexuality. Stokely Carmichael, the chief architect of the Black Power movement in the United States, routinely referred to Fanon's writing in his public speeches on Black Power, and for many others in the United States and throughout the African diaspora, Fanon's writings were read and discussed as living scriptures. In fact, Fanon's work, including *Black Skin, White Masks* and *The Damned of the Earth*, stirred transnational liberation movements among subjugated peoples and their political efforts to end colonialism and apartheid and segregation.

Fanon's broad appeal stems in part from how precisely he dissected race within the subtext of the body and colonial domination, and through the lens of psychoanalysis, sexuality, and to some extent Marxism. Through his writings, Black subjugation emerged not only as political and economic injury to a colonialized and racialized people; it also manifested itself in and through the body, and that subjugation and injury was based on normative beliefs in the moral, intellectual, and aesthetic inferiority of black bodies in particular and of blackness in general. For such reasons, like Du Bois's *The Souls of Black Folk*, Fanon's approach captured the political and moral imagination of the African diaspora. It revealed the tragic nature of Black existence under colonial rule and white domination.

Retrieving the body as central to the narrative of black subjectivity is critical for understanding Fanon and his significance in philosophy and Africana studies. As Lewis R. Gordon argues brilliantly in *What Fanon Said: A Philosophical Introduction to His Life and Thought*, Fanon lifts Black subjectivity from the epistemic sphere of "experience" or "pure exteriority" and places it within the realm of embodied knowledge with an "inner life" capable of producing knowledge. It is a form of knowledge, writes Gordon, that requires a "renewed understanding of human possibilities" based on a "conception of radical criticism that challenges the dominance of philosophy as the ultimate critical theory and arbiter."[11]

In *Black Skin, White Masks*, Fanon described to his reader the time a young white boy called him *nigger* as he stepped upon a train's platform. The "force of language froze Fanon in his tracks," writes Gordon, and created a moment of piercing reflection upon the social nature of blackness.[12] Though he was in medical school pursuing a career in psychiatry at the time of the encounter, his training had not prepared him to address the psychosocial dynamics of Blackness. For the first time, it appears, Fanon could see and feel the social ontology of Blackness: how the cultural perceptions and demonization of Blackness preceded his existence, erasing his individuality and collapsing Fanon into the category of the "problem," the *Black*. "The idea is to imagine being wholly taken over, seized, in the presence of the object. What is rich about the example is that the seizure, so to speak, is also an act of seizing; the boy's experience of being ensnared, dried up, and laid out in a world of ice-cold exteriority."[13] The encounter left Fanon facing an ethical dilemma: he could dismiss the boy's comments as an innocent moment that said more about his individual family and social location than of his own inclination, or he could embrace the moment as real and as how society sees Blacks.

By choosing to interrogate the child's racism, and his response to it, Fanon discloses what many others had stumbled over but ignored in their exhaustive efforts to understand the *nature* of anti-Black racism: black subjectivity as possessing an interiority, an inner life. "Fanon announces the experience of a world that denies his inner life; he examines this supposed absence *from the point of view of his inner life*. The paradox of black experience is thus raised: Black *experience* should not exist since blacks should not have a point of view."[14] Gordon's insight into Fanon's thought is novel: black bodies matter, and not because of any constitutionally protected right; instead, they matter because they are in possession of knowledge and capable of producing new epistemic resources for (re)imagining and transforming oppressive social contexts.

Gordon's examination of Fanonian interiority places the thinker alongside W. E. B. Du Bois, another major thinker who imagined Black subjectivity as possessing knowledge and consciousness of the world through his formulation of double consciousness. As Gordon put it, the "interplay of ironic dimension of sight and thought of doubled doubling" are critical hallmarks of Fanon's thought.[15] Instead of describing the crisis of souls as rooted in what Du Bois characterized as identity, Fanon described it as a problem emerging from desire. "By adding the dimension of what blacks want, Fanon raises and expands the question of the subjective life of blacks, of black consciousness, that parallels the Freudian question of women—What do women want?"[16] The insertion of desire is "prereflective and reflective." According to Fanon, any investigation into Black life requires what he called "ontogenic" (the individual subject), "phylogenic" (based on the species), and "sociogenic" (that which emerges within the social context) approaches. Both Du Bois and Fanon struggled to construct a "critical consciousness," but their approaches, Gordon suggests, diverge.[17] One wonders, however, if Du Bois's yearning to invent a "truer" self from the collision in double consciousness stems from an interior desire to acquire, replace, and insert a political and erotic power over whites, especially white men.

Still, Fanon is distinctively unapologetic in his biting criticisms of Freudian-based psychoanalysis of sex and sexuality. Indeed, Fanon illumines in our language the "failure of a special kind, that which emerges from the retreat from the public sphere of language to the supposed private sphere of sexual intimacy."[18] What Freudians ignore, says Gordon, is that one cannot "escape the social reality principle of antiblackness through a loving whiteness."[19] This does not foreclose interracial relationships, but it does highlight the pathology that emerges when the "basis of the liaison" is rooted in the intoxication with whiteness.

Frantz Fanon was born in 1925 on the Caribbean island of Martinique and died in 1961. He served in World War II, attended medical school in Lyon, France, and later supported the Algerian resistance movement. *The Damned of the Earth* is one of Fanon's most important works, if not the most visible text among social activists and intellectuals. Written at age thirty-five, and in a mere ten weeks, the book grapples with cultural and political implications of colonialism and offers a vision for imagining human existence beyond white subjugation. In his interpretation of the text, Gordon focuses on the misreading among scholars and activists of Fanon's call for revolutionary violence. Gordon is clear: any disruption to the social conditions in colonialism and apartheid, for instance, demands an individual and collective struggle that is violent by virtue of its disruption to the social order. This kind of revolutionary violence creates the conditions for embodying freedom. "Although one's liberty license, or absence of constraints could be handed over by another, it is the struggle for liberation that actually engenders one's freedom," he says.[20] Indeed, revolution is the only way toward freedom and liberation. Reformist politics, which may, for instance, assume liberation and social justice can be acquired by replacing whites with Black and Brown bodies, fails to understand oppression and its systemic role in reinforcing itself both among the colonized and colonizer. Gordon summarizes the point aptly: "Eliminating colonial occupation is not identical with achieving independence."[21]

Fanon's recognition of colonialism's wide reach, from material resources to the consciousness of the colonized, reflects the burden of ethics that fuels his thoughts. Gordon teases out this point in his analysis of Fanon's writings. The double consciousness of the colonized, for instance, emerges in Fanonian thought as a struggle "for the ethical to emerge, for ethics and morality, proper, are relationships between human being or in terms of demands placed on living in a human world."[22] Within this context, it is not surprising that Fanon ends with a prayer directed at humankind and designed to transform the ethical burden into human action. "Although not *the* universal, because of the fundamental incompleteness at the heart of being human, the paradox of reaching beyond particularity is the simultaneous humility of understanding the expanse and possibility of reality and human potential."[23] This is the prayer Fanon offers to the subjugated: the awakening and subsequent embodiment of a new kind of humanism.

BAKER AND HUMANISTIC ACTIVISM

Our second thinker, Ella Baker, the political philosopher Joy James calls a "'brilliant strategist'. . . . Her 'organizational work' expanded U.S. democracy as well as helped to redefine and radicalize the roles of intellectuals and activists in the civil rights era."[24] Baker's politics and ethical leanings emerge from "her upbringing in Christian service," Du Bois's Talented Tenth, and the Black Baptist Missionary Movement.[25] She internalized from her New York organizing in the 1930s a radical and progressive political ideology and praxis that emphasized "deliberative politics, non-hierarchical decision making, and participatory democracy." Her ideal leader would "listen, facilitate, share, and lead in equal measure when appropriate, but most importantly, always remember that he or she was firstly a member of the group."[26]

Humanistic ethics is embedded, for instance, in Malcolm X's effort to rally African leaders to bring before the United Nations human rights violations against the United States for condoning more than "four hundred years" of violence and discrimination against African Americans. This ethical framework emerged in his 1964 address "To Mississippi Youth," where he argued that desegregation had nothing to do with "moral enlightenment or moral awareness" but stemmed from global pressure: "No, the only time that cycle [of segregation] was broken even to a degree was when world pressure was brought to bear on the United States government. They didn't look at us as human beings— they just put us into their system and let us advance a little bit farther because it served their interests."[27]

Moral suasion, as Malcolm X indicated, would not help end Black oppression if African Americans were not human, and if they were not human, they were not redeemable. Another form of critical reflection was needed, a discourse or practice that would interrogate racial injustice transnationally. Though Malcolm X did not explicitly name ethics as a discursive site for interrogating Black subjugation, his move toward framing racial injustice in the United States as a matter of human rights depends on the implementation of ethical practices at the individual and group level that foster and sustain critical reflection and creative exchange.

The ethical framework in Malcolm X's writings becomes more apparent after his departure from the Nation of Islam and subsequent iconic role in etching out the terrain of post–civil rights Black nationalism not as a reinvention but as a reframing of three important epistemic resources he drew on throughout his intellectual and spiritual life: Black women's radicalism, religious ecumenism, and a Black working-class ethos.[28] Though not always illuminated by the activist-intellectual in his public speeches and in the scholarship of the mostly male interpreters of Malcolm X's thought, these resources are critical to understanding his deepening pan-African perspective. It is unlikely that Malcolm X would have discovered the intellectual narratives, spiritual resolve, and courage needed to recast Black nationalism by incorporating human rights as a deliberate extension of political freedom if he had focused strictly on "manhood" and "African nationality" without forging a link to Black feminist thought, religion, and the Black working class.[29]

Though I believe Malcolm X's move is novel, some leading historians disagree with my position. Wilson Jeremiah Moses, for instance, in his prolific literary analysis of the jeremiad in African American religious and political traditions, resists identifying Malcolm X's interest in human rights as unique or reflecting a creative development in his political thought. Instead, according to Moses, Malcolm X's motivation for "abandon[ing] civil rights" emerges, in part, from an African American intellectual tradition among writers and activists "who had internationalized their struggle by lecturing abroad on the defects of American democracy."[30] According to Moses, the "followers of this tradition had hoped to profit from the moral vulnerability of a nation self-conscious of its destiny as a 'City on a Hill.'"[31]

I agree with Moses, at least partially. Malcolm X's move did represent a return to a radical Black political tradition that predated the civil rights movement, but I disagree with Moses's suggestion that leftist thinkers like Malcolm X were attempting to exploit the nation's "moral vulnerability" at a time when the world had grown increasingly suspicious of America's international political endeavors. Malcolm X was unabashed in his position on America's moral standing: the country was amoral and could not muster sufficient evidence to the contrary. As early as 1961 in a speech delivered at the Harvard Law School, Malcolm X called America "wicked" and claimed it was on the verge of experiencing God's wrath for its treatment of Blacks. "We are living in the Day of Judgment right now. Our American slave master must answer to God, the judge. God is striking this country with tornadoes, storms, floods, rain, hail, snow; and terrific earthquakes are yet to come."³² Had Malcolm X continued to appeal to apocalyptic rhetoric and theological reasons for America's "decline," Moses's argument would be justified. But by all accounts, Malcolm X's conversion to orthodox Islam and growing interest in African independence from colonial rule, which began when he started traveling to Africa and the Middle East beginning in 1959, was far more deliberate than Moses depicts. For instance, a year prior to his censuring, Malcolm X began articulating in his public speeches the need for African American solidarity with Africans and grappling with African American social and economic power as necessary resources for achieving freedom, especially for those committed to an integrationist agenda. The move is subtle but nonetheless noteworthy. Malcolm X remained committed to African American independence within the context of the Nation of Islam's theology of separatism. However, he began expressing nontheological reasons to justify the Nation of Islam's position. In his 1963 speech, "Twenty Million Black People in Political, Economic, and Mental Prison," Malcolm X's primary objections to integration were political and economic reasons, not simply theological ones. The move offers a glimpse into Malcolm X's increasing intellectual frustration with Nation of Islam's theology, which was primarily focused on separatism without any critical attention to international politics and capitalism's role in fostering economic and racial inequality. The religious and political positions of Malcolm X after his departure from the Nation of Islam had been developing several years prior to his split with his spiritual father and community. However, after he started his own organization, he grew increasingly confident in his new beliefs. Malcolm X's expanded religious and political perspectives were intentional and increasingly guided by his emerging ethical imagination.

That ethical imagination stems from two epistemic narratives from Malcolm X's biography and inform my understanding of the role of humanistic ethics within his thought: his parents' Black nationalist religious and political teachings and his relationship with Black feminists. Malcolm X grew up in a religiously ecumenical home among family members who were deeply committed to Black nationalism. His father, Earl Little, was a Baptist preacher and staunch supporter of Marcus Garvey's popular Universal Negro Improvement Association (UNIA). His mother, Louise Little, was also active in the UNIA and introduced Malcolm X to global culture and politics and influenced his worldview. Fluent in five languages, she acquainted her children with French and Caribbean literature, emphasizing their Caribbean heritage in their upbringing.[33] In "Black Popular Culture and the Transcendence of Patriarchal Illusions," Barbara Ransby and Tracye Matthews maintain that Malcolm X's political organizing was undergirded by "grassroots women organizers, who were the very backbone of groups like SNCC [and the] Mississippi Freedom Democratic Party" and who were heavily involved in articulating and executing political positions.[34]

From Black feminists, Malcolm X learned a great deal about Western imperialism, African history, and socialism. In "'If You're in a Country That's Progressive, the Woman Is Progressive': Black Women Radicals and The Making of the Politics and Legacy of Malcolm X," Erik S. McDuffie and Komozi Woodard offer a substantive and nuanced account of Black women's role in shaping Malcolm X's intellectual activism. Turning to "biographical accounts of him" by Black women in diaries, public archives, and oral histories in an attempt to counter Manning Marable's portrayal of Malcolm's thought in *Malcolm X: A Reinvention*, they argue that Malcolm X was "committed to a Black radical agenda, and that women of color radicals such as Vicki Garvin,

Queen Mother Moore, and others were central to helping him rethink and develop an even more expansive position on Black liberation in the United States and globally."[35] Along with teaching Malcolm X the importance of understanding Africa in relationship to African American slavery and segregation, Black women like Vicki Garvin, who played a central role in Reverend Adam Clayton Powell Jr.'s election to the New York City Council and U.S. Congress, were, according to McDuffie and Woodard, resources Malcolm X relied on to expand his political mobilizing in Harlem and abroad.[36] McDuffie and Woodard see the influence of Black women's thought on Malcolm X's political imagination in particular during the last two years of his life, when he traveled to Africa for extended periods of time:

> If Malcolm's international travels and exchanges with female revolutionaries of color overseas altered his global vision, they certainly also transformed his gender politics. Underscoring the ways women of color were sometimes ahead of him on political matters, due in part to his encounters with them Malcolm came to reject the Nation of Islam's patriarchal gender politics and began to adopt a progressive gender outlook that appreciated women's status as the barometer by which to measure democracy at home and overseas.[37]

Malcolm X's public speeches during that time seem to pull from the fragments of the ethical narrative developed during his childhood, which fed his relationship with Black feminists and radicals during his years in Harlem. Nonetheless, many of Malcolm X's speeches remained deeply steeped in gendered language and gender biases. Yet as his interest in international affairs expanded, his speeches took on a reflective tone and engaged in political issues that went far beyond the American narrative of the white/Black racial binary. These signs of his expanded political agenda spoke to the ethical challenge he was increasingly waging against democracy.

His critical reflection on democracy raises a serious challenge to contemporary political liberal visions of it. A "weak" political liberal vision assumes that reasoned debates, in which citizens bandy about justifications for their decisions based upon established rules, will lead to just ends. But the degree to which racial and gender biases might impede rational discussions is often not taken into account, particularly if they are fueled and justified by religious reasons and moral beliefs. A "strong" political liberal vision assumes that reasoned debates alongside a political tradition that emphasizes and cultivates trust might create the conditions for building a just society. Both weak and strong liberals seem to suggest that twentieth-century American democracy, framed largely by political liberalism and its rights and equalities, seem to suggest that political actors will act according to just, democratic principles and rules. Malcolm X's late speeches indicate otherwise.

Unlike many of his peers, Malcolm X anticipated the dangers of appropriating the familiar political vocabulary of liberty, rights, and democracy for pragmatic, political goals. Malcolm X was clear: American democracy had emerged from the same ideas that sustained American slavery and segregation, which could only mean that it was fundamentally flawed and that any attempt to revive its ideals and fundamental principles without careful attention to racial violence and subjugation would fail. Uncritical assessments of democracy's potential would camouflage structural divides and silence internal and external critics of American empire. Malcolm X exposed the limits of liberalism and attempted to carve out a new political ethos fashioned by the political and social circumstances facing democracy's victims.

In part Malcolm X attracted an audience from a range of political, economic, and social contexts because the charisma and conviction he embodied *represented an ethical imagination.* He was a living example of how Blacks might answer the existential question of who they were in an anti-Black society. While Malcolm X did not provide specific responses to this question, his speeches helped his hearers to imagine a possible relationship between ethics and democracy.

To build the case for taking seriously Malcolm X's ethical imagination, I first examine his early speeches and identify contrasting and overlapping themes that reflect his ethical commitments and the moral fabric of his thinking. I then investigate his understanding of Black nationalism as a political tradition that encompasses human rights. Finally, I explore the two basic components of humanistic ethics: reflective action and creative exchange.

EARLY SPEECHES: MASCULINITY, RHETORIC, AND BUILDING A MOVEMENT

William W. Sales Jr. conveniently divides Malcolm X's political thought into three periods: 1952–1962, when he adopted the theology of the Nation of Islam; 1963–1964, when he became involved in African American politics and founded Muslim Mosque, Inc.; and 1964– 1965, when he embraced pan-African internationalism and global politics.[38]

Malcolm X first attempted to extend Elijah Muhammad's empire among the working poor and the neglected prison population. He focused on legitimizing the Nation of Islam as the true religion for African American freedom. A central component of the religion's theology is the Yacub creation narrative, the story of an evil Black scientist who, thousands of years ago, created white people—a race who are evil by nature. In his speech "The Black Man's History," Malcolm X elucidates this story:

> I just wanted to point out that the white man, a race of devils, was made six thousand years ago. . . . The only reason God didn't remove them [at God's appointed time] was because you and I were here in their clutches and God gave them an extension of time to give the wise men of the East the opportunity to get into this House of Bondage and "awaken" the Lost Sheep. Once the American so-called Negroes have been awakened to a knowledge of themselves and of their own God and of the white man, then they're on their own. Then it'll be left up to you and me whether we want to integrate into this wicked race or leave them and separate and go to our own. And if we integrate, we'll be destroyed along with them. If we separate, then we have a chance for salvation.[39]

This theological explanation of white racism reinforced the insanity of white racism. "The point was not so much Yacub as it was a racial Manichaeism that the story constructed: white is evil, Black is good. This account offered an easy explanation of white racism: white people oppressed nonwhites because of genetic programming."[40]

This narrative is important for three reasons. First, it provides theological support and justification for believing that Blacks were the creators of civilization and whites were the devil. Second, the story distinguishes the Nation of Islam from previous iterations of Black nationalism by rooting its ideology of separation theologically. Third, the creation story gave Malcolm X the theological language with which to condemn integration as a barrier to Black liberation and freedom as well as to justify the need for a separate nation for Blacks.

The early speeches were also jeremiad in tone. Malcolm X routinely referred to the pending doom facing the nation and to how the only way African Americans could save themselves was to separate from whites.[41] At a 1960 freedom rally in Harlem, he reminded the audience of the looming tragedy awaiting society:

> The Western World today faces a great catastrophe. It stands on the brink of disaster. Mr. Muhammad says the only way our people can avoid the fiery destruction that God Himself will soon unleash upon the wicked world is for our people to come together among themselves in unity and practice true brotherhood.[42]

Then, at his first speech at Harvard Law School in 1961, Malcolm X continued with the jeremiad motif. This time he suggested that Black oppression was divinely planned. "The miserable plight of the twenty million Black people in America is the fulfillment of divine prophecy."[43] Malcolm X reminded the people that God had promised to choose someone from "among the lowly, uneducated, downtrodden, oppressed masses, from among the lowest element of America's twenty million ex-slaves," to redeem God's people.[44] Of course, this person was Elijah Muhammad. "Now, today, God has sent Mr. Elijah Muhammad among the downtrodden and oppressed so-called American Negroes to warn that God is again preparing to bring about another great change, only this time it will be a final change"[45]—by which he meant the restoration of Black people to their original and ordained status. White rule would come to an end, and God would "close out the entire old world, the old world where for the past six thousand years most of the earth's population has been deceived, conquered, colonized, ruled, enslaved, oppressed, and exploited by the Caucasian race."[46]

During the next two years, Malcolm X spoke on topics otherwise ignored by Elijah Muhammad. He was unusually critical of Black politics and African American leadership in a 1963 speech he delivered in Detroit called "Message to the Grassroots."

Here, Malcolm X outlined his critique of the civil rights political strategy in his analogy of the "field Negro" and the "house Negro." He used the distinction to mark the boundaries between Black nationalism and the civil rights movement. "The house Negroes—they lived in the house with master, they dressed pretty good, they ate good because they ate his food—what he left."[47] The house Negro grew into the traditional leader of the civil rights movement. The field Negro, on the other hand, was beaten and mistreated by his master; of course, he disliked the slave master and was prepared to fight. In the context of simmering political and personal disputes within the Nation of Islam and the growing jealousy among some over Malcolm X's increasingly heroic public status, this address is another indication of the shifts in Malcolm X's politics. Edward Curtis IV makes an apt observation regarding the growing chasm between Malcolm X and Elijah Muhammad: "While Malcolm continued to defend Elijah Muhammad and his version of Islam throughout 1963, it is clear that his separation from his spiritual father had already begun."[48] According to Curtis, he had begun to have doubts about Muhammad in the late 1950s, when the Nation of Islam faced fierce criticism from a number of Sunni Islamic groups from abroad for its use of Islam to justify racial separation.[49] Rod Bush is more direct about Malcolm X's growing skepticism of Muhammad's teaching.

> Malcolm's efforts to internationalize the struggle for freedom, justice, and equality for Black people was at odds with Elijah Muhammad's antipathy for foreigners and his focus on the Lost-Found Nation in the wilderness of North America. The effort to make the struggle for civil rights a struggle for human rights to be adjudicated in the World Court got Malcolm in trouble.[50]

In fact, after 1962, his speeches are less about justifying Muhammad's teachings and more about Malcolm X's own criticisms of

Black integrationist politics and American foreign and domestic policies. The ethical turn had begun. He was encouraging people to broach questions of what ought to be the case and what might be possible.

The clash between his commitment to the Nation of Islam and his growing interest in international politics created the political and religious conditions that transformed his jeremiad rhetoric into a radical ethical discourse, both particular and universal in nature. To be sure, Malcolm X was fundamentally a race man, focused primarily on the plight of African Americans, and he remained heavily invested in a separatist agenda. But his interest in the particular plight of African Americans did not negate his interest in human rights and his desire to link African American political struggles to the global fight to end imperialism.

His intellectual and personal relationships to radical Black feminists and Womanist thinkers informs Malcolm X's maturing political view of pan-Africanism and global politics. Not that his thought is proto-feminist per se. However, as he shifted away from the strict political teachings of the Nation of Islam and as he began to consider the economic and class-based sources of racial inequality in the United States and abroad, he was engaged in serious conversations with thinkers such as Shirley Graham Du Bois, Maya Angelou, Vicki Garvin, Alice Windom, and Queen Mother Moore—all of whom were involved in pan-Africanism and women's rights long before Malcolm X expressed a serious interest in exploring racial oppression in relationship to colonialism and imperialism.[51]

But just because Malcolm X was indebted to the work of these Black women does not mean that he was a feminist. Indeed, Patricia Hill Collins and Farah J. Griffin appropriately question the usefulness of reclaiming Malcolm X's thoughts for purposes of dismantling gender barriers and exposing Black women's social injustices. Malcolm X's understanding of gender, which was heavily influenced by the strict and narrow constructions of women's role in the Nation of Islam, was limited throughout much of his life. Malcolm X viewed women in several ways. There were women "who challenged male authority, often by using their sexuality for their own gain," which Collins describes as the Eve archetype.[52] There were women who sacrificed for their families at all costs, which Collins calls the Madonna archetype. And finally, there were women who were the subject of the "protection of promise" discourse within Malcolm X's speeches, as Griffin puts it, that spoke to the need to protect Black women from sexual, physical, and emotional assault.

In short, Malcolm X's conception of gender was complicated. It reflected an earnest desire to honor and "respect" Black women, but the framework was far too narrow, according to Patricia Hill Collins, to be of any use in Black women's liberation: "Malcolm X's treatment of gender reflected the widespread belief of his time that, like race, men's and women's roles were 'natural' and were rooted in biological difference. Like his essentialist definition of race, Malcolm X held equally essentialist notions about gender." Still, Ransby and Matthews have discovered evidence of Malcolm X grappling with his sexist views. He admitted the following in a 1965 letter to his cousin-in-law:

> I taught brothers not only to deal unintelligently with the devil or the white woman, but I also taught many brothers to spit acid at the sisters. They were kept in their places—you probably didn't notice this in action, but it is a fact. I taught these brothers to spit acid at the sisters. If the sisters decided a thing was wrong, they had to suffer it out. If the sister wanted to have her husband at home with her for the evening, I taught the brothers that the sisters were standing in their way; in the way of the Messenger, in the way of progress, in the way of God Himself. I did these things brother. I must undo them.[53]

Malcolm X's religious and political conversion clearly played a significant and sustained role in his intellectual life. This brief excerpt reflects his ongoing questioning and analysis and provides a glimpse of his changing gender politics.

What remains at issue is the political framework Malcolm X used to shape his understanding of human rights in general and African politics in particular. Some scholars suggest that even the globalist lens he adopted after leaving the Nation of Islam was male centered. In *Black Empire*, Michelle Ann Stephens considers the epistemic contours of Black internationalism during the 1960s and asks whether the move toward pan-Africanism was just another way to expand Black men's leadership. "The black global imaginary described here was also inherently masculine, created to fit the needs of a new and modern Black male subject entering onto the stage of world politics."[54] Malcolm X was indeed limited by the gender biases of his religious training, the gendered language he used to describe freedom, and the overall internationalist framework he employed in his expanded political vision. But we should not let this limitation lead us to ignore the usefulness of his ethical and creative imagination for imagining and developing radical practices.

RELIGION, BLACK NATIONALISM, AND BLACK RADICAL TRADITIONS

Elijah Muhammad and the Nation of Islam's version of Black nationalism emerged in opposition to integration. With its focus on morality, self-empowerment, and economic mobility, the Nation of Islam eschewed political involvement. According to Dean Robinson, for Muhammad, "the so-called Negroes of the United States were lost—they knew nothing of their original identity, of their true religion, or of what they needed to build a Heaven on Earth. Further, they wasted their time on political struggles. Allah would solve the problem of white racism, with His vengeance."[55]

What distinguishes Malcolm X's thoughts from, say, that of Marcus Garvey and Elijah Muhammad is the extent to which he imagined human emancipation as a process of diving into particular historical narratives and normative philosophies in order to loosen the chain that binds us to histories and narratives we did not create. The historical memory of slavery and its subsequent role in reinforcing and reifying Black subjugation would not be shattered, Malcolm X insisted, as long as Blacks idealized integration and political rights as the route to success. Gaining a seat in a historically segregated workplace, state legislature, or college would not alter the fundamental systems that initiated Black subjugation. Integration gave Blacks new access but without the fundamental power to reconstruct or reimagine the table at which they sat.

The mature Malcolm X drew on Black nationalism as a starting point for criticizing American democracy. "I'm one of the 22 million Black people who are the victims of democracy, nothing but disguised hypocrisy. . . . And I see American through the eyes of the victim. I don't see any American dream; I see an American nightmare."[56] The backdrop to this nightmare is segregation, which forced Blacks to work in and endure what he characterized as menial positions. The nightmare ended, albeit temporarily, in the midst of the Cold War. The war allowed Blacks slowly to free themselves from segregated contexts. They landed better jobs, and eventually their educational and social opportunities expanded.

The milestones some African Americans gained carried little significance for improving their overall conditions. Political efforts to sustain liberty and rights were meaningless, according to Malcolm X, without the economic and social power to protect them. In Malcolm X's vision, economic mobility was a form of embodied power:

> If we own the stores, if we operate the businesses, if we try and establish some industry in our own community, then we're developing to the position where we are creating employment for our own kind. Once you gain control of the economy of your own community, then you don't have to picket and boycott and beg some cracker downtown for a job in his business.[57]

Initially, he believed separation would allow Blacks to secure economic power and mobility, but over time he modified his position.

As early as 1960, at a freedom rally in Harlem, Malcolm X began exploring the topic of human rights in relation to African American political struggles. "As collective masses of Black people we have been deprived, not only of civil rights, but even our human rights, the right to human dignity . . . the right to be a human being!"[58]

As Malcolm X distanced himself from the teachings of Elijah Muhammad, he began to address Martin Luther King Jr., and his political visions in his speeches. "While he continued to reject integration and to advocate separation," James Cone says, "Malcolm concluded that the return to Africa or the creation of a separate state in the Western hemisphere was 'still a long range program.'"[59] He still wanted to expand the struggle for liberation by compelling African Americans to consider the limitations of a U.S.-based political agenda. "For Malcolm, it was clear that the U.S. stage was a white stage. If one looked at the plight of African Americans as a problem of human rights and not civil rights, then one moved to the world stage, where Blacks were a part of the dark majority of humankind."[60] The shift in African American politics, Malcolm X suggested, would give African Americans the political and ethical resources to develop a broader political project than one based on white political acceptance and economic benevolence. Malcolm X wanted Blacks to change the fundamental conditions and terms by which African American imagined freedom and democracy.

HUMANISTIC ETHICS

Malcolm X desperately yearned to reframe the epistemic narratives through which African Americans imagined themselves and that informed political and racial subtexts. The most striking manifestation of this yearning emerged in the Oxford Union debates in England, where, standing on the world stage, Malcolm X called for a renewed resistance against American racism and imperialism. He called it "extremism, in defense of liberty."[61] This, said Saladin Ambar, represented Malcolm X's most reflective account of revolution. All human beings who are, or have been, subjugated and oppressed by their government or society are justified in using extremist tactics, said Malcolm X:

> So my contention is that whenever a people come to the conclusion that the government, which they have supported, proves itself unwilling, or proves itself unable to protect our lives and protect our property, because we have the wrong color skin, we are not human beings unless we ourselves band together and do whatever, however, whenever, is necessary to see that our lives and our property is protected, and I doubt that any person in here would refuse to do the same thing were he in the same position, or should I say were he in the same condition.[62]

Malcolm X refrained from his usually biting jabs against the nation. Instead of justifying Black revolution by referring to the "white man's" evil soul or incarnation as the devil, he drew on the language of rights and liberty to characterize how the national government had failed to "protect" the "lives" and "property" of African Americans. He used the language of political liberalism to raise a critical question: How can one not support a revolution against such political atrocities? Malcolm X aptly observed that revolutionary behavior is contextual, and that one ought to examine the historical and social circumstances of the revolution before determining its merits. Whites would not be justified, he suggested, in calling for political resistance to efforts to implement civil rights legislation because that would not be extremism in defense of liberty.

In his Oxford talk, Malcolm X also criticized U.S. involvement in the Congo. Whereas the media had reported it as humanitarian assistance, he labeled it "criminal activity." The nation illicitly relied on its standing in the world, Malcolm insisted, to justify its involvement in the Congo's internal political strife. The death of "Congolese women, Congolese children, Congolese babies [is] extremism, but it is never referred to as extremism because it is endorsed by the West, it is financed by America, it's made respectable by America."[63] This kind of extremism, Malcolm X continued, was manifested in the nation's bombing of Hiroshima.

Malcolm X's criticism of the U.S. involvement in the Congo was noteworthy, as it pointed to his growing knowledge of African affairs. Kevin Gaines maintains that it also shows Malcolm's increasing political sophistication. "Malcolm noted the double standard by which the State Department and the Western press condoned the slaughter of Congolese under the cover of humanitarianism, yet condemned the rhetorical advocacy of self-defense by Blacks as a means of protest against unredressed white violence in the South."[64] Not only did Malcolm X link racial injustice to American imperialism, but he also showed how America manipulated its world power to serve narrow self-interests.

His condemnation, in effect, invoked the question of the ethical, implying that individual behavior and group actions are accountable to laws that transcend the nation-state or cultural context. "In this new phase in Malcolm's political understanding, unrestrained power is the devil within humanity, not the blood that courses through the veins of whites."[65] Ambar calls this Malcolm's political conversion. "For while Islam had confirmed the universality of the human condition, the Black struggle in America and around the globe validated the specific attention to racial equality. Human beings had rights and those rights could be fought for without respect to race, but they could also be fought for, and indeed had to be fought for on occasion, with respect to race."[66] Malcolm X's Black nationalism informs and contextualizes the struggle for human rights as embodying an ethics that should protect positive and negative freedoms. All nations, America in particular (according to Malcolm X), ought to be held accountable for crimes that violate human rights as outlined by the United Nations' adoption of the Universal Declaration of Human Rights in 1948.

Malcolm X's criticism illuminates his personal moral struggle to make sense of Black subjugation, and from this moral struggle emerges a framework for imagining humanistic ethics in which critical reflection and creative exchange play essential roles.

Humanistic ethics assumes political actors are reflective. Malcolm X's distinction between the Uncle Tom or house Negro and the field Negro is hyperbolic, but it's apt for my understanding of the reflective component of humanistic ethics. Both the house

Negro and the field Negro possess double or triple consciousness, and both are at war with their multiple identities. Reflection and critical engagement with their social and political contexts create the conditions for the emergence of reflective political actors who are interested in engendering ethical practices.

Humanistic ethics calls political agents to engage the lived world, not simply through rational debates on justice but by joining movements and involving themselves in transnational political struggles. Without this engagement, Blacks cannot assume or understand different viewpoints or conceptualize the world from the underside apart from an *ideal* perspective. During his world travels, Malcolm X came to see that poor and working-class African Americans would remain stuck at the bottom if they did not find a way to shed their American identity and American-centered racial politics. Finding freedom would become possible, according to Malcolm X, when Blacks joined transnational political movements.

It is only as political actors engage the world through critical reflection and sustained action that conditions emerge for a creative exchange, by which I mean the development of a novel idea or strategy. A case in point was Malcolm X's attempt to mobilize African leaders to bring charges against America for violating the human rights of African Americans, which set the stage for his ethical imagination to take shape. His strategy was to create a distinct link between Africans and African Americans as a way to generate support among the leaders for his proposal. The language he retrieved to frame his overall argument accomplished his goals. His speech acts created a new political landscape through which to see and hear voices otherwise ignored in the political mainstream. When he referred to Blacks as Afro-American, he engaged in a creative act. It was "a defiant assertion of the expansiveness of Blackness as the basis for demands for national citizenship, for international affiliation, and ultimately, for a radical democratic politics universal in its applicability."[67]

* * *

In the last chapter of his autobiography, Malcolm X shared his intimate feelings about his political work:

> I must be honest. Negroes—Afro-Americans—showed no inclination to rush to the United Nations and demand justice for themselves here in America. I . . . had known in advance that they wouldn't. The American white man has so thoroughly brainwashed the black man to see himself as only a domestic "civil rights" problem that it will probably take longer than I live before the Negro sees that the struggle of the American black man is international.[68]

His tone is rather pessimistic here, but indeed, Black freedom on American soil would not be realized during his lifetime. As he reflected on his political life, he acknowledged a truth he had never articulated: African Americans were Americans, and as long as they remained in America they would never pursue a real political fight against the place they called home.

> The black man was scarred, he was cautious, he was apprehensive. I understood it better now than I had before. In the Holy World, away from America's race problem, was the first time I ever had been able to think clearly about the basic divisions of white people in America, and how their attitudes and their motives related to, and affected, Negroes. In my thirty-nine years on this earth, the Holy City of Mecca had been the first time I had ever stood before the Creator of All and felt like a complete human being.[69]

In America, African Americans were (and are) locked in a racial prison. As Blacks, their identities were defined in opposition to whites and whiteness. Of course, Blacks could free themselves by changing their names, reframing their identities. To do so, Malcolm X implied, required some kind of radical action, a kind of suspension of judgment that would permit Blacks to see themselves in tension with the normative white gaze. In a practical sense, this is what happened when Malcolm X traveled to Africa and the Middle East. There, he could "feel like" a human being. But as long as African Americans placed their faith in political rights and narrow visions of American democracy, they would never know what it felt like to be a whole human being. What it takes to feel like a human involves a practice of intentionality, reflection, and creation. It involves this framework for building a new political agenda based on humanistic ethics.

5

HUMANISTIC NATIONALISM
AND THE ETHICAL TURN

Before Martin Luther King Jr.'s 1967 Riverside Church sermon in which he called on Americans to join in decrying the Vietnam War and America's involvement in it, SNCC's International Affairs Commission in New York City and the Third World Women's Alliance had already been advocating for human rights activism in Vietnam and South Africa.[1] Black women activists such as Frances Beal and Mae Jackson designed, developed, and led conversations around imperialism, global racism and sexism, and anti-colonialism among SNCC's New York, Washington, DC, and Atlanta offices. The increasingly global political strategy focused on topics ranging from Palestinian rights and South African apartheid to political struggles in the Caribbean.[2]

SNNC's human rights activism offers a rare glimpse into the organization's political philosophy. As Beal and others organized conferences, drafted position papers, and traveled to Africa and the Caribbean, members introduced the term "humanistic nationalism" to underscore its commitment to Black Power as well as human rights activism in the Third World. The rhetorical move is significant as it gives us a unique insight into the political aims and aspirations of the organization's radical turn in the mid-1960s. Its political imaginary is informed by dispossessed Black bodies and designed both to heal and reclaim the "grammar of Black suffering," to imagine humanism and humanistic strivings from within the Du Boisian veil. Humanistic nationalism appeals to a consciousness and history, as I construe the category, that seeks freedom and justice through universal (humanism) by way of the historical specificity of gender, race, class, etc. I call this move to humanistic nationalism *the ethical turn*[3] *in radical politics*—not ethical in terms of right or wrong actions or decision-making based on divine command theories or ethics of duty (deontology); instead, it is ethical in the sense of an intentional effort toward communal and collective freedom and justice by way of the individual attaching his or her political struggle to communal mobilizing against, for instance, colonialism. In the face of dehumanizing and violent assaults following the Voting Rights Act of 1965, SNCC members lost faith in securing freedom and justice in the United States. Turning to Third World alliances and human rights activism, members sought to find new transatlantic homes, metaphorically or literally.

Whether one agrees with the strategic move or not, the turn to humanistic nationalism symbolizes the ongoing epistemic inventiveness of a people to discover liberation through nonviolence and cross-cultural alliances. Black Power, within the context of humanistic nationalism, unfolds a story of pursuing freedom and justice through reinventions, appropriations, and discoveries from places discarded as inferior, primitive, or irrational. For instance, Anglo-American philosophical liberalism bracketed religion, Africa, African retentions, and scripture as relics of the past. For its followers, social contract theory, assimilation, and the unencumbered political self were the legitimate sources for defining the terms of justice and freedom. Black Power took a different and uncharted path.

The ideological shift I am outlining here reflects the ethical turn within U.S. Black political struggles during the mid to late 1960s. As I construe it here, the ethical turn is the ongoing recentering of Black subjectivity as central, necessary, and foundational in any humanistic endeavor to imagine, interpret, and invent existential and epistemic legitimacy. The movement from the periphery to the center disentangles humanism, God, and power from discourses and political structures that dominate and oppress based on moral and political beliefs in one group's superiority over another. The architects of Black Power understood the role of nonpolitical beliefs in creating the infrastructure needed to maintain political and economic subjugation. To combat both the political and moral justifications for oppression, Black Power turned to "revolutionary ethics" to establish the philosophical justifications for Black independence, group consciousness, and self-reliance. The ethical turn translates into a new comprehensive political vision some SNCC members called "humanistic nationalism."[4] Burdened by the psychic assaults, brute force from the state and nonstate actors, and legal apartheid, Carmichael and SNCC supporters turned inward in an effort to address the universal problem of domination, social cooperation, and oppression.

Unlike previous Black political movements in the twentieth century, Black Power incorporated aspects of competing traditions within Black political life to establish a general understanding of the movement's political philosophy. Achieving this political feat involved taking seriously the concerns of the Black church, without a commitment to its theological ends, embracing the transnational influence on and emergence from within U.S. Black politics, and incorporating self-reliance as a tool for developing humanism and humanistic activism. The political and theological substructure framing Black Power underscores the comprehensive approach that Black Power and the Black radical left employed as they attempted to translate *Negro problems* into a vocabulary comprehensible to an entire nation and to leaders constrained by a political vocabulary of rights, individual liberty, and equal opportunity.

EXPANDING THE BACKDROP TO BLACK POWER

General characterizations of Black Power portray it as a separatist and anti-white political movement intended to reject American liberalism. More recent scholarship challenges such notions and reexamines its relationship to traditional civil rights politics. What has become known as "Black Power Studies" fundamentally aims to provide a more nuanced historical account of Black Power's prominent, but often overlooked, role in shaping Black political thought in general and American democratic strivings in particular. Guided by Peniel Joseph, Rhonda Williams, and other scholars, Black Power Studies recasts Black Power as a political movement that "redefines and deepens American democracy."[5] Within this narrative, Black Power has emerged as an intrinsically American, democratic, and loosely liberal political philosophy.

I take issue with one fundamental political claim of Black Power Studies: that Black Power deepens American (liberal) democracy. While Black Power does invoke a political vocabulary that includes liberal principles of justice and equality, its anti-colonial and anti-racist criticisms of American empire fundamentally challenged and rejected *political* liberalism's account of democracy as primarily the achievement of equal rights, arguably the bedrock of the civil rights political agenda. Yet without an analysis of structural power and its role in maintaining and widening economic and political disparities, equality and rights in the abstract would almost always be undermined by institutions and individuals in power. The moral problem of Blackness further complicates political liberalism and Black Power's role in "deepening" American democracy. In far too many instances, whites have demonstrated a propensity to work against their own economic and political interests rather than join in solidarity with Blacks. Dating back at least to Reconstruction, most barriers impeding interracial coalitions stemmed from racist beliefs in Black inferiority and racist beliefs regarding Black sexuality and masculinity. How do we account for these irrational conceptions of Blackness within politics? Activists such as Stokely Carmichael and Ethel Minor[6] invoked power as a discursive category both to defeat white supremacy and to encourage a Black nationalist rhetoric of self-help and self-determination.

The case for power in the broadest terms is evident in the post–civil rights context. Following the decline of the civil rights movement and the rise of Black Power and Black nationalism, many civil rights leaders in the 1970s extended their alliance with government and private-sector enterprises to implement the rights-based political agenda and philosophy framed most prominently by Martin Luther King Jr. and the scores of people participating in marches and boycotts across the South. In a few short years, monumental change was evident in three specific ways: the emergence of Black mayors in the largest and fastest-growing cities in America, affirmative action in higher education, and integration in both corporate America and public schools. Yet in spite of these advances along with landmark court cases and the success stories of individual African Americans, the American dream was still out of reach for the vast majority of Blacks.

Nearly a quarter of a century later, Black elected officials and a handful of social programming had neither solved W. E. B. Du Bois's "Negro problem" nor alleviated anti-Black racism as manifested within the resegregation of secondary education, imprisonment of nearly half of the African American male population, and increasing police shootings of mostly unarmed Black and Hispanic women, men, and children. In almost all areas of African American life, the rights-based strategy of political liberalism had proven inadequate for ameliorating Black political suffering and subjugation.

Black Power offered a corrective to a voting-rights strategy isolated from a deeply woven economic and political infrastructure to promote, sustain, and advocate for African American communities at the seat of empire, where capitalism and liberal politics collided and overlapped in the American context.[7] Within the context of counter-publics, Black Power sheds light on a philosophical tradition best characterized by what the philosopher Lucius Outlaw describes as "black theorizing" of both Black life and the human condition, which almost always emerges as a "form of social praxis."[8] Far from idealizing Blackness as a static category, SNCC activists, especially Black women, translated Black suffering into a tool to determine the social and political needs of the communities they were serving. This explains, in part, the origins of the 1964 Mississippi Summer Project created by the SNCC, an effort aimed at teaching voting-rights education alongside a Black history curriculum. "One of the purposes of the Freedom School idea," the Project described, "is to train and educate people to be active agents in bringing about social change. In order to accomplish this purpose, it is necessary to provide an educational experience that is geared to the needs of the students, that challenges the myths of our society, that provides alternatives, and directions for action."[9]

SNCC's freedom schools and mobilizing efforts are a backdrop for understanding humanistic ethics. Designed and developed to disrupt, dismantle, and rebuild political and cultural expectations, humanistic ethics is not only a model but also a form of social praxis.

DEFINING HUMANISTIC NATIONALISM

What is this humanistic nationalism? Records show that SNCC members mentioned the term *humanistic nationalism* during the 1967 central committee meeting in the Atlanta office. Though no one there identified its origins, nor defined it, one of the sources for the idea may have been the Jewish philosopher Martin Buber. His book, *On Zionism*, explores nationalism within Zionist writings and especially within the works of Theodor Herzl, the "father" of modern Zionism. What Buber calls "nationalistic-humanism" reflects both the literal and metaphorical Zion and signifies the emergence of a new society informed by love of all humankind. "Zion is only Zion when this ground is preserved. . . . This concrete geographical Zion is only then truly Zion if it realizes the prophetic meaning which once filled out the name, if, therefore, its new construction is built on the foundation of human love," he writes.[10] While Carmichael and others were interested in Zionism and how it might translate to Black freedom, they do not name Zionism or Buber as a reference point. To some extent, then, I am linking Zionism as one starting point for humanistic nationalism based on SNCC's ongoing interest in Zionist literature when I piece together a definition of the category in conversation with Carmichael's early speeches, prior to his name change in 1969[11] and SNCC's meeting notes in James Forman's papers.

Humanistic nationalism[12] begins the long and tedious work of addressing the enduring legacy of the Negro problem or what Frantz Fanon calls the "zone of nonbeing" within Black political thought. Unlike the Negro problem, Fanon's zone of nonbeing is an "existence without being. To exist is to stand out, but, as [Fanon] learned, doing such as illegitimate meant a violation of being."[13] To exist, then, is to find oneself in a perpetual sense of "self-illegitimacy," an ongoing awareness of one's negation and absence in the world. Carmichael articulated a similar philosophy of existence on how to become an "antiracist racist."

> The fact is that all black people often question whether or not they are equal to whites, because every time they start to do something, white people are around showing them how to do it. If we are going to eliminate that for the generation that comes after us, then black people must be seen in positions of power, doing and articulating for themselves."[14]

One of the sure ways to assess Blackness is to detach it from the white/Black binary in the United States and locate it firmly in the anti-colonialist context. Fanon pushed against that binary through a "dialectical movement to a critical Black consciousness,"[15] a hermeneutical lens both Fanon and Du Bois employed to assume an essential *Blackness* in order to detangle and rescue it from the normative colonial or white gaze. Freeing *Blackness* from racial domination and oppression meant toppling *whiteness* from bad faith, scientific racism, and biological determinism. This move makes humanism both the starting point and telos of any political struggle.

The implications of this move are noteworthy. Human flourishing,[16] and more specifically human dignity, had until now been tied to achieving rights and acting reasonably upon them in the public sphere. This changes with humanistic nationalism. Within this context, humanistic nationalism detaches human dignity from a rights-based political agenda and locates it within the ethical. The move toward humanistic nationalism established an untenable tension in SNCC's political agenda, with SNCC seemingly locked between America's narrowly restrictive racial white/Black binary and the group's growing Black internationalist agenda. Alongside this tension sat another deeply burdensome matter. Unlike immigrant groups, citizenship was not simply a matter of securing public rights. Obtaining full citizenship, especially among politically liberal Blacks in the nineteenth and twentieth centuries, was linked to achieving human dignity. Here's the question I propose we pursue: *How ought I respond to state-sanctioned violence against me?* This question inserts ethics and ethical thinking into the liberal political framework. I do not mean ethics as in Kantian duty or ethics as in deeply held virtues. The tradition of ethics to which I am appealing can be found in African American religion in general and radical biblical hermeneutics in particular. From this context, ethics emerges from a Black religious tradition that Tracey Hucks and Dianne Stewart call a "provisional and dialogical" framework for engaging the tension between our idealized norms and what Charles Mills calls our "naturalized rights."

This ethical social praxis is one based on the following assumptions: First, our available tradition is the necessary and legitimate starting point for imagining oneself in relation to society; second, our individual and collective starting points are familiar, flawed, and in need of modification; third, in this deliberative context, we enter knowing that our beliefs and actions may be contested and proven unacceptable; fourth, the deliberative space aims to remember, dismantle, disrupt, and reassemble the dead bodies from our living past, knowing we can never escape history but only find meaningful ways to live with it; and finally, if a goal can be achieved within this deliberative context, it is that the ethical turn aims to illumine our weaknesses, strengths, vulnerabilities, and potential future.

Ethics means disrupting, dismantling, and reconfiguring. It is about imagination, movement, and balance. The spirit of ethics I am imagining is most evident in the politics of respectability and Black separatist nationalism as evident in the Nation of Islam. These divergent but overlapping traditions all push people to move beyond or to transgress white supremacist views of Blackness as well as to develop political and economic strategies to free the people. This link between Blackness and political and economic freedom must not be underestimated. The link is a reminder of what political theorists often ignore: the degree to which Blackness as a form of humanism and the longing to be seen and treated as human haunts Black intellectual and religious production. In these traditions, two forms of ethics are consistent: African American normative ethics and virtue ethics. Conversely, the traditions develop ethics in opposition. The politics of respectability imagines ethics as either latent in the natural law of Victorian ideals or as a heuristic tool for training the people—especially the Talented Tenth. Both strands assume a kind of ethics of accommodation. By contrast, Black separatist nationalism envisages ethics in the following ways: first, as a meta-ethics that frames and highlights white immorality and liberalism's political bankruptcy; and second, as directly tied to a political and cultural care of the self that is evident in the aesthetics and what people eat and consume.

Let's not think about ethics in terms of right or wrong, good punishing evil, and good people acting kindly or justly. Instead, let's conceive of it as the act of disrupting, dismantling, and reconfiguring. It is about imagination, movement, and balance. The spirit of ethics that I am imagining is most evident in the politics of respectability and in the Black separatist nationalism of the Nation of Islam. These two divergent but overlapping traditions reflect efforts to incite the people to move beyond or to transgress white supremacist views of Blackness as well as develop political and economic strategies to free the people. This link between Blackness and political and economic freedom cannot be understated: it is quite simply the longing to be seen and treated as human.

Carmichael and SNCC were aware of these multiple views of what ethicists might characterize as duties, responsibilities, and obligations. What is often called revolutionary ethics in the SNCC archives is linked to individual behavior and worldview—all linked in turn to self-examination, critical revaluation of social and cultural norms, and reimagination of race/gender and human aspirations. This is evident in three early stages or problems facing the turn to Black Power: the role of whites in SNCC, the relationship between Israel and Palestinians, and the role of Black internationalism within domestic politics. The debates and deliberations over these issues cultivated a rich but understudied ethical tradition in Black radical politics.

The ethical turn in Black radical politics is therefore significant for three reasons: First, it discloses Black Power's political faith in humanism and human rights activism; second, the move exposes the important but rarely explored shift in Black-church prophetic traditions and Exodus motifs in Black political philosophy; third, the ethical turn inserts ethics as a performative tool for disrupting, dismantling, and reimagining political possibilities and political agency.

FRAMING HUMANISTIC NATIONALISM

In what follows, I outline humanistic nationalism as depicted in the early writings of Stokely Carmichael and the letters and essays on Black Power in SNCC's archives. As I envision it, humanistic nationalism brings to light four critical claims that are necessary to develop ethics as a foundational resource for underscoring political agency and deliberative models in African American political thought: One, non-ideal theory serves as the starting point for disrupting the racial contract. The demand for moral and political self-determination as characterized in Black Power is such a starting point; two, the (Black) self stands in tension with community. In other words, traditions and norms that inform community will shape and guide political agency and deliberation, but participants are not obliged to restrict their commitments to, let's say, racial uplift ideology or the Exodus tradition; three, Black Power reifies Blackness in an effort to negate normative beliefs in Black inferiority. As it reimagines the (Black) self, tradition, and community, it transforms strong commitments to "Blackness" into strident beliefs in transnational politics and humanistic virtues, beliefs, and commitments; and finally, freed from the constitutive norms of the racial contract, at least conceptually, human dignity and respect are no longer rooted in political justice. Instead, human dignity is earned and achieved through political action, care and compassion, and reflective subjectivity.

The suspension of justice and the turn to freedom together disrupt the normative commitments to the politics of respectability, Black liberation theology, and racial uplift ideology. Instead, Black Power cultivates a political vision of recovery and repair/reformulation in a quest for African Americans to become human. This process requires a suspension of judgment, ignoring racist legal codes and turning a blind eye to cultural norms. Prior forms of Black politics, like racial liberalism and traditions within Afro-Christianity, required Blacks to live in and with "bad faith." Black Power shatters bad faith through a complete rejection of whiteness. Instead, it embraces Blackness.

Yet this move is not about essentializing Blackness or whole-heartedly rejecting whiteness but about disrupting the political status quo.

In a political system characterized by white racial privilege, Black inferiority, and a complete erasure of gender, I suggest that human dignity, and for that matter humanness, can only be embodied within those who are phenotypically white, or those who knowingly and actively choose the racial contract as a political ideology and weapon against nonwhites. In this white political system, Black and Brown bodies are subhumans, inferior subjects of the state. Without political or economic power, African Americans in particular cannot obtain human flourishing, dignity, or respect without handing over their humanness to the gods of capitalism, religious fundamentalism, misogyny, and xenophobia. Individual Blacks can become the exception through education and wealth, but the group as a whole will remain locked in a subordinate moral and social class known as a "dark ontology," the unacknowledged vestige from Enlightenment in which Africans were nonpersons and thereby outside the parameters of rights-bearing individuals.[17] "This is the social ontology of the world of slavery, colonialism, and segregation, where concrete individuals are seen as raced and colored and treated accordingly."[18] We see SNCC grappling with the racialization of social structures by appealing to the grammar of Black suffering vis-à-vis humanistic nationalism to achieve far more than political rights. By reimagining human dignity and respect beyond the category of rights, humanistic nationalism offers a counter tradition through which deliberation in general and ethics in particular may serve as viable resources.

As a social praxis, humanistic nationalism involves three steps: first, grappling with the ongoing clash between the weight of tradition and the constant but shifting encumbered self; second,

reorienting political (and moral) values through a critical evalu-
ation of the familiar, both in terms of politics and comprehensive
values; and third, developing new political vocabularies in conversation with existing discourses. In *Black Power: The Politics of
Liberation*, Carmichael and Charles V. Hamilton assert the guiding principles that seem to undergird humanistic nationalism:

> Our basic need is to reclaim our history and our identity from
> what must be called cultural terrorism, from the depredation of
> self-justifying white guilt. We shall have to struggle for the right
> to create our own terms through which to define ourselves and
> our relationship to the society, and to have these terms recog-
> nized. This is the first necessity of a free people, and the first right
> that any oppressor must suspend.[19]

As one can see from this, the existential concerns are far more
daunting than classical Afro-Modern political thinkers such
as Frederick Douglass or Maria Stewart articulated. Achieving human dignity is an impossible goal within liberalism. Yet
somehow SNCC members do not appear to see a contradiction between voting rights and Black Power. Nonetheless, the
employment of Black Power signaled the doom of racial liberalism and, by extension, gestured to the demise of white participation within SNCC.

Carmichael linked these two—the erosion of racial liberalism
and white allies—in an essay printed shortly after his Mississippi speech. "Negroes are defined by two forces, their blackness and their powerlessness," he wrote in "Toward Black
Liberation."[20] To overcome these forces, Carmichael said, Blacks
need to "reclaim our history and our identity from the cultural
terrorism and depredation of self-justifying white guilt." As he
saw it, liberal philosophy established itself on a fundamental

contradiction: liberal doctrines were established in conversation with and based on political justifications of Native American subjugation and African slavery. This created the economic and political contradictions of liberalism prior to the Black social protest movements in the nineteenth and twentieth centuries.

In a speech delivered in 1968, Carmichael lays out a guiding "ideology" for the emergence of a new people, one freed from the racist white/Black binary. In "A New World to Build," he encourages his audience members to look inward before imagining the contours of liberation. In doing so, they will discover a necessary but often overlooked social fact: "Black people are a colonized people."[21] He establishes two dialogical moves for dismantling colonization: entertainment and education. What Carmichael characterizes as entertainment is better described as performance, the discursive and inventive rhetorical strategies typically inaugurated during social protests. Pejorative terms and categories such as "Whitey" and "burn this city down" symbolize rhetorical weapons designed to perform a menacing "Blackness" to a white audience. This form of public engagement, Carmichael asserts, illustrates a necessary "sort of catharsis" to repair the psychological distress among a disinherited people.

Carmichael also calls for transformative education, one that can prepare the people for "revolution."[22] Retrieving ideas from Frantz Fanon's *The Wretched of the Earth*, he exhorts audience members to reject aesthetic values and historical narratives premised on the inferiority of Blackness and by extension Africa, African Americans, and the Third World. Instead, he urges them to embrace education as a form of "reestablishment and the reinforcement of values and institutions of a given society"[23]— specifically African American "communitarian" traditions, the third principle of this educational model in Black communities.

Revolutionary education is a form of "undying love." On the one hand, it involves self-defense—protecting community members from violent attacks from racists as well as from state actors such as police officers. On the other hand, it is a necessary response, he suggests, when overthrowing racists regimes and governments.[24] Undying love is a tall order as it generally refers to heroic acts such as standing up to and against state actors and taking part in nonviolent protests.

What specifically links his speech to humanistic nationalism is the argument for transforming the "Negro" into a Black man. Carmichael overstates the distinction but it is nonetheless worth mentioning. The Negro symbolizes the self-hating person, despising any forms of Blackness, whereas the Black man is liberated by virtue of "his" love for and revolutionary commitment to African American communities.[25] Carmichael's descriptive account of the "Black man" is gendered and masculinist; conceptually, however, the idea of transforming oneself from self-hatred to self-love and community-love symbolizes the potential to move away from harmful practices and beliefs to those that cultivate and produce meaning, wellness, and well-being for all.

Black Power shifts the terms of the debate and introduces humanistic activism into the public sphere. It is a move away from the politics of respectability to humanism and human rights. Many scholars have missed this point because they have focused instead on the rise of Black nationalism and Afrocentricity following Black Power. Humanistic activism is tied to three important themes: the freedom schools, self-determination, and moral egalitarianism. In what follows, I focus on self-determination as developed at Booker T. Washington's Tuskegee Institute, an educational model often referenced by Carmichael and Black Power activists.

THE TUSKEGEE MODEL OF
SELF-DETERMINATION

An example of self-determination emerged within Booker T. Washington's racial uplift model at Tuskegee Institute. What we learn both from the freedom schools and Tuskegee's model of self-determination became the moral and philosophical backdrop of Black Power's unprecedented political engine. Unlike the civil rights agenda, which relied on weaponizing Black bodies—mostly women and children—to compel legislative action at the federal and state levels, Black Power focused largely on empowering Black bodies with history and political philosophy to fuel or motivate their political self-determination. The latter fuels action at the ground level, replacing or at the very least reducing the amount of power wielded by those in leadership positions. In the abstract, the model or conception of SNCC's leadership reflected a liberal, deliberative model—a universal acceptance of the reasonable claims of rights-bearing citizens. But we can't look at the 1960s in the abstract. It was a time of deep racial hatred, often perpetuated by unreflective citizens who took for granted a social contract designed to benefit whites at the expense of Black and Brown bodies.

CONTEXTUALIZING THE ETHICAL TURN

My interpretation is that what happened in the first iteration of Black Power was not completely linked to racial solidarity, which puts me at odds with Tommie Shelby's provocative reading of Black Power in *We Who Are Dark*. In Shelby's account, Carmichael and Charles Hamilton invoked Black Power because the "continuing racism and black poverty demanded greater black solidarity."[26] I agree with Shelby's claim—but not with the conclusion of his argument: that racial solidarity is ineffective, in part because "*most* people do not freely make *great* sacrifices for people with whom they do not share intimate bonds." If this were true, it would preclude elite Blacks from sacrificing in meaningful way for the Black poor. I think Carmichael's insistence on imagining Black Power in the context of humanistic nationalism and human rights assumes that collective power is dependent upon an ideal far greater than racial solidarity. Put differently: I believe that Carmichael's first iteration of Black Power calls into question the substantive value of this group solidarity. Carmichael's call for solidarity represents a form of negation that is intended to decenter Blackness in an attempt to create a humanist consciousness. From this I want what I call "reflective improvisation" to underscore and extend humanistic nationalism as a model through which to piece together new concepts of humanism.

Toni Cade Bambara's criticism of Black male chauvinism and sexism during Black Power is also reflective of the ethical imagination undergirding humanistic nationalism. She illuminated Black women's invisibility within the leadership ranks in an effort to expand the possibilities both for women *and* men in politics. Bambara's philosophy aimed to strengthen what she called "political consciousness,"[27] another term for critical Black consciousness that incorporated a dialectical engagement both within Black political organizations and without. "In other words, we are still abusing each other, aborting each other's nature—in the teeth of experiences both personal and historical that should alert us to the horror of a situation in which we profess to be about liberation but behave in a constricting manner; we rap about being correct but we ignore the danger of having one half of our population regard the other with such condescension and perhaps fear that the half finds it necessary to 'reclaim his manhood' by denying her peoplehood."[28] Bambara, who at the time of *The Black Woman*'s publication was still named Cade, realized correcting sexism and patriarchy involved substantive action, what she framed as "purging." The literary writer envisioned the purging as a needed outcome on the road to creating "a new identity, a self, perhaps an androgynous self, via a commitment to the struggle."[29] Cade explores Fanon's *A Dying Colonialism* to imagine new values and paradigms for defining family, gender,[30] and "a commitment to Blackhood."[31] The ethical revolution Bambara calls for is intentionally reflective and dialogical.

Reflective improvisation is borrowed from the idea of double consciousness. The reflective dimension of double consciousness is not strictly tied to reason, as in the capacity to differentiate and distinguish, for it is also linked to categories such as conjure and revelation. In other words, conjure is evident in double consciousness insofar as the language of double self and "doubleness" creates the cultural conditions in which self-critique is normalized and the possibility of transforming the self and public become evident. In a broad sense, my understanding of conjure, which is borrowed from Theophus H. Smith's *Conjuring Culture*, involves manipulating and transforming the immediate contexts and narratives citizens find themselves facing. The transformation of the double self into a "truer" self involves the suspension of judgment as citizens explore their epistemic resources in such a way as to bracket familiar resources when they explore the nuances of a given debate or text. It also involves hearing what is revealed when the text (or person) speaks. As I am using the term, revelation in the Du Boisian context is not a divine message, only the discourse that emerges when individual political actors pursue their truer self. In fact, double consciousness is a symbol of what it takes to achieve democratic principles insofar as it denotes the individual struggle that is required in public life to achieve democracy. As Anthony Bogues reminds us in the *Empire of Liberty*, human beings "must struggle to construct and invent *ways of life* that allow us to practice forms of democracy."[32]

Double consciousness offers us three important points concerning moral agency that are worth considering: First, public cultures contain the moral language, narratives, and traditions needed to cultivate practices of self-interrogation. The evidence for this may emerge, for instance, at the dinner table as an elder recounts the Exodus narrative, possibly while listening to a vocal artist's reinterpretation of a classic love ballad, or during a visceral reaction to a favorite reality show. Self-interrogation does not need to follow a procedural model or ritual in a formal sense; self-interrogation is a fundamental component of human agency. At issue, however, is the degree to which moral actors can comprehend what is revealed in that self-interrogation. In the Du Boisian sense, moral agents by "nature" experience ongoing moments of feeling torn by and conflicted over their competing and overlapping identities, and the "nature" of moral agency is equipped to handle the existential crises moral agents are doomed to face. Second, moral agency, choosing to act in the multiple forms of public spheres, is intertwined in the search for a truer self. As moral agents affirm and challenge the norms and expectations of culture, the truer self unfolds. Third, moral agency discloses the spiritual strivings of a people, their hopes, aims, and fears while searching to materialize their democratic dreams and aspirations. Spiritual strivings reveal what far too many political liberals refuse to name: the moral dimensions of political commitments and cultural norms.

Reflective improvisation introduces narrative as a framework for measuring the "truthfulness" of our political claims, the depths of our democratic aspirations and the weaknesses of our moral commitments. This approach fundamentally alters the collective sense of who we are and what we *think* we ought to pursue. Reflective deliberation assumes we are free, equal, *and* vulnerable and prone to cling to the familiar in times of uncertainty. If we want to preserve critical pluralism within our democratic traditions, we ought to open ourselves to new models of deliberation and modes of public discourse that reflect the rich complexity of our political and moral beliefs and take advantage of epistemic diversity.

* * *

As I envision it, the insertion of the ethical compels us—and even *condemns us*—to envision the role of subjectivity (and individual narrative) in political struggles. It compels us to imagine political subjects as more than rights-bearing persons—as persons seeking human dignity and a deep sense of belonging even as they remain bound by public laws and cultural beliefs.

Why ethics? Because it has everything to do with character and customs, both of which have dogged Black life in the United States. The idea that Blacks are human, that they possess feelings and character and have a viable and robust tradition or traditions, is relatively new in the Western mind. In light of this, I choose to talk about Black radical politics in terms of ethics, or more precisely, the ethical turn in politics. We can trace this ethical turn to a number of events and circumstances. In religion, the hermeneutical approach to biblical interpretation and the Black church as counter-public are two fine examples of the materialization of ethics in Black life. In Black political philosophy, Black women's efforts to legitimize their womanhood and agency illumines the embodied response to subjugation, a kind of ethical response to rape, violence, and subjugation. This is what I mean by ethics, an ethical worldview guided and shaped by the following assertion made by Toni Morrison:

> Most of us are plagued by a sense of being worn shell-thin by constant repression and hostility as well as the impression of being buoyed by visible testimony of tremendous strides. There is repetition of the grotesque in our history. And there is the miraculous walk of trees. The question is whether our walk is progress or merely movement.[33]

What is important to keep in mind is that political actors rely on ethical subjectivity as a resource for self-critique and self-repudiation and to challenge or access the political goals toward which they strive. This reduces or minimizes the chances of reinforcing hegemony. Put differently: Black radicals rely on an external, metaethical framework for measuring their political pursuits.

Why is ethical subjectivity important? Because it reminds us of both the limits and possibilities of human existence. Ethical subjectivity disrupts normative, familiar ways of being. This is important not only for understanding radical practices but also for trying to imagine how we are informed by previous traditions. Daniel Boyarin, in *Intertextuality and the Reading of Midrash*, suggests that the text is always constituted in and through the "conscious and unconscious citation of earlier discourse" that will inform the reading and interpretation of subsequent generations. His arguments regarding the "cultural codes" and hermeneutics are far more germane to the work on ethics. On the one hand, I agree that cultural codes and norms "constrain" the "production" of texts." On the other hand, I disagree with his notion that readers cannot produce new texts.[34]

This kind of work that ethical subjectivity demands is not navel-gazing. It is not some kind of individualistic moral remedy that does not take into account radical praxis. Ethical subjectivity is quite radical and can only happen within community. This is the ongoing work that must happen within radical political groups to prevent their reinscription into the old ways of being.

It is commonplace to think of ethics as virtue, and therefore as normative and prescriptive. At least for Black women in and after Black Power, the decisions to engage in political life, sometimes at the risk of so much loss, were guided in the general sense by ethics, and more specifically by ethical subjectivity, of self and community.

Why is this important? Because it provides a different perspective on Black radical politics. It is not simply secular, antiestablishment, and devoid of examination of the individual. From the perspective of Black men, maybe this is the case. But Black women's writings show a different perspective. They focus a great deal of attention on agency, intentionality, and regulation. In such writings, there seems to be an awareness both of the limits of authority and the limitless bounds of individual agency within the group. For writers as politically different as Amiri Baraka and Ralph Ellison, there was a sense among Black men during and after the Black Power era of the need to acquire power as a means of signifying one's human status, one's manhood. For Ellison, it was a means of illuminating one's invisibility. To do so was a sign of one's power and ability to lift the veil and expose one's voice. Baraka, on other hand, wanted power to define the terms of Black existence and to do so in contexts created by Black hands. Both writers imagine power as acquisition and signification. Among Black radical feminists, we see something else. For them, power does not begin through acquisition but through disrupting narratives of the self, and using the fragments of the disruption to reconstruct or remold the nature of social narratives, and hence the nature of social being.

6

SNCC's PALESTINIAN PROBLEM

I n 1967, SNCC's secretary of communications, Ethel Minor, was the lead writer of one of the most consequential news-letters in the mid-twentieth century by a Black U.S. political organization. Entitled "Third World Round Up: The Palestine Problem: Test Your Knowledge," the essay appeared in the June–July issue of the *SNCC Newsletter*. It expressed unequivocally SNCC's anti-war position, condemned "European Jews" for set-tling in Palestinian land, slayed the state of Israel for its brazen relationship with the apartheid-led government of South Africa and other "colonial powers," and denounced Israel's treatment of Palestinians and Arabs. Minor framed SNCC's criticisms of all these groups and countries in thirty-two questions designed to introduce "facts" to an audience with (presumably) minimal knowledge of Israel and Palestine. What was an effort by the international community to respond to the Holocaust and solve the question of Jewish landlessness became "a world problem," a crisis of Palestine, said Minor's article.

The backlash against the article was swift and widespread. Prominent civil rights leaders and Jews condemned it, refer-ring to it as another form of anti-Semitism and racist ideology. According to Whitney Young Jr., the prominent president of the national urban league, SNCC's statements were an "unfortunate distortion of history and logic (with) anti-Semitic overtones. Negro citizens are well aware of the contributions made to the drive for equal rights by Jewish citizens. Negroes have been the victims of racism for too long to indulge in group stereotypes and racial hate themselves."[1]

The national media, especially leading newspapers including the *New York Times* and the *Washington Post*, eviscerated SNCC for participating in foreign-policy debates, especially for doing so by criticizing the major Western powers for alleged human rights violations. Along with calling the organization anti-Semitic and anti-American, the media interpreted SNCC's position as naive and "not well thought out." There's some debate as to whether the document reflected SNCC's "true" and full beliefs about Israel and Palestine, for it was a working paper, designed to stimulate debate and discussion among the executive committee before SNCC released its official public statement on the Middle East. Soon after parts of the essay were leaked to the media, SNCC published the compete document in its newsletter.

SNCC's response to the Six-Day War surfaced as the organization grappled with the role of whites in the organization, and particularly their visible leadership positions. What an interesting set of paradoxes: diving into transnational politics while cleansing one's own organization of whites, most of whom were Jewish! How do we make sense of this glaring move in light of the group's growing human rights agenda? On the one hand, SNNC's rhetorical move reflects what Frantz Fanon describes as a violent end to the colonizer's stronghold on the natives. This internal revolt by some members of SNCC, unfortunately, complicated the group's understanding of political solidarity. In personal writings found in the James Forman archives, members expressed their deep admiration of and trust in Jews because they too had faced ongoing hatred, persecution, and death—the ghostly signs of the tyranny of white supremacy. But soon after white Jews assimilated in America's mostly Protestant middle-class suburbia, performed whiteness, and appeared to be no longer "the Jewish problem" in American society, many SNCC members changed their political views of Jews and the viability of a sustained political relationship with them. Clayborne Carson characterizes this move as the final chapter of the "relationship" between Blacks and Jews in SNCC.

CLASH OF POLITICAL IDEOLOGIES

The Brown vs. Board of Education court case in 1954, as well as the efforts to dismantle Jim Crow in the South in the 1950s and 1960s, galvanized a small but sturdy and resilient group of Black women from different socioeconomic backgrounds to pull the nation with their dogged strength toward tangible democracy for all. The passage of the Civil Rights Act of 1964 and the Voting Rights Act of 1965 signaled to many the burgeoning of a new political momentum unwitnessed by the nation since Reconstruction.

Emerging alongside federal political victories was a chilling narrative, one ignored by most but foretold by the radical arm of Black politics in the 1960s. Malcolm X, Ethel Minor, and Stokely Carmichael, to name a few, proclaimed from pulpits and in published editorials harrowing accounts of white violence against Blacks in the South as signs of the potential crumbling of the recent legal victories. As they watched violent responses to anti-colonialism in the Third World, and the steady violence against Blacks in the South, their faith in their nation's desire and willingness to protect Blacks against white backlash was nearly non-existent. Their skepticism about their nation, and for that matter all colonial powers, had everything to do with economic and moral dimensions of anti-Black racism. First, what was the financial reason for protecting Blacks? Unlike slavery and segregation, there were financial reasons for ending those horrific systems (at least on paper.) Second, "the Black" remained a national problem that needed to be silenced and maintained, rather than eradicated and reimagined. Third, Black Power advocates also believed that Black liberation would not surface through legislation, presidential executive orders, or court decisions but emerge from a collective Black struggle against gender, race, and class exploitation to produce a new social world and a new humanism. The historian Christopher Lasch suggests that Black Power's radicalism was a response to the fall of the civil rights movement. I disagree. Black Power's shift to Third World politics, as well as its emphasis on economic power, self-love, and political independence, triggered the decline of a civil rights agenda that focused narrowly on integration and voting rights. Ethel Minor noted in a 1966 SNCC newsletter piece that despite the landmark political victories, the federal government as well as white vigilantes remained laser focused on SNCC and its radical arm. "This country can no longer tolerate us. As usual in the United States, when black people become too strong, there is always an attempt to exile, jail or kill him. Every black leader who became a leader of the black masses with an international perspective, has either been physically destroyed, exiled or harassed throughout his lifetime."[2]

Minor's retort against the backlash Black leaders and organizations face when they link African American struggles to global struggles against white struggles foreshadowed SNCC's collapse following its public criticism of the 1967 Israeli–Arab War. For all the discussion around the group's skewed foreign policy and anti-Semitism, which needs to be explored and condemned, what is too often overlooked is the degree to which Black Power advocates sought to build a political platform based on anti-war and human rights activism. Yes, the path was fraught with mishaps. But the journey unveils the peculiar search for freedom as struggle, negation, and expansion. Put more concretely: Black Power advocates imagined African American freedom in relation to the struggle for freedom and liberation across the globe, including Africa and South America. This vision is far more in line with King's Beloved Community than was evident in the civil rights movement.

A number of scholars have already explored the historical conditions and circumstances that led to this "rift." Peniel Joseph and Clayborne Carson characterize the deteriorating relationship between Blacks and Jews in SNCC as a natural progression given the organization's increasing radicalism and "separatist" leanings. I am not so much interested in the historical political encounters between Blacks and (white) Jews or in exploring the historical origins or merits of SNCC's criticism of Israel; Keith Feldman's *A Shadow Over Palestine: The Imperial Life of Race in America* offers a sufficiently detailed and provocative historical account of SNCC's engagement with Israel and Palestine. Instead, I want to focus on the political reasons and subsequent consequences for SNCC's solidarity with the Palestinians. As I will attempt to unfold, the Palestinian debate was a necessary epistemic and existential move for SNCC and its Black radical arm as it linked together the lived experience of Du Boisian double consciousness and Fanonian violence as epistemically and existentially necessary for the emergence of a new humanism, a world in tension with the white/Black racial binary. Indeed, in the chapter I highlight the implicit ideological tension within Black Power's turn to human rights activism in the Third World.

In the face of what can be characterized as a tension between ideal and nonideal theory, the world as imagined versus the world *as is*, SNCC's radical arm crafted a Third World political strategy based on normative commitments to anti-colonialism, diasporic coalition-building among African descendants, and global cultural nationalism.[3] "The Palestinian Problem" is a direct result of SNCC's ideal understanding of revolutionary politics—by way of disentangling *Blackness* from W. E. B. Du Bois's "Negro problem" and imagining themselves outside the U.S. white/Black racial binary and within a Third World context. This tension is terribly important as it points to the friction within SNCC regarding how best to solve ongoing social injustice and economic disparities. Should one imagine an ideal society to start the necessary work of restorative justice and freedom? Or is it better to start with the nitty-gritty, the lived experience of oppression?

Investigating the philosophical nature of Black Power's support of Palestine brings one face-to-face with ongoing concerns of political solidarity, political expediency, and political ideals. This highly complicated debate should not be reduced to a facile tension between idealism and pragmatics. But why did Black Power advocate for the human rights of Palestinians at the expense of their own political welfare? Let's assume Blacks and Jews were never in an "alliance" or "relationship." Yet the disproportionate support of Jews within the civil rights movement, SNCC, and legal efforts to end school desegregation, for instance, would suggest some kind of allyship. In the face of growing political opposition to voting rights and school desegregation, why would Black Power advocates risk losing bodies and resources for a political struggle discovered primarily through textbooks and political philosophers—and on the other side of the world?

Along with the philosophical tensions in SNCC's Third World agenda, the organization's decision to expand its political reach into international strife at the risk of losing allies, American Jews, and mainline Black leaders from civil rights organizations reflects a strategy that jeopardizes known risks and benefits for an unknown future. Indeed, why would SNCC join in an alliance with Palestinians and Arabs, for instance, when there was no clear economic or political benefit to them? SNCC's growing demands for Black Power should have expanded the call, I believe, for cross-cultural and racial solidarities in light of its deepening criticisms of America as an imperial nation-state. The move to alienate its allies—American Jews in particular—seems to work against the broad political goals of transnational solidarity that sat at the heart of aligning Black Power with human rights activism. In most instances, political obligations are long-standing, enduring, and immobile when the aim is to achieve pragmatic political goals. This is sometimes the prudent path to pursue in moments of extreme social oppression and political subjugation. In the case of SNCC's political solidarity with Jews, we see a different approach. Sometimes, and possibly only on rare occasions, do historical circumstances and events place limits on political solidarity, compelling political actors to pursue untraveled paths in resolving political impediments and philosophical differences. When certain "truths" or "beliefs" are violated, political actors may be inclined to pursue new political paths by suspending the pragmatic and heeding political moves that are far more ideal than otherwise pursued or imagined.

WHY PALESTINE?

SNCC's siding with Palestine and Palestinians is a story of transnational solidarity, a tale of a group's effort to show accord with a suffering people in the Third World, a way of being salt eaters.

It is also a narrative of people struggling to achieve "freedom" in and through the dismantling of "Blackness" as it was construed through the white/Black binary, namely, Blackness as inferior to whiteness. The focus of my exploration is that by claiming a transnational alliance, African Americans inserted themselves into a global imaginary, superseding or transgressing the confines of the master-slave dialectic and claiming political subjectivity or identity within the Third World Alliance. The reader can then understand freedom from within the confines of existence under looming threats of violence, an apt characterization of living "coloniality." To this end, the reader can recognize the force of rhetoric and the body as epistemic weapons within the empire. Put differently, Black folks have survived more than four hundred years of discrimination and racial domination in part because they have found counter or alternative means for understanding and executing freedom. The alliance with Palestinians is especially curious in light of the historic encounters between Blacks and (white) Jews in the United States and given African Americans' relationship to the Exodus story.

Palestine is far closer to African American political thought than one might imagine. Not only did the Exodus story capture the imagination of enslaved Africans, but early twentieth-century Black leaders turned to Zionism to help inform their own understanding of Black nationalism and strategies for liberation. Marcus Garvey, Edward Blyden, and Martin Delany are some of the early Black nationalists to engage Zionism and show support for the state of Israel. Left-leaning African Americans found within Zionism resources for Black freedom. Indeed, "some of the most principled left-wing internationalists of the first half of the twentieth century, from Du Bois to Paul Robeson, also backed the quest for Jewish nationhood. To them, the movement seemed consistent with progressive global commitments."[4]

DREAMING OF ZIONISM

Early in their careers, Pan-Africanists such as Edward Blyden, W. E. B. Du Bois, and Marcus Garvey constructed a vision of Black emancipation by appealing to many sources, including early iterations of Zionism.[5] Du Bois admired the socialist and nationalist appeals for Jewish liberation and the creation of an independent homeland for Jews. In a 1919 editorial advocating for African American involvement in reimaging and rebuilding Africa entitled "Africa for Africans," Du Bois justified his call for the "colored American to emigrate and to go as a pioneer to a country which must, sentimentally at least, possess for him the same fascination as England does for Indian-born Englishmen," based on his attraction to Zionism. He noted, "The African movement must mean to us what the Zionist movement must mean to the Jews, the centralization of race effort and the recognition of a racial front. To help bear the burden of Africa does not mean any lessening of effort in our own problem at home. Rather it means increased interest."[6] Similar to early Zionist tropes, Africa surfaced in the minds of Black intellectuals as a symbolic idea of how to develop transnational political aspirations. Far from what later advocates would call a back-to-Africa movement, Du Bois's exhortation was ethical, a way of beckoning African Americans to envision their politico-economic destiny as dependent upon African independence from colonial rule. In an unpublished 1948 essay, "The Ethics of the Problem of Palestine," Du Bois referred to Palestine as a problem for the world to solve, especially as Western nations grappled with the double problem created by modernity: the Holocaust and the question of "original possession" of Palestine. Du Bois reflected in 1950 on the dire need for both groups to think long and hard about possibly joining political forces for their mutual benefit.

Acknowledging historic and ongoing economic barriers to building wealth among African Americans, Du Bois recognized imbalanced economic power as a fundamental impediment to developing a robust coalition between Blacks and Jews. He nonetheless wanted the groups to join forces in their pursuit of a homeland in light of ongoing discriminatory laws and violence against them. Du Bois noted, "And on the world scene, the Negro people have an obligation to support the fight for a free Israel as the Jewish people have an obligation to support the fight for Africa." The "united Negro-Jewish struggle" for emancipation is deeply intertwined in Black political struggles, Du Bois observes. Pointing to the three "Jewish immigrants" who joined John Brown's group of abolitionists in 1855 in Kansas, Du Bois sketched a brief narrative of their unified political efforts.[7] Du Bois framed the early context in which Blacks in the United States and the Caribbean engaged Jews, Zionism, and Israel. As Israel attempted to gain political, military, and economic standing after 1948, the wide-ranging acceptance of Zionism as a paradigm for Black political struggles began to wane. Increasingly, left-leaning Black activists interpreted Israel's shift away from seeing itself as a utopian homeland to that of a nation-state facing issues of sovereignty, war, and economic (in)stability, issues compromising the socialist origins of Zionism.

Religious appeals to Judaism's adherence to the law and orthodoxy also played a decisive role in attracting Blacks to Zionism, especially in northern cities like Harlem, where Blacks converted to "Black Judaism." Many of the early-twentieth-century Black Jews could trace their religious lineage back to "Hebrew Christian" churches, where they continued to believe in Christ while also celebrating Passover and Saturday Sabbath.[8] "Calling themselves Israelites, Hebrews, Canaanites, Essenes,

Judaites, Rechabites, Falashas, or Abyssinians (Ethiopians), they were founded primarily by West Indian immigrants. Influenced by close contact with the Ashkenazic Jewish communities, their ministers often learned some Yiddish and Hebrew, and abandoned the Christological trappings of the earlier congregations. They still claimed a hereditary link to the biblical Israelites, but were more open to positive relations with "white" Jews."[9]

Stokely Carmichael was introduced to Zionism during his years at the Bronx High School of Science, where he developed friendships with left-leaning Jewish students who identified as "progressive and socialist." "Here I learned to sing 'Hava Nageela' and to dance the hora."[10] It was not until he was a student at Howard University that he stumbled upon writings exploring the "rights and resistance" of Palestinians, most notably in the Nation of Islam's official newspaper, *Muhammad Speaks*. Carmichael suggests the framing of the Israel/Palestine problem was largely in opposition to other media, which he says routinely characterized the Palestinians as "terrorists." What is most compelling about Carmichael's narration of his understanding of Middle East politics is his portrayal of the competing sides of the debate. On the one hand, his Jewish friends back in high school seemed to be uncritically pro-Israel; on the other hand, the Nation of Islam (NOI) offered a counter narrative of the conflict but was not necessarily transformative in its thinking about global politics in general and the Middle East in particular. However, shortly after Malcolm X's assassination in 1965, Carmichael and his fellow SNCC members stumbled upon an African American who would fundamentally shift the political focus of SNCC away from a domestic civil rights agenda to a transnational political outlook focused on human rights activism. Along with the study of Israel and Palestine, the group

turned to books on apartheid in South Africa, and in this particular examination of global politics sits the heartbeat of SNCC's
biting attacks against Israel and its link to imperial powers during the rise to statehood.

THE PALESTINIAN PROBLEM

More than a decade after Du Bois's glowing characterization
of Zionism and the "unified Negro-Jewish struggle," the Black
leftist arm of SNCC inaugurated sweeping organizational and
thematic changes to one of the most successful student organizations to emerge in the mid-twentieth century. Two fundamental political agendas drove the organization: politico-economic
self-reliance and human rights activism against colonialism. The
pull toward self-reliance influenced by observing the economic
and cultural success of Jews in the United States called for a new
political strategy in the rapidly changing civil rights agenda.[11]
Whites, including those who identified as Jews, were asked (and
in some cases forced) to leave the organization to make room
for a Black leadership that favored Black Power as its primary
tool for achieving political and economic emancipation. Second,
Black women in particular pushed the left arm of SNCC to
think about domestic politics in the context of colonialism and
transnational struggles to end Western imperialism.

WHO IS ETHEL MINOR?

No one played a bigger role in shaping the internationalist agenda
of SNCC and the Black Power movement than Ethel H. Minor.
The former advisor to Malcolm X spearheaded, and many believe

wrote, SNCC's infamous essay "The Palestinian Problem," an
unedited rebuke of the Arab–Israeli Six-Day War in 1967. Minor
encouraged young Black activists to travel outside the United
States to meet and engage with freedom fighters in the struggle
against colonialism and Western hegemony. Indeed, Stokely Carmichael's travels to places like Ghana and Guinea were prompted
by her urging; she accompanied Carmichael on many of his trips
abroad and co-wrote or edited his speeches on colonialism, Black
Power, and human rights activism. Minor also defended Carmichael against critics who deemed his travels as futile. When
Carmichael left the United States for an extended period of time
to consult with the exiled leader of Ghana, Kwame Nkrumah,
Minor defended the face of Black Power against the "white press"
that portrayed Carmichael's trip as self-imposed or an attempt
to abandon the movement. Instead, she described his trip as an
effort to materialize Black Power's vision of self-determination
through a separate homeland where the economic, political, and
cultural interests benefit, protect, and enhance human flourishing for Blacks. She explained, "Carmichael recognizes that black
people in the United States—African-Americans or Africans in
the United States—needed a land base, one which we can relate
to on a concrete basis of history, ancestry and kinship. The majority of our forefathers, who were slaves, came from the 'gold coast'
area of West Africa, which is now Ghana."[12] For what is known
of her public life as a writer and activist, Minor imagined Black
freedom within a global and African context, where she believed
the problem of anti-Blackness was far less insidious and rampant.

Born in 1938 in Chicago, she graduated from the University
of Illinois in 1959 and wanted to work for the United Nations,
but the color and gender lines prevented her dream from mate-
rializing. Instead, she traveled to Colombia, South America.
"I was trying to escape from a country that offered me limited

opportunities," she said in the late 1990s in one of the few interviews she ever granted. "I wanted to work at the United Nations, but when I got my degree . . . the U.S. government was not hiring 'colored girls' to represent this country."[13] In Colombia, she was a schoolteacher.[14]

Soon after Minor's return to the United States in 1962, Malcolm X's biting words in a television clip captured her imagination. His message resonated with her own political and religious convictions of what was needed to "save" a people demanding full citizenship rights through a political strategy of nonviolence, mostly in the form of bus boycotts and sit-ins throughout the South. His approach, though, didn't fulfill the ends she believed would liberate her people: freedom through land ownership and Third World solidarity. But the words of Malcolm X, one of the most mesmerizing speakers and political visionaries of her generation, beckoned Minor to join the NOI. She said, "Malcolm was a like a truth-bearing angel from heaven."[15] When Malcolm X was removed from the leadership role of Harlem's Mosque No. 7 in 1964, Minor left with him to establish the Organization of Afro-American Unity, where she served as his secretary.[16] Minor encouraged Malcolm X to travel to the Middle East to envision Islam through a global lens. After his assassination a year later, she returned to Chicago to write for *Muhammad Speaks*. She also continued her activism through the local chapter of SNCC. Shortly after Carmichael's Black Power speech, she met him, and he recruited her as the organization's executive director. She relocated to its Atlanta headquarters. After she joined SNCC, Minor served as Carmichael's editor and speech writer. When Carmichael broke away from the organization after his Black Power speech, Minor seems to have cut ties with the organization as well. In doing so, she devoted her full attention to a transnational political agenda that formed the foundation of her political life since her undergraduate studies. She left the United States for three months to spend time in Guinea, where she was a political strategist working with Nkrumah, Sékou Touré, the Guinean president, according to a 1972 interview with the Howard University student newspaper *The Hilltop*. Little is known about those conversations or who funded her trips.

Soon after returning to the United States, where she spent time in Washington, DC, the avowed Pan-Africanist delivered speeches throughout the area. Howard University was likely a second home, since Black Power was institutionalized among the student body. For instance, students sporting African attire, Afros, and natural hair protested in front of the Embassy of Portugal in 1972 following Portugal's aerial strikes in Tanzania. Student activism on campus had also heightened. This activism extended to a small number of faculty members who would play a significant role in the 1990s during the rise of Afrocentrism. In fact, her cousin Dr. Frances Cress Welsing, author of the widely popular *The Isis Papers: The Keys to the Colors* and a foundational voice of Afrocentrism, was an assistant professor of psychiatry at the renowned institution. For these reasons, Minor would have found a welcoming audience among the school's student body and a fraction of the faculty.

In a 1972 speech at Howard, Minor chastised Blacks who felt distraught in the aftermath of the Black Power movement. At issue was the apparent lack of a central leader or a coherent political vision of next steps for the people. She encouraged the audience to remain diligent. "People are easily disillusioned. If people don't see a structured organizer or leader at rallies, they feel nothing is going on."[17] The time was ripe, she suggested, for deepening political struggles against structural and systemic racism, classism, and neocolonialism. The political struggle did not warrant a new charismatic leader or "personality" to direct the new political agenda. Minor's speech was bold, and she did not mince words. She warned the crowd against worshiping and immortalizing figures such as Louis Farrakhan, Carmichael, and Jesse Jackson. The ongoing desire for a charismatic leader stemmed from the increasing corporatization of Black politics within the media, which substituted politics for "entertainment."

Minor's transnational, specifically Pan-African, political imagination played an outsized role in "centralizing" the shift to anti-colonial and anti-apartheid movements away from a laser focus on acquiring voting rights to secure the unfulfilled promises of democracy. Her vision was part of a broader political imaginary. Brenda Gayle Plummer reminds us that "international activism has been a strategy that African-descended people have employed historically to address their oppression in the United States."[18] Indeed, since the founding of SNCC in 1960 at Shaw University in Raleigh, North Carolina, Fanon Che Wilkins asserts the internationalist vision was a significant component of its political vision. What downplayed a coherent or systemic internationalist project was the group's decentralized format, which allowed local SNCC groups to determine the strategic vision based on the particular concerns of the local community. SNCC "organizers saw their local efforts as inseparable from larger international movements engaged in similar and sometimes overlapping struggles for freedom and self-determination."[19] Though Wilkins argues SNCC's internationalist vision informed and shaped its domestic policies, the internal struggle at the Atlanta headquarters following Carmichael's 1966 speech suggests global politics played a secondary role in its day-to-day operations. To be sure, left-leaning SNCC members developed long-term relationships with African and Arab students, as indicated by correspondence between SNCC and groups such as the Arab-American Student Alliance.

SNCC's PALESTINIAN PROBLEM

SNCC's members framed Israel's war with an Arab nation as a problem of ethics based on the unintended consequences of war against Palestine and its people. To this end, SNCC criticized Israel's use of war to justify securing both safety and land. The problem here, according to SNCC, is that this strategy mirrored those cultivated by Christian missionaries to enslave and subjugate the peoples of Africa and the Caribbean. Far more than criticizing the tactics of war, Black Power activists condemned "occupation," European Jewish immigration to Israel as signs of an ongoing war between colonizers and the Third World. Guided by political expediency between friend and foe, acquisition of natural resources and military might, both wars (1948 and 1967) foretell a narrative of Black Power that advocates wanted to avoid: a European Jewry supported by new friends (South Africa) and old foes (Great Britain) against a steadily declining Palestinian nation.

Three fundamental points frame the SNCC's criticism of Israel: First, the article claimed that Zionism "created the 'State of Israel' by sending Jewish immigrants from Europe into Palestine . . . to take over the land and homes belonging to the Arabs" without any concern for the Palestinians. The point highlights a fundamental racial tension that SNCC wanted to exploit, that is, European expansionism within Palestine, albeit among European Jews. The move here sets the stage for a European over the subaltern binary, one that would make sense within the context of U.S. racial codes and colonialism in Africa and the Caribbean. Second, in its formation, Israel, according to SNCC, received "maximum support" from former colonial powers such as Great Britain and the United States. Here, the point may have been overstated but it nonetheless speaks to a key component of SNCC's argument: that Israel is forever bound to and by states

that solidified their "democracies" through economic exploitation and the political subjugation of Black bodies. Why is this
important? Because it sets the stage for understanding the moral
backdrop to SNCC's concern. At issue is not the emergence or
the justification of a homeland for the Jewish people; instead,
SNCC is questioning Israel's alliances with "colonial powers" as
a way of legitimating itself.

The third fundamental point of the article's argument is the
"Palestinian Problem." According to the newsletter, the problem
of Palestinians predated 1948; in fact, it is traced back to 1897,
when the Zion Congress set in motion plans to make Palestine
a homeland for Jewish people. Subsequently, as the newsletter
indicated in question four of its thirty-two questions, Palestine
became a "world problem" in 1917 when Great Britain introduced the Balfour Declaration, which noted for the first time a
major political power's support for a "homeland" for Jews. This
final point is noteworthy for two reasons. On the one hand, it
builds support for SNCC's primary argument regarding Great
Britain's support of European Jews over and against Palestinians.
On the other hand, SNCC acknowledges that the "Palestinian
Problem" was not created by the establishment of Israel; instead,
Palestine, similar to Du Bois's "Negro Problem," was produced
when its future was negotiated and determined by the economic
and political conditions of colonialism.

The layout of the article is also noteworthy. The article is presented around two cartoons, which are arresting, staggering, and
flagrant. In one cartoon, a Black hand brandishing a machete
with the words "liberation movement" etched on the blade
dangles in the center of a noose. The uncharacteristic depictions
by SNCC of Israel and Jews represent capitalism as an inherent doctrine of Judaism, triggering for its reader generations-old
tropes of Jews as unethical moneylenders and financiers. In one

picture, a bald soldier wears a patch over his left eye. His shirt has the Star of David on the collar and each shoulder is adorned with dollar signs. The second cartoon is far more diabolical. A hand with a tattooed Star of David holds a rope in the form of an upside-down *U*. At each end of the rope is a noose wrapped around the necks of two men. One appears to be a Palestinian or Arab and the other an African American.

As far as one can tell, SNCC was irate by this relationship between Israel and colonial powers as necessarily fueling and leading to Israel's turn to war to settle border disputes. To be sure, Carmichael was especially angered by Israel's relationship with South Africa. As he described it in his autobiography, the discovery "that the government of Israel was maintaining such a long, cozy, and warm relationship with the worst enemies of black people came as a real shock. A kind of betrayal."[20] This "betrayal," which suggested a preexisting political and cultural intimacy between Blacks and Jews, Carmichael linked to Israel's turn away from what he called "principled Zionism" to a form of Zionism he did not recognize.

PALESTINE AND BLACK POLITICAL THOUGHT

"The Palestinian Problem" essay is significant within Black political thought for at least two reasons: First, the article details rather boldly SNCC's political shift away from domestic concerns of voting rights to transnational concerns of sovereignty and human rights activism. Second, the emphasis on colonial power and the empire mark a direct attack against the United States and its hegemonic role in global politics. Keith Feldman calls the article a "groundbreaking rhetorical and imaginative work to remap the relationship between domestic movements for racial justice in the United States and transnational struggles for liberation in Israel/Palestine."[21] This political shift seems to be fueled by a reemergence of Black internationalism among left-leaning SNCC activists who are calling for Black Power. To be sure, Feldman's magnificent archival work details the increasing political turn to global politics, and especially the focus on the Israel/Palestine problem. He argues that SNCC's remapping of Black political thought foregrounds the rise of the "New Left racial politics," which unfolded into postcolonial critiques of political subjugation happening in places such as Algeria, Palestine, and South Africa. Along with SNCC, widespread condemnation of colonialism and apartheid ranged from the Black Panther Party to the Black Arts movement. "Indeed, some of the most durable critiques of the colonial occupation of Palestine have emerged through the embattled post-civil rights spaces imagined by SNCC in 1967. That is the article's oft-forgotten future."[22]

One of the most striking elements of Feldman's essay is his analysis of SNCC's critical engagement with and employment of the phrase "permanent state of war." Feldman frames it as an analytic category to underscore the extension of SNNC's move away from a rights-based political agenda to a political philosophy aimed at disclosing power—economic, political, and cultural—as both the discursive and structural tool developed and delimited to maintain and secure the "Western" among resource-rich "Third-World" nations. This otherwise amorphous but far-reaching category is evident in economic policies and public laws that too often impede and create social contexts blighted by poverty and crime, leaving working-class and Black and Brown populations trapped in a vicious cycle of political and economic despair.

June Jordan describes the point in her seminal essay, "For My American Family." Here, Jordan moves beyond civil rights motifs of racial uplift and the politics of respectability to explore the structural and internal implications of the "war" on Black families, detailing its disciplinary reach. Jordan highlights clearly and without hesitation the multilayered dimensions of power and how it frames the internal and external war against Black families. The sociopolitical scope of subjugation, as Jordan notes, encapsulates the framing of anti-Black racism within the context of global politics that emerges with Black Power. As Feldman rightly argues, this turn away from the civil rights agenda "asks us to take seriously the counterhistorical strategies used by artists, scholars, and activists to articulate substantive forms of freedom, equality, and self-determination 'located in the fine meshes of the web of power.' "[23]SNCC's phrase "permanent state of war" is an indication of its increasing return to one of the organization's founding principles of human rights, human rights activism, and subsequently humanistic nationalism. Beyond appealing to the abstract universal rights that would have been well known in the ratification of the United Nation's 1948 Universal Declaration of Human Rights, SNCC's humanistic appeals were designed to tackle colonialism's lingering presence in establishing justice, freedom, and liberation by cultivating an ethical turn in radical politics.

THIRTY-TWO QUESTIONS ON ISRAEL

After the infamous article "The Palestinian Problem: Test Your Problem," apparently a draft that was not intended for publication, only internal discussion, was leaked to the press, SNCC published it in its newsletter. The article raised thirty-two questions as a context for unfolding its interpretation of Israel and Palestine. Here, I focus on three of them: First, the claim that Zionism "created the 'State of Israel' by sending Jewish immigrants from Europe into Palestine . . . to take over the land

and homes belonging to the Arabs." Second, the claim that the state received "maximum support" from former colonial power such as Great Britain and the United States. Third, the claim that the "Palestinian Problem" began in 1897, when the Zion Congress set in motion plans to make Palestine a homeland for Jewish people. This tension is terribly important as it initiates a conversation on how best to solve ongoing social injustice and economic disparities. Should one imagine an ideal society to start the necessary work of restorative justice? Or, is it better to start with the nitty-gritty, the actual lived experience of oppression?

STRANGE BEDFELLOWS: AMERICAN ZIONISTS AND BLACK POWER

Marc Dollinger suggests that Black Power fueled American Zionism by advancing ethnic nationalism as a response to oppression. "Black Power gifted American Jews [with] a new appreciation and enthusiasm for Jewish nationalism, redefining what it meant to be an ethnic American and inspiring an unprecedented growth in American Zionism. If African Americans could advocate for black nationalism, so too could Jews press for their version of sovereignty."[24]

How do we explain the Jewish response to SNCC's move? It's a difficult narrative. Michael Staub says the Holocaust was a guiding narrative, and Israel saw as a threat to Jewish identity any political moves that seemed to question the legitimacy of Israel and its subsequent use of force to defend itself. In addition, he writes in *Torn at the Roots: The Crisis of Jewish Liberalism*, In Postwar America the class between Gentile culture and African American traditions placed Jews in a peculiar and somewhat ambiguous political and social role. On the one hand, some inner-city Blacks, according to Nathaniel Podhoretz, ridiculed Jews for being Jews; on the other hand, they were alienated within the public-school setting. This tension placed a curious kind of problem on urban Jews: Do we pursue social justice for Blacks at the peril of our own social existence?

In an insightful article, "Black-Jewish Universalism in the Era of Identity Politics," Clayborne Carson beautifully captured the growing tension between Blacks and Jews during the 1954 to 1965 period of the civil rights movement. As he described it, the divide emerged as non-elite Blacks embraced what he called the "identity politics" of the Black Power movement, while Jews dived deeper into assimilationist models of political reform. "In an era of identity politics and cultural conflict, the universalistic values and cosmopolitan perspectives which had characterized the civil rights movement exerted less and less influence over national politics and over the attitudes of African Americans and Jews."[25] That schism would set the stage for the fallout over the development of the state of Israel.

Carson characterized the decline of Black–Jewish relations as an extension of the "worldwide decline of transracial, trans-cultural, and transnational movements seeking to realize egali-tarian and democratic ideals."[26] For Carson, Black Power sat at the center of the storm. "The increasing militancy of the civil rights movement exposed tensions that existed between African Americans and Jews regarding the usefulness of interracial political strategies and ultimately brought to the surface doubts about the assimilationist values that pervaded liberal racial reform efforts."[27] Prior to Black Power, Blacks and Jews, accord-ing to Carson, found common ground in the reformist racial politics steering the National Association for the Advancement of Colored People. The principles seemed to create an alliance between them: expanding citizenship to all, "extending political rights for former slaves," and racial integration.[28]

188 ∽ SNCC'S PALESTINIAN PROBLEM

I agree with Carson that Blacks and Jews could not come to terms about the best response to Black Power. However, I disagree with his analysis of Black Power as a symbol of the decline of universal and cosmopolitan ideals within Black political thought during the rise of Black radicalism. In fact, Black Power reinforced humanistic ideals that were latent in SNCC.

One of the fundamental political ideologies steering SNNC was Booker T. Washington's racial uplift philosophy and model of self-reliance. When members went into the Deep South to register Black voters, they emphasized the need to empower the people with the necessary resources so that they could determine their own political destiny. As a student organizer, Carmichael would often refer to Washington and his legacy of the Tuskegee Institute.

Black Power, then, emerged from a sense of self-reliance as a starting point for building economic and political power. This was the lesson SNCC's members learned from Jews. Yet as Blacks struggled for political rights and acceptance, they soon discovered that their Jewish allies had become members of the economic and political establishment.

Carson's characterization of Blacks and Jews assumed both a historical and theological connection, one burdened by and destined to fight against oppression and hegemony; because the nature of their discrimination has been rooted in their ontology, both groups' response to their existence has been to turn toward ethics.

PERMANENT WAR

Dollinger raises an important point: What if nonviolence had been the primary political strategy for solidifying Israel as a nation-state? This important question, he suggests, was never answered when Rabbi Allan Levine raised it with David Ben-Gurion.

According to Dollinger, "in retrospect . . . the independence of Israel could have been achieved without terror and violence or by the same direct nonviolent method used by those of us involved in the struggle for freedom and civil rights in the United States."[29]

The creation of the State of Israel and its 1967 war with Arab nations cemented the long wall placed over Palestine and Palestinians throughout much of the late twentieth century. What may be considered an unintended consequence of Zionism's quest to achieve "manhood" after generations of displacement, dehumanization, and the subsequent death of six million of its own beloved community set in motion an enduring war between two historically despised people—Jews and Palestinians.

Torn by what they saw as the increasing Black nationalism within the SNNC, the efforts to remove whites from leadership positions within the organization, and the ongoing criticism of liberalism and American capitalism, Jewish SNCC members slowly left the organization, signaling the decline of relationships between Blacks and Jews. Marc Dollinger called this the beginning of a "new identity politics-based consensus . . . [based on the] continued disagreements over Israeli government action and the right of Palestinians to enjoy their own national self-determination."[30]

As left-leaning members of SNCC witnessed ongoing violent attacks in the United States against Blacks in the South as they attempted to "democratize" the nation through voting, public integration, and seeking public office, they turned to transnational thinkers and organizations such as Frantz Fanon and the Arab American Student Association to find new resources and tactics to defeat anti-Black violence as well as to think globally about their own political struggles. What they discovered was glaring: the fight against colonialism and apartheid in Africa looked very much like the Black struggle in America. That is,

Blacks in the African diaspora were already trying to defeat political and economic structures either controlled or substantively influenced by Western liberalism and capitalism. Without substantive military or economic power, the struggle for political and economic liberation seemed to be doomed as long as they relied on a liberal vocabulary of equality and justice as the *primary* weapon of defense. Within the political global context of colonialism and anti-Black subjugation, Black Power activists embraced a thicker political vocabulary, one established and guided by humanistic ethics. This category reflects the discursive efforts to build a theory of freedom based on the guiding principles of self-representation, transnational political obligations, and economic independence, all of which demanded varying forms of socio-political dismantling, disruption and rebuilding of structures, and narratives and traditions that informed how one might respond to the world.

ETHICS AND THIRD WORLD ACTIVISM

Black Power's criticisms of the civil rights movement's emphasis on voting rights as the (only) necessary step to equality and freedom underscored an ongoing debate within Black political thought over the appropriate uses of justice. One way to understand the problem is to turn to what Nelson Maldonado-Torres calls "decolonial justice"[31]: it attempts to dismantle the "longstanding patterns of power that emerged as a result of colonialism, but that define culture, labor, intersubjective relations, and knowledge production well beyond the strict limits of colonial administrations."[32] Decolonial justice is guided by a "non-ethics of war," a way of denaturalizing race as ontological, subhuman, and the problem.[33] Without this fundamental feature, decolonial

justice would reinscribe normative beliefs in race as static, natural, and biological—in short as necessary starting points for justifying why a certain race of people can be condemned as evil
and subsequently murdered, imprisoned, or segregated without
any substantial cry and involvement from local or external publics. This comprehensive understanding of justice is what we
keep in mind when thinking through Black Power's criticism of
the Israel/Palestine problem. Yet Black Power activists did not
criticize the necessary grounds for Israel's existence. Instead,
they criticized state actors for adopting colonialist tactics to
defend the state and in doing so creating the conditions for an
ongoing war with a dispossessed people. And as long as war was
the primary means of protecting Jews against anti-Semitism,
the fledgling state would go down a path traveled by colonial
empires, a path on which democratic or decolonial justice is substituted for colonial justice.

Many scholars forget that a central factor driving SNCC's
response to Israel was its anti-war position. At issue, then, is
the use of war to solidify a nation-state based on a (liberal) ideal
and theory of justice. One might imagine, on the one hand, the
creation of Israel as a symbol of an ideal, a normative commitment by Great Britain and the United Nations to secure the
future of Jews in a Jewish state. On the other hand, one can
see how SNCC activists retrieved nonideal theory, the socio-
political legacy of slavery and segregation, to argue against war
and the subsequent displacement of Palestinians. By locating
the debate between Blacks and Jews within the family debate
of ideal versus nonideal theory, I show how contemporary liberal philosophy fails to offer an adequate definition of justice
that will adjudicate social conflicts and wars that are fundamentally, though only in part, rooted in ontological claims of
irredeemable differences.

WAR AND THE COLONIALITY OF JUSTICE

Five decades after Black Power, Nelson Maldonaldo-Torres developed the concept of the "coloniality of being" to imagine the possibilities of justice as an "exchange" rather than a series of "impositions." As he argues, Fanon and anti-colonial writers and activists fought against "coloniality," the "long-standing patterns of power that emerged as a result of colonialism, but that define culture, labor, intersubjective relations, and knowledge production well beyond the strict limits of colonial administration."[34] The move was born from an examination of colonialism's profound scarring on two critical sites of inquiry: being and power. On the one hand, "colonial relations of power" describes the "areas of authority, sexuality knowledge and the economy" within postcolonial contexts and exposes the "coloniality of power" in the formation of contemporary forms of domination and exploitation. Coloniality of being, on the other hand, decodes how anti-Blackness renders Black and Brown bodies the *damned* of the earth, bodies that are, as Fanon and Du Bois note, a social *and* an ontological problem. Indeed, the coloniality of being "indicates the emergence of a world structured on the basis of the lack of recognition of the greater part of humanity as givers, which legitimizes dynamics of possession, rather than generous exchange."[35] Writing against political liberalism's abstract ideal of justice based on equality and equal economic opportunity, Maldonaldo-Torres digs into the beast of colonialism by exploring "the lived experience of colonization and its impact on language," rather than employing an ideal theory to imagine the socio-political possibilities in a postcolonial context.[36]

For this reason, race, gender, and critical racial theory are necessary epistemic sources for developing a "decolonized justice," a justice based on exchange and eradicating the "normalization of the extraordinary events that take place in war."[37] This emphasis on war symbolizes the ongoing forms of *routine* abuses such as police killings of unarmed Black bodies and cruel immigration policies that include placing immigrant children in animal cages.

Decolonized justice aptly frames the epistemic lens that is guiding the "New Left" and, subsequently, compels modern readers to take seriously the humanistic strivings and ethical turn that underscored Black Power. This framing contextualizes broad analytic tools that fueled political struggles at the dawn of Black Power and anti-colonialism throughout the Americas and Africa. Liberation and freedom struggles deliberately focused on a body politic, a focus that included analyzing both the psychic and bodily violence against colonialized and castigated bodies. Liberalism's rights-based approach and emphasis on equality were secondary motivations for struggling against hegemony. As least for Black Power, embodied freedom and power fueled and motivated the struggle against political and economic subjugation. For these reasons, Black Power as a political phi-losophy encompassed a literal and imaginative turn away from white supremacist notions of the "Black and Blackness" to a substantiated human informed and shaped by self-love, com-munity, economic empowerment, and institution-building. A nagging question persisted with SNCC's new political agenda: How best to build a freedom movement without becoming fundamentalist? This question surfaced as Carmichael and his peers gained the attention of the NOI and the Honorable Elijah Muhammad. The two groups' cautious alliance was established on a clear understanding of the cultural differences between Black Power and the NOI. As Carmichael notes in his auto-biography, he respected the organization immensely but was always put off by its "authoritarianism and fundamentalist views on leadership and democratic participation within the group."

The point here is noteworthy as it highlights the ongoing struggles within Black power to cultivate the particularity of "Blackness" as an analytic category for exploring justice and freedom, without necessarily foreclosing the possibility of imagining deploying "Blackness" to think through humanism and humanistic visions of the social world. What Carmichael learned from the NOI's comprehensive philosophy of liberation is telling: Black people needed to be healed from the generations of violent torment of white supremacy. A comprehensive intervention was needed, and Black Power's emphasis on self-love was undoubtedly in response to Malcolm X's public admonishments against self-hatred. Subsequent iterations of Black Power through, for instance, Audre Lorde and Toni Cade Bambara, aimed to expose the extent to which Black self-hatred materialized from the enslavement and subsequent subjugation of Black and Brown bodies based on the colonizer's desire of the other's body, which always led to the metaphorical or literal carnage of those bound by the colonizer's normative gaze. Notwithstanding the psychic aspects of colonialism and anti-Black racism, what is clearly evident here is the discursive use of power employed by the colonizer as well as its multifaceted effects on the subjugated and the conceptual framing of the socioeconomic possibilities beyond colonialism and subjugation.

With this backdrop, it becomes easier to see Carmichael's vision of Black Power as a new political movement and philosophy designed to "advance our people's interest while avoiding narrow nationalistic regimentation or religious fundamentalism."[38] What Carmichael conceptualizes anticipates a decolonized justice based on his engagement with the works of thinkers and politicians such as Fanon and Kwame Nkrumah.

Such decolonized justice establishes a new hermeneutical lens for investigating Black Power's Israel/Palestine "problem" by focusing on the remnants of the "coloniality of being" that inform and guide Israel's emergence as a state and world power. At issue for SNCC is the process of *state-making*; by this I mean political strategies and tactics retrieved to establish a homeland within an existing colonial territory. The ethical question that Lewis Gordon argues surfaces among Blacks in an anti-Black world, *What shall I do*, seems to be guiding SNCC members as they reflect on two important points: the historic longing among many African Americans for a Black homeland vis-à-vis early-twentieth-century Jewish Zionism and the resurgence of Black internationalism and human rights activism within the Black Power movement, which necessarily suspiciously viewed the immigration of European Jews to a land populated by Brown people.

The tension here is glaring. It is one divided by nationalist leanings and humanistic strivings and explored through a decolonized justice. In other words, Black Power's indictment of Israel had everything to do with its conflicted stance on nationalism and desire to renounce imperial powers (Great Britain and the United States) as it established a Third World alliance.

When SNCC started debating the Middle East dilemma in the mid-1960s, it was nothing out of the ordinary, as the group had always discussed international issues. Indeed, during its founding conference at Shaw University, the group outlined its political obligations to "Third World politics and proposed ways to demonstrate its solidarity with Africa." Malcolm X and others had paved the way for such a move as many Black artists and leaders traveled regularly to Africa and the Middle East prior to and after SNCC's founding.

In this SNCC is representative of the leftist tradition within twentieth-century Black political thought, which includes figures such as W. E. B. Du Bois, Anna Julia Cooper, and Frantz Fanon. The tradition emphasized the degree to which Black subjugation was inscribed within the political, social, *and* moral fabrics of Western society. Indeed, the *problem people* were by nature inferior and consequently they were born into a world behind a veil that circumscribed their existence. Political and economic reform alone would not solve the Negro problem. "From the day of its birth," Du Bois wrote in *Black Reconstruction*, "the anomaly of slavery plagued a nation which asserted the equality of men, and sought to derive powers of government from the consent of the governed."[39]

SNCC grew increasingly aware of the perils of Blackness and its inability to solve the problem through a rights-based approach that only discussed domestic racism. In a speech at the organization of the Arab Student Convention in Ann Arbor, Michigan, Stokely Carmichael, chairman of SNCC, began carving out a plan to reimagine Black political struggles in the United States by turning inward and then pushing beyond familiar terrains. Put differently: Black Power, the growing theme of SNCC in the mid to late 1960s, imagined power through a reification and negation of Blackness. This is a turn toward subjectivity. Carmichael described it like this:

> Now we find that black people in the United States are colonized people, as differentiated from exploited people. . . . Colonized people are not only exploited because of economic wealth, but their culture, their values, their languages, their entire way of life are stripped from them and they are forced to identify with the oppressor.[40]
>
> [Black power is the struggle to achieve] our humanity. . . . It is not just a fight to change systems, it is a fight for our very humanity, our freedom to live, to have the type of culture and language we desire, and to live and function and enjoy the wealth of the earth.[41]

Though at some point in the speech he called for an armed revolution, Carmichael seemed to be speaking rhetorically. He concluded with a call for deeper subjectivity, which, he said, can only materialize when the social conditions create the context for the emergence of individual and collective freedom.

SNCC's deployment of Black Power and its increasing efforts to join human rights activism elsewhere in the world are curious representations of how those disempowered economically, politically, and militarily respond to human degradation within the context of empire. Such moves reflect ethical subjectivity. I am not suggesting that SNCC grew less concerned about domestic issues or the problem of Blackness when it turned to international crises. On the contrary: the retrieval of Black Power demonstrated their core commitment to the specific realities facing Blacks in the United States. And yet this singular commitment to Blackness empowered them to embrace and join in struggles to improve human dignity, self-determination, and social access throughout Africa and the Middle East. I wonder if the radical inward turn was in fact an effort to escape what the philosopher and political activist Cornel West calls the normative white gaze?

SNCC's experience reminds us that any discussion of American democracy and imperialism demands a discussion of ethical subjectivity—the competing and overlapping ways in which bodies secure freedom while remaining imprisoned and subjugated by the reigning political order. How else can we imagine Black struggles without questioning the merits of the struggles' deep and long-lasting tradition of nonviolence and reconciliation? In other words, if the ethical focus is removed from historical reflections of late-twentieth-century Black political struggles within an anti-Black society, we may see only the demise and destruction of a people.

But the insertion of the ethical compels us, and dare I say *condemns us*, to envision the role of subjectivity in political struggles—this idea of imagining actors as more than rights-bearing persons but as persons seeking dignity and a deep sense of belonging even as they remained bound by public laws and cultural beliefs that legalized and justified their oppression.

One of the most striking lessons that we can learn from SNCC's move away from traditional civil rights activism is the degree to which our political aspirations must be tailored by and subjected to the ethical traditions that are germane to the group at hand. If not, our efforts to find political freedom and liberation based on ethical subjectivity will always be at risk of reinforcing the very hegemonies we are attempting to debunk. Indeed, the inclusion of ethical subjectivity does not guarantee that old oppressions will not resurface but sheds light on the limits *and* breadth of our political aspirations.

As we think about ways to deepen our discussion of religion's role in shaping American imperialism, the relationship between SNCC and Jews is a compelling narrative to consider. Indeed, it raises some questions we struggle to face: Will group identity always supersede political solidarity? Under what conditions will we risk the pragmatic for political goals that may not immediately benefit us but are nonetheless noble and necessary in fulfilling the need for dignity, shelter, and worth for the stranger, the alien, and dispossessed? The experience of SNCC is a cautionary tale about what happens when one pushes the boundaries of the political. Empire always strikes back, and the steady fragmentation—and some say decline—of SNCC's once towering reputation never recovered after its turn to Black Power and human rights activism. Maybe this decline is the price of claiming and striving toward human subjectivity, the Du Boisian tragic soul-life in and through which freedom is discovered and possibly even destroyed.

7

THE RELIGION OF BLACK POWER

They always laughed whenever Floyd John Hood asked them to look into the brown bowl. As they sat at the kitchen table in the one-room shack and stared at the crystals, rocks, and small figurines, their laughter would almost always shift to tears, or collapse into a frozen stillness or give way to what Floyd called "a shivering tongue," what can be best described as a relentless rambling of indecipherable words. When the shock wore off, Floyd would decode what had been said and then ask the person sitting across from him a series of questions. After his reading, he walked outside to his nearby garden, where he placed his left hand in the dirt. Known to everyone in the community as "Top Hat" and "the physician," he sometimes returned to the kitchen with herbs or flowers for the person; other times he came back empty handed. This concluded the reading. Top Hat's clients then paid him the best way they could: money, tailored clothing, a truckload of fresh fruits or vegetables, and, on rare occasions, with live animals such as cattle. From all over Alabama, women and men, black and white, traveled in the 1930s and 1940s to the rural town of Marion, nearly seventy miles south of Birmingham, to seek Top Hat's advice to solve a marital strife or personal challenge, locate stolen livestock, or receive a remedy to cure an illness.

This is the narrative that my late grandmother, Mary Kate Johnson, shared in a number of conversations as she approached her death at the age of ninety-one in 2016. She spoke of Top Hat with deep fondness, duplicating many of his home remedies when friends and relatives called with physical ailments. She even possessed his gift of discernment and interpretation. I recall throughout my childhood the countless phone calls that asked for "Sister Kate" or "Sister Johnson" to interpret a dream. While it was not until decades later that I possessed the words to capture what I witnessed and overheard, I always knew my grandmother's faith was both eclectic and fundamentally rooted in bodies: faith in the body to heal itself, faith in the body to withstand physical violence, and faith in the body to move mountains, literally.

Whenever we found ourselves at the kitchen table, religion would inevitably surface. One day on a visit home from graduate school, I decided to stoke the fire. I knew she did not believe women should be ordained clergy, but I wanted to challenge her in a polite way. When I asked her whether she attributed her religious convictions and deep faith to a particular minister or family member, she said it was my great-grandfather, Top Hat, who had played the most significant role in shaping her religious faith. At this point in the conversation, I was confused. "Grandma," I implored, "you don't believe in women preachers, but you condone the work of a conjurer, someone you said rarely (if ever) stepped into a church. This doesn't make any sense." She looked at and through me with fiercely dark eyes. "Terrence," she said, "he was a kind and gentle man, and helped everyone he could. I don't understand how the Bible's condemnation of women preachers has anything to do with the work Top Hat did for others. Why are you so confused? It makes plenty sense to me."

The tension I interpreted between my grandmother's disapproval of women preachers and her favorable view of my great-grandfather's "conjure-work," did not exist within her religious orientation and moral imagination. As I probed deeper into her convictions, I discovered that what she believed the Bible said regarding women preachers had nothing to do with her affirmative belief in women's authority in and outside the church. Without saying so, she had employed what Lewis R. Gordon called a hermeneutical turn within her religious imagination, a move that allowed her to acknowledge doctrinal and cultural teachings without obscuring her own interpretive lens. Indeed, there was a normalcy in my grandmother's understanding of gender roles in the church and conjure work in Black religion that I find compelling and, to be frank, challenging to understand. It was a complicated but commonsense understanding of religion that disrupted the binary between the old and new, institutionalized and noninstitutionalized, and African versus Christian, as Black Power did, too. The tension between my great-grandfather's conjure business and my grandmother's vision of the Black church may seem counterintuitive, but it in fact aptly characterizes what Yvonne Chireau in *Black Magic* calls "vernacular religion," the "contrast between official doctrines of institutional religions . . . and the vast territory of behaviors that human beings may invest with religious meaning."[1]

Burdened by the Du Boisian question of "How does it feel to be a problem?" or what I have called the "moral problem of Blackness," Blacks like Top Hat and my grandmother in the mid-twentieth century found themselves grappling with the double consciousness of being both subalterns and knowledge producers within a white supremacist society. Cast behind the veil of Blackness, to borrow from Du Bois, Blacks were an invisible presence to most whites, commodities born for the sole purpose of maintaining white economic, political, and social dominance. And yet within the veil, they built long-standing independent religious, educational, and cultural traditions that were sustained by narratives and circumscribed by practices and habits. The epistemic vitality within the veil stemmed, in part, from what I characterize as the sacred subjectivity of Black vernacular religious narratives and traditions. By this I mean what Dianne Stewart and Tracey Hucks describe in their groundbreaking essay "Africana Religious Studies" as "sacred subjectivity communicators"—women and men who reformulated and reconstituted moral and religious vocabularies from the collision between Christianity and African traditions in the New World. Indeed, African slaves and their descendants arrived in the New World, I believe, with preexisting knowledge and vocabularies that did not die in slavery and subsequent encounters with white supremacy. The knowledge they possessed was evident in conjure, divination, and elaborate burial rites, to name a few, that emerged as long-lasting traditions. As these traditions expanded, new moral vocabularies emerged alongside cultural rituals that normalized the diversity of Black religion and religious expressions.

The singular importance of Black religion is undeniable. Indeed, Black religion's understanding of scripture as a talking book, as an encounter between an individual and God or a community and the prophets of the Hebrew people, fundamentally transformed how enslaved people imagined religion, themselves, and the New World they were forced to build. By inserting themselves within an otherwise dead text, one deployed to demarcate their oppression and subjugation, they breathed life into the ancient scrolls through new applications and interpretations of a foreign God. The Bible was probably the single most important text among the enslaved, and it served as a reference point in political debates long after slavery ended. In fact, Allen

Callahan goes so far as to argue that the Bible is the "book of slavery's children."[2] For the approach to scripture among the enslaved was fundamentally at odds with standard interpretations employed by (white) Christian enslavers. Callahan argues that slaves imitated what they heard in white sermons—but it did not prevent them from creating a new theological and hermeneutical starting point. The shift, in part, had everything to do with how they were introduced to the Bible. Most slaves studied the Bible through oral recitations and subsequently memorized scripture before they had ever laid eyes on the text. "It was through the human voice, then, and not the printed page, that the Bible came to inhabit the slave's inner world."[3] Afro-Christians relied on this hermeneutical turn to push against the anti-Blackness, to make sense of their human passion in and through their tattered and beautiful souls.

Without conjure and Black folk traditions, Black Power and Black radical traditions would have lacked the conceptual and imaginative space to engage anti-Black racism beyond the white /Black binary and political liberal tradition. The legacy of the *talking book* and of African Americans reading and writing themselves into biblical narratives establishes a political paradigm for *reading* and "reenvisioning" texts such as the U.S. Constitution and the Declaration of Independence. Writings from David Walker's *Appeal* and Martin Luther King's "Letter from Birmingham Jail" establish a framework for the hermeneutical turn in Black politics and the emergence of Black Power. As Theophus Smith argues in his noteworthy *Conjuring Culture: Biblical Formations of Black America*, "indigenous African and extra-Christian elements were also at work in the success and character" of biblical hermeneutics and religious orientation among nineteenth- and early-twentieth-century African Americans. The "conjurational performances at the level of social history employ biblical figures with a curative intention (as materia medica), and for purposes of reenvisioning and transforming lived experience and social reality through mimetic or imitative operations."[4]

As Smith aptly notes, the "innovation" of Black conjure is its pragmatic import on the "social imagination and political performances" of African Americans. This is not to suggest that religion is primary or necessary within Black political thought; rather, Black religion contains the conceptual tools to undercut racism, gender oppression, and classism when it is used to expand who might enter and engage historically dogmatic and dominating texts and traditions.

To this end, Black religion offers a compelling counter-narrative to the widely popular Afropessimism. As noted by Lewis R. Gordon, Afropessimism challenges the viability of Black liberation or freedom from the white/Black binary. "The world that produced blacks and in consequence Blacks is, for Afropessimists, a crushing, historical one whose Manichaean divide is sustained contraries best kept segregated."[5] Within Afropessimism, Blackness as a racist invention assumes two fundamental starting points: that the social world is anti-Black and that Blackness is inescapable.[6] Conceptually, Frank Wilderson III, for instance, is correct when he asserts, "Blackness and Slaveness are inextricably bound in such a way that whereas Slaveness can be separated from Blackness, Blackness cannot exist as other than Slaveness."[7] The ideology of white supremacy reinforces and recreates Blackness not only as an aberration of whiteness but as a morally and epistemically oriented in unfreedom or "slaveness." However, the social and performative elements of Black religion, specifically conjure, underscore the extent to which Blackness is reoriented, redefined, and reimagined both conceptually and through the lived experience of African American religion and religious practices.

Imagining African American religions as sacred subjectivity traditions opens the conceptual space for disengaging Wilderson's

slaveness from Blackness, one in which the divine and sacred
are within arm's reach and the priestly role is inhabited by sin-
ful, human flesh. Building upon Frantz Fanon, William R. Jones,
Alice Walker, and Anthony Pinn, what I call sacred subjectivity
symbolizes a heuristic tool in which conjure might reassemble the
shattered pieces of Black bodies torn asunder by white supremacy. Sacred subjectivity involves two important moves: First, it
involves an awareness of one's body and soul; second, it assumes
an ethical question: Will one choose to look at the brokenness?
This latter question also involves acknowledging the degree to
which bad faith (which Lewis R. Gordon characterizes as choosing to see and accepting the consequences of what one chooses
not to see) offers a sobering corrective to the theological claims
of God's role in the lived expression of liberation. As Gordon
brilliantly notes, "efforts to rationalize black suffering as part of
a divine theological plan are flawed . . . because of an unwilling-
ness to regard the multi-evidentiality of suffering and the historical situation of black people"[8] in white supremacist contexts. This
point underscores the intensely intimate, painfully subjective turn
or awareness of the price of emancipation from within Black religion: How do we explain unmerited and unjustified Black suffering? He imagines human angst, the tragic nature of Black life,
and the folly or whimsical nature of human will, desire, and longing through a community's self-understanding of scripture. It
is not a matter of whether humans will suffer but when and for
how long. With this move, conjure erases God's sovereignty from
day-to-day human interaction, limits any subsequent God-talk
in delimiting human will, and peers into the existential path of
humankind. What I am creating is unnerving, I know—a bru-
tally candid and sordid narration of human passion, sorrow, and
joy. God's presence is constant, shifting, and wholly absolved of
any responsibility for human action. Similar to Anthony Pinn's

nontheistic theology, conjure orients itself "through the centrality of the body and the embodied self's presentation in time and
space adds marker[s] of the religious."[9] God, then, emerges as a
symbol through which humans can interpret their past, imagine
the future, and understand immediate circumstances. It is the
caretakers of scripture, of God's "word," who are responsible for
unmerited suffering and pain. For it is through their misreading
of scripture and haste in appealing to scripture to address and
ameliorate anti-Blackness that religion and the sacred are blamed
for Black suffering. And yet, sacred subjectivity remains constant
in the vocabulary, symbols, and aesthetics of African American
literature, philosophy, and political thought. What I am pro-
posing builds upon classic understandings of slave religion and
Afro-Christianity.

SLAVE RELIGION

Albert J. Raboteau's *Slave Religion: The "Invisible Institution"
in the Antebellum South* is singularly the most important historical text for exploring and understanding the relationship
between Christianity and Africanisms during American slavery.
Raboteau's towering historical examination of Black religion
continues to define and demarcate the epistemic boundaries of
African American religions and foster innovative research and
scholarship regarding the religious cultures, traditions, and practices of African descendants in the South. Without his careful
detail to the archival data and robust theoretical understanding
of competing religious traditions, we would have a warped view
of religion and African American religions in particular.

What I identify as the three most noteworthy contributions
to the field by *Slave Religion* I characterize here broadly, but

they nonetheless speak to the scope and depth of Raboteau's exemplary scholarship. First, he outlines a conceptual framework for imagining both the geographic and epistemic terrain of African slaves and their competing religious and philosophical traditions. This move allows Raboteau to explore specific tribal religious, ethnic, and cultural origins, which provides sufficient justificatory grounds for linking slaves and their religious practices back to Africa, while also illustrating the universal religious orientations that were embedded within competing ethnic groups. Second, Raboteau portrays slave religion as a living tradition, one in which the "fundamental religious perspectives of Africa have continued to orient the descendants of slaves in the New World" without overshadowing the novel religious inventions developed by African-descended people in the Americas.[10] Third, Raboteau explores the link between "institutional" and "noninstitutional" forms of religious expression to justify a bold move within his work: like my grandmother he claims that conjure "could, without contradiction, exist side by side with Christianity in the same individual and in the same community, because for the slaves, conjure answered purposes which Christianity did not and Christianity answered purposes which conjure did not."[11] This is a critical point of entry for me into his work but a position I am struggling to understand. Indeed, why is Raboteau inclined to argue for the coexistence and compatibility of these disparate traditions? My inclination is that a sacred subjectivity approach to African American religions might extend his project and possibly allow readers to embrace new religious traditions that are evident in slave religion but distinct from Afro-Christianity.

As I attempt to decipher the significance of religious sacred subjectivity within the ethical and moral traditions of African American religions, *Slave Religion* is a necessary starting point

for my study. However, what I define as the post–Christian religious strivings among Blacks at the turn of the twentieth century may disrupt some of the Christian theological boundaries
inscribed within Raboteau's portrayal of the religious expression
of slaves as a primarily Christian endeavor. As he describes it, "in
the peak experience of conversion, slaves felt raised from death
to life, from sorrow to joy, from damnation to election."[12] This
Christian transformative experience is critical to the history
of Afro-Christianity and deserves careful scrutiny. But there
is another tradition at work among the slaves that created an
enduring discourse evident in the twentieth century, a tradition that Yvonne Chireau eloquently describes as the "strange
fluidity" with which Blacks have moved between Christianity
and conjure, and divination and Black magic. The fluidity that
Chireau characterizes in her book, I want to suggest, stems from
a discourse rooted in a tradition of religious sacred subjectivity,
which brought overlapping and competing vocabularies and
conceptual schemes into expression and investigation as New
World Africans articulated their moral imaginations and religious identity within the confines of slavery and subjugation.
This sacred subjectivity approach assumes that the primary goal
of our scholarship is to examine the meaning-making within
Black religion and its rituals, discourse, and traditions.

To some, this may look like a form of navel gazing. But it is
something else—a disruption of the normative white gaze that
rewards scholarly productions that show a rugged compatibility
between the slave and nonslave, the civilized and the brute, the
Christian and the savage. For justifiable reasons, many scholarly
endeavors of Black religion have attempted to shed light on the
deep resilience and fierce efforts among Blacks to debunk beliefs
in their subaltern and subhuman status. *Slave Religion* mag-
nificently portrayed African traditions as legitimate epistemic

resources, a noteworthy move in the late 1970s. I wonder, though, if too many of us have focused on Raboteau's effort to shed light on the real and viable traditions within slave communities as a means to overdetermine slaves and slave religion. Indeed, exploring and examining Black religion primarily as a subversive tool has led to dangerous results: First, the political end to which Black religion strives, in some scholarly instances, have been conspicuously liberal and pragmatic; second, the emphasis on politics, most notably the Exodus narrative, has nearly decimated an entire field of scholarly interest in Africa within African American religions and conversely has created a preoccupation with the vitality and validity of Africanisms in the New World. If we shift our attention to creating new methods for exploring the meaning-making of Black religion without the explicit worry of the Exodus narrative or of Africa, we will in fact discover rich and varied political traditions and deeply ingrained memories and the rememory of Africa while accomplishing what to date remains a lingering hope: assuming that Black religion is already at the center without need for laudatory justifications or peer approval. The recentering of Black religion, borrowing from Toni Morrison's literary analysis of Black vernacular language and marginality, attempts to address the concerns raised by scholars such as Chireau, Hucks, and Stewart in regards to expanding the epistemic terrain of African American religions.

CONJURE

Conjure, then, is an extension of the slave religion, especially of the hermeneutical moves these slaves and their descendants invented as they inserted themselves into scripture. I call this move a hermeneutical extension, a way of imagining new meanings within the narrative accounts of human suffering and flourishing in antiquity. By making this hermeneutical extension, and imagining new meanings for their lives, African descendants created a set of practices that gave life to a material culture that allowed them to invent and perform their sacred subjectivity. Sacred subjectivity was constant but shifting throughout Black religion and religious expressions. It surfaced when the individual or group attempted to produce life in and through the holy texts, songs, and rituals they engaged. This dialogical exchange assumed that the participant had direct access to the text—as long as she mastered the norms of her given community. This religious encounter underscored ethical subjectivity, a way of manipulating, transforming, and producing new life.

As you might imagine, I am attempting to carve out a space between two major extensions of and subsequent challenges to Raboteau's thesis: that is, between the compatibility thesis (Chireau) and the indigenous religious cultures thesis (Stewart and Hucks). On the one hand, Chireau argues, "historically, many black Americans have not separated magical beliefs from religion, seeing that the two exist as necessary counterparts."[13] Put differently: African slaves assumed Christianity and Africanisms were compatible. On the other hand, as Stewart and Hucks argue in "Africana Religious Studies: Toward a Transdisciplinary Agenda in an Emerging Field," the long-lasting traditions of Africanisms in Black religion suggest that slave religion included counter-religious traditions and values that were epistemically and philosophically distinct from Christianity.

I want to differentiate my work by extending Chireau's project and suggesting that the fluidity examined between Christianity and, say, divination, is indicative of a distinct tradition, one reflecting not simply a fluidity of religious expression but of the sacred subjectivity nature of Black religions. Like Stewart and

Hucks, I want to push for a "transdisciplinary" approach to the academic study of African American religions, one in which the indigenous religious cultures thesis serves as a guiding framework for evaluating traditions and practices. (To be clear, Raboteau set the original framework for this transdisciplinary method.)

However, I want to rethink what Hucks and Stewart call the "ritual theological continuity between African and Black communities in the U.S."[14] As Stephanie Smallwood asserts in *Saltwater Slavery*, African slaves found themselves in a "transatlantic exile . . . [without] the return journeys, correspondence, and other means of contact by which migrants shaped networks of social and informative exchange between their origins and destinations."[15] I believe there is a disruption of Africa as a formative site of continuous interaction in the New World. What am I saying? That the African gods were reinvented because there was not a continuous and sustained relationship with the continent. That because the slave ship ended most direct familial contact with Africa, and prevented the circular nature of narratives to remain in contact with the motherland, there was a one-dimensional understanding of African culture among the slaves. This does not mean the religious cultures died. Instead, narratives and traditions—the stories slaves inherited and passed along and the discourses that sustained narratives and established practices—took on new and unique discursive roles in the New World. Conjure and divination, for instance, emerged there because Africans carried with them a preexisting knowledge and working vocabulary of them. The traditions thrived and influenced generations of African-descended people, in part because the narratives behind the traditions were modified and shifted when new practitioners inherited the practices. In other words, as a symbol Africa becomes generative for disrupting, decentering, and rebuilding religious meaning. As a formative site, the

New World may or may not correspond to the historical cur-
rents or trends within Africa.

The sacred subjectivity of Black religion assumes two fundamental notions: first, it takes into account a vibrant tradition of
code-switching, the insertion of competing, overlapping, and
sometimes seemingly contradictory vocabularies and conceptual
schemes both to comprehend and express religious meanings of
the subject under examination. Second, this approach locates the
"originary" space of Black religion not only as in the symbol or
site of Africa but also within the interiority and practice of formerly enslaved peoples. One of the most dynamic expressions of
sacred subjectivity materializes in Black theology of liberation.
Unfortunately, the first iteration of Black theology of liberation
dismisses any meaningful account of interiority and leaves unaddressed the question of Africa.

BLACK POWER AND
LIBERATION THEOLOGY

James Cone's groundbreaking *Black Theology and Black Power*,
published in 1969, lays the groundwork for understanding Black
radicalism within Afro-Christianity in the twentieth century.
Cone retrieves the rhetorical forces of Black Power to develop
what would become nearly a half-century-long project of Black
liberation theology, one engaged in highlighting a God of liberation for African Americans, primarily, and the poor and disenfranchised, secondarily. His liberation theology begins with
Black Power, where the theologian interprets the message of
the New Testament within the political struggles of the 1960s
to liberate African Americans. "This work, then, is written with
a definite attitude, the attitude of an angry black man, disgusted

with the oppression of black people in America and with the scholarly demand to be 'objective' about it."[16]

For Cone, Black Power is "Christ's central message to the twentieth-century America."[17] While the message of scripture is timeless and does not change, Cone notes that every generation must bring the specific circumstances of the moment to the pages of scripture. Cone builds the case for Black Power's theological viability by appealing to three important points: First, both Christianity and Black Power are philosophies that fundamentally and wholeheartedly aim to liberate humankind.[18] Cone envisions the gospels providing the evidence to support this image of a liberating Jesus freeing the oppressed, wounded, and incarcerated. Second, the gospels of the New Testament bear witness to God's promise to walk and coexist with humans in the present moment.[19] "For the gospel proclaims that God is with us now, actively fighting the forces which would make man captive."[20] Christians are charged, therefore, to join God in fulfilling scripture on earth. Third, Cone argues, freedom and justice are "interdependent." For without justice, "a man's freedom is threatened."[21] Justice for Cone is entangled in the being of God, specifically as being is found in God's righteousness within history and "the historical events of the time and effecting his purpose despite those who oppose it."[22] To justify what Cone believes is God's liberating hand in history, he must link God's righteousness to African Americans. Since God reveals divine righteousness to the poor, oppressed, and powerless, especially within the Exodus story in the Hebrew Bible, according to Cone, God must remain "true to himself" by extending righteousness also to African Americans—the oppressed and disinherited of Cone's generation. "It is within this context that men should be reminded of the awesome political responsibility that follows from justification by faith. To be made righteous through

Christ places a man in the situation where he, too, like Christ, must be for the poor, for God, and against the world."[23] Cone places an enormous political burden upon the Christian church and Christians, for to follow Christ is to stand in solidarity with African Americans and join in their political struggles against white supremacy and its analogues.

ANTI-BLACK RACISM, LIBERATION, AND CHRISTIANITY

Certainly, Cone's *Black Theology and Black Power* fundamentally alters the content of and epistemic resources used to examine theology in late-twentieth-century American religion and Christianity throughout Africa. Certainly, his scholarship is significant. However, Womanist theologians and scholars of African American religions have raised deep concerns regarding the scope of liberation within his project as well as his understanding of race and gender. Here, I am interested in two aspects of the criticisms: Cone's link between freedom and justice, and the fact that instead of using Black sources to inform his understanding of Black Power's political cry, he reads Black Power through Anglo-Christianity.

Cone connects freedom and justice in *Black Theology and Black Power*, saying that they not only overlap but that they are fundamentally dependent upon God's righteousness. He defines liberalism as proceduralism without "conflict" or "risk."[24] This definition extends itself to Cone's understanding of justice as equal protection under the law. Within this liberal framework, all rights-bearing citizens are equally protected and guaranteed equal access. Freedom, according to him, is subsequently dependent on justice. "Where there is no justice in the land, a man's

freedom is threatened."[25] Cone's definition of freedom suggests that slaves cannot be free or execute freedom in meaningful ways unless justice has been rendered. As I have suggested
elsewhere, Frederick Douglass's fight with Edward Covey is the
starting point for Douglass's freedom, a freedom he earned with
his hands through struggle.[26] Without this framework, Cone is
fatalistic about slavery and assumes that life and freedom did not
begin until after the Emancipation Proclamation. This is certainly not the case.

Cone also fails to embrace Black epistemic resources as sufficient and knowledge-generating unless they are examined and
displaced into Christian sources. He writes that Negro spirituals
are not "protest songs" but composed to help "make a psychological adjustment" within a white supremacist society. The point
is partially convincing. On the one hand, as theologian Howard
Thurman notes, the "religious folk songs" during slavery were
indeed "born" from the "genius" of African American religions
that taught every slave that he or she was a child of God.[27] For
Thurman, Negro spirituals symbolized "a monument to one of
the most striking instances on record in which a people forged a
weapon of offense and defense out of a psychological shackle."[28]
Naming slaves as a child of God was a radical move, both during and immediately after slavery ended, as it threatened the
legitimacy of anti-Blackness, enslavement, and Jim Crow. To
this end, Thurman believed that the axiom empowered enslaved
Christians to read against racist and sexist biblical interpretations but that it also led to disruptive and transformative African
American biblical hermeneutics. For instance, Thurman's grandmother, a former slave, grew tired of white ministers quoting
Paul the Apostle's "Slaves, be obedient to your masters"[29] when
she was a slave. Consequently, upon emancipation his grandmother did not allow Thurman to read to her Paul's epistles to

the early church. His grandmother's hermeneutics of suspicious, an extension of the slave's interpretation of the Exodus, transformed Thurman's hermeneutical approach to the Bible and to religion in general. It, too, played a broader role in transforming Afro-Christianity and African American biblical hermeneutics.

This brings me to the next subtext of the tradition—that Negro spirituals represented the creative genius of the enslaved, namely their refusal to die in slavery. Freedom was evident in their resistance.

> This is the discovery made by the slave that finds its expression in the song—a complete and final refusal to be stopped. The spirit broods over all the stubborn and recalcitrant aspects of experience, until they begin slowly but inevitably to take the shape of one's deep desiring. There is a bottomless resourcefulness in man that ultimately enables him to transform 'the spear of frustration into a shaft of light.' Under such a circumstance even one's deepest distress becomes so sanctified that a vast illumination points the way to the land one seeks.[30]

Thurman calls this discovery the interior place where humankind finds God. I think this point can be extended to include the slave's agency, the creative epistemic resources slaves developed to define freedom. It was a freedom without justice but nevertheless a freedom in which African Americans could construct a life independent of white supremacy, where counter-publics are produced to fight for political rights, but also a place where they can be made whole and heal themselves. All of this points to a Black radicalism, a tradition delimited by struggle against hegemony and one toward a political and spiritual wholeness.

Cone's writings changed the nature and direction of religion following the assassination of Malcolm X and Martin Luther

King Jr. His iconic *Black Theology and Black Power* retrieved the
political rhetoric of Black Power to underscore the movement's
religious dimensions as well as to disclose the epistemic value of
imagining faith, oppression, and Jesus through the wrenching
narratives of Black subjugation and resistance. In an undeniably
prophetic claim, Cone carved out the literal space within public life to engage the religious dimensions of the civil rights and
Black Power movements.

Cone's project offers a theological and philosophical corrective, J. Kameron Carter argues, to existing unencumbered
"white" theology or theologies that avoid grammars of Black
suffering and oppression. Carter suggests that the brilliance of
Cone's project is Black theology's claim regarding the "concrete-
ness" of Being. Cone's "black liberation theology comes to the
threshold of an intellectual program that theologically disrupts
modernity's analytics of race."[31]

Yet the problem is that this disruption ends up denying or
marginalizing the faith of Black people, especially as that faith
emerges within non-Christian traditions such as conjure, divination, and voodoo. By placing liberation within the hands of a
God, Cone leaves unanswered William R. Jones's concern about
how God is or can be liberating within a modern world birthed
and sustained by anti-Black racism and the subsequent subjugation of Black bodies. If Cone had worked through Black Power's
ethical turn to Pan-Africanism and human rights activism, liberation might have become for him secondary to human flourishing in and through ethical subjectivity.

This is significant because sacred subjectivity seeks to emancipate the people from the problem of Blackness, of romantic
notions of the state, and tired notions of human finitude. Sacred
subjectivity is about stripping oneself of believing that one sits
on the margins or stands on the political periphery. By this

I mean African American religions, especially the monotheistic traditions of Christianity and Islam, offered the infrastructure to construct educational, political, economic, and social platforms that would allow Blacks some semblance of safety and social life in an anti-Black society. But as Blacks demanded a greater role in the broader society, these segregated contexts could not contain the knowledge emerging from them. So when Black Power expanded the political struggle to include Black freedom, Black interiority, and the acquisition of political rights, it did so in a way that transformed religious knowledge into a new self-expression that was rooted in the reliance on human agency and ancestral agency rather than on a single suprahuman source (such as God). In fact, the publics had a difficult time interpreting Black Power because the language either was so unfamiliar and revolting that folks could not interpret Blacks' motives, or the rhetoric exposed the untold secrets or feelings that others rejected Black Power merely as a way to retaliate against the perceived traitors.

Black Power gave voice to the moral and political links between racism and rights, shifting the strict divide between public and private. Black Power created a messy conflict by collapsing two worlds. "There were spaces and places in which a single person could enter and behave as individual within the context of the community."[32] The best example of this is within Black churches. Morrison explains: "It is a very personal grief and a personal statement done among people you trust. Done within the context of the community, therefore safe. And while the shouter is performing some rite that is extremely subjective, the other people are performing as a community in protecting that person."[33] This messy entanglement between the public and private is noteworthy. Benjamin Elijah Mays and Evelyn Brooks Higginbotham have written eloquently on the Black church as a

distinct institution within African American life and have imagined it as a counter-public.

The Black Power era raised several challenges to this counter-
public. Indeed, at least during its infancy, the era reflected what
was rather uncommon in many Black churches: the privileging
of unabashed Blackness. Certainly, many churches prided themselves on the rememory of Black history, but they often did so
within the context of a politics of respectability: constructing
Blackness and Black accomplishments as equal to the best of
Anglo-American culture. Black Power cast a veil over the politics of respectability. It reified the distinctiveness of Blackness—
of Black aesthetics, virtue, and communalism—as a privilege. It
also accomplished what the Black church had not: it transferred
the rite of mourning, loss, recovery, and rememory of Blackness
from the margins to the center. Black Power was the public sign
of Black faith inserted into politics.

This radicalized African American Christianity and possibly
foreshadowed its decline by retrieving Black faith as a political
tool for designing religious subjectivity. It displaced Jesus, or
rather bracketed Jesus, and placed political salvation within the
hands of the people, particularly those who were conscious or
struggling to attain Black consciousness.

In a strange sense, the ethical turn may only be possible in
counter-public spaces such as the Black church or SNCC, where
doctrine and norms inform the working vocabulary invoked.
Afro-Christianity informs public rhetoric rather than reflects
the doctrine or strict theological rules, political habits, and moral
beliefs within the counter-public sphere. Joseph Washington
is correct when he writes rather polemically in 1964 that Black
Christianity is in fact *not* Christianity. Black Christians don't
adhere to static religious doctrinal tradition, as may be the case in
Protestant mainline denominations. The prevailing view among

scholars such as Washington and Cone is that the nature of white supremacy impeded any effort to create Afro-Christian doctrines and dogmatic practices that resemble Catholicism and Anglican, for instance, due to the church's ongoing efforts to address political, social, and economic concerns that both federal and local governments often ignored. Indeed, the institution functioned as the primary social, cultural, economic, and political fabric of Black communities during slavery and segregation. Even within Black Islamic communities such as the Nation of Islam and among U.S. practitioners of indigenous traditions like Yoruba, Black religion has been designed to address the wholeness of Black life.

From the struggle to free the enslaved from the psychic and physical violence of slavery, to imagining worlds, societies and communities in, beyond, and against white supremacy, Black religion, and specifically the Black church, has been an undeniable factor in Black politics and political thought. As far back as Phillis Wheatley's poetry and the abolitionist movement, religion, religious symbols, and language have found a comfortable home in the language developed to fight oppression and subjugation. Without the Black church, which often provided the public space and intellectual resources for sustaining political groups, organizations like Marcus Garvey's Universal Negro Improvement Association and the Nation of Islam would have floundered. Interestingly enough, the Black church's focus on religion and politics nurtured a liminal yet formidable structure that enabled Christian and non-Christians alike to use the church's resources to benefit a wide range of resources.[34] This counterpublic's unprecedented approach to religion and politics led to the emergence of complex moral beliefs and traditions, some of which stood in tension with Christianity. One such moral tradition is the ethical turn within Black radical politics that this book has described.

Against this backdrop, Cone's Black theology of liberation reinterprets Christianity through "Black experience." But it fails to develop an understanding of suffering, liberation, and the cross through the epistemic value of Blackness as expressed in ethical subjectivity. Why is this important? Not only does Black theology of liberation create what Victor Anderson calls a heroic understanding of Blackness, it also ignores the humanistic traditions within Black religions. Cone's Black theology identified God as the source of liberation and the subsequent response to Carmichael's demand. In *Black Theology and Black Power*, Cone characterized Black Power as an "inward affirmation of the essential worth of blackness."[35] The inward affirmation is a critical element for understanding Black Power, but the ethical implications of Carmichael's call for humanism and humanistic nationalism remain unanswered in Cone's powerful text. The ethical turn addresses two significant debates facing Black theology and racial liberalism. First, within this context, Black Power both anticipates and provides an answer to Victor Anderson's criticism of Black theology's ontology problem. Whereas Anderson argues that Blackness in Black theology is "always bound by white racism and the culture of survival," the ethical turn creates the conditions for imagining Blackness as a resource for thinking in and beyond traditions, a way of discovering, inventing, and disrupting self-imposed and self-construed narratives. Anderson's major concern with Black power and liberation theology, the "black survivalist culture and black revolutionary self-assertion," reflects two interventionist moves in "black collective consciousness." But Anderson fails to acknowledge Carmichael's effort to retrieve Black Power as a way to demystify and disrupt Blackness as an ontology and representative of a people. Instead, he portrays Black Power as both a hermeneutical invention and ethical move to transcend racial laws and codes.

Second, Black Power exposes the limits of racial liberalism. The question of which party one should support cannot be answered in isolation but instead must be examined alongside the question of how it feels to be a problem. In turn, this question cannot be answered if one is not willing to articulate what remains unspoken. Lifting the veil on the Negro problem demands an ethical response.

As we can see, Black Power articulated not only the limits of liberalism but also the degree to which bad faith was required or needed to participate in a system. It exposed the lack of freedom within liberalism. Within these Black counter-publics, the radical left pursued freedom, ethics, and aesthetics, "Black magic," and God. Black Power recognized what Benston calls the body as an essence/ontology and "representation." Ontology recognizes the humanity and sacred subjectivity of the body. Representation takes into account the social constructions of Blackness and thus the limits of such categorization.

Black Power, nonetheless, created a "structural and emotional" distance from the politics of respectability and rights-based politics, allowing Black leftists to invent, disrupt, and reimagine human agency within a nation-state. The internal debates reflect what Kim Benston calls the tension of the "communal self," one "that is both prior to and consequent to individual expression."[36]

FANON AND BLACK LIBERATION

Cone's Black theology also ignores the force of Frantz Fanon, the diviner of sorts. Fanon articulated the global sin of anti-Black racism—the centuries' long moral and aesthetic disdain for Blackness. Writing from Lyon, France, Fanon exposed the despair and dread oozing from his divided Caribbean and

French-influenced identities. He exposed the sexual, political, and psychoanalytic angst facing the Negro, particularly a highly gendered Negro.

In his much acclaimed book on the effects of colonialism on subjectivity, Fanon examined philosophical problems of subjectivity, authority, and ontology in certainly unfamiliar and possibly even unacceptable terms for traditional students of Western philosophy. He investigated the problem of Blackness in autobiographical points of references, centering his rhetoric within his Caribbean identity as a way of exposing the limits of colonialism and its configurations of race, sexuality, and culture. But this should not negate the epistemic value of his project.

Fanon peered into the soul, the abyss of nothingness. With his pen, he constructed a framework for a new humanism. It is a political-moral vision—but it is not without ethics. He calls for Negroes to acquire a subjectivity, and for him this act allows them to become universal. He explores this humanism within a white/Black binary of the colonizer and the colonized, managing this duality within a Hegelian-like dialectic. But the dialect does not end in Absolute Spirit but in a kind of Absolute action. This action is dependent on a critical agent, a reflective one. This agent is aware of the tragic past but is not bound, conflicted, or torn asunder by its ghosts. Instead, the agent dances with the ghosts. They divine the past as a way of seeing the present more clearly.

Fanon's is a transnational account. He puts anti-Black racism on a global scale. The African diaspora heritage looms large as he narrates the encounters between the ambiguous "white" and faceless Black (wo)man. Without essentializing the effects of colonialism's role in shaping local racial identities, he nonetheless gives a broad account of the ways in which white supremacy defines the racial and sexual subtexts of Black bodies.

Fanon divines a transnationalism and diaspora heritage that are strikingly familiar and embraced within the late-twentieth-century civil rights movement in the United States. Fanon the diviner explains the rage, violence, and psychosis that occurs more than a decade following the French publication of *Black Skin, White Masks*. It is more than the dread Blacks carry. It is a narrative of identify formation—of how colonialism locks groups within impenetrable boundaries.

Borrowing from literary critics such as Henry Louis Gates Jr., who appropriate African diasporic themes to renarrate the Black Atlantic journey in postmodern contexts across the Americas, I locate Fanon as an exemplary diviner, one whose ear bends with each echo whispered by the ancestors and who gives birth to the whispers in his analysis of the social world and context at hand. In short, Fanon sees what most are too stubbornly afraid or lacking the courage to articulate: the credulous nature of a racialized and gendered capitalist society that obliterates Black sexual and racial subjectivities. This is the nonexistence that looms throughout *Black Skin, White Masks*. "A feeling of inferiority? No, a feeling of nonexistence. Sin is Negro as virtue is white. All those white men in a group, guns in their hands, cannot be wrong. I am guilty. I do not know of what, but I know that I am no good."[37] This kind of psychoanalysis is missing from discourses on colonialism and the problem of Blackness—the feeling of nonexistence that is both internalized and manifested in the flesh, within embodied political interactions in public and private life.

In spite of the nonexistence, the Black nonetheless glimpses at her soul through traditions:

> I feel in myself a soul as immense as the world, truly a soul as deep
> as the deepest of rivers; my chest has the power to expand without

limit. I am a master and I am advised to adopt the humility of the cripple. Yesterday, awakening to the world, I saw the sky turn upon itself utterly and wholly. I wanted to rise, but the disemboweled silence fell back upon me, its wings paralyzed. Without responsibility, straddling Nothingness and Infinity, I began to weep.[38]

The glimpse of the soul causes her to weep, a weeping of joy, pain, love, violence, and hope.

There is a kind of nihilism that lurks near the periphery of colonized people's traditions, discourse, and imaginations, a nihilism Fanon's woman expresses above. This nihilism comes from a realization that Blacks may never overcome Blackness, that their bodies forever align them to a complex narrative. For Blacks, there's this perennial sense of fear of one's body and this desire for white men and women. For Black women, there's aesthetic inferiority emerging from the gross exaggerations of her sexuality and of masculine strength. This is why weeping is terribly important because their being is never accepted—by themselves or the other. Similar to Du Bois's double consciousness vis-à-vis tragic soul-life, the soul is found in struggle. Not because it is sui generis redemptive or salvific but because struggle is the only way out. Only by pushing beyond familiar landscapes may Blacks discover a life, a narrative in tension with white supremacy.

The text serves as a psychoanalytic and philosophical blueprint for decoding and deconstructing the politico-ethical imaginations of the humanistic rhetoric that emerged in transnational movements to free Blacks from colonialism, segregation, and apartheid. Cold War racism against Black troops, burgeoning Third World struggles for freedom, and the rejection of Blacks at home together created the conditions for new conversations on race. A growing number of Blacks used America's racist political and economic policies as a launching pad to join political struggles outside of the United States. Communism and socialism are clearly important in this period. Yet what scholarship on African American ethical theory and liberationist movements often overlooks is the degree to which African Americans retrieved the dominant rhetorical sources to amplify their own internal struggles as well as to bolster their alliances to the African diaspora. They retrieved the American jeremiad as a resource for three things: to advance an internal critique of the nation-state, to develop a legitimate platform to criticize Black politics and religion, and to employ a model of cosmopolitanism that tied one directly to the heart of the nation's democratic tradition. This politico-ethical imagination that retrieved aspects of the exceptionalist motif encapsulated African diaspora discourse (according to Dianne Stewart) and Black religious rhetoric to imagine a post–white supremacist world, or what is commonly called a postracial world.

The Damned of the Earth is critical for understanding the possibility of ethics and sacred subjectivity. Fanon's closing prayer gives us a glimpse of his ethics: "The Third World today faces Europe like a colossal mass whose aim should be to try to resolve the problems to which Europe has not been able to find the answers."[39] Indeed, "humanity is waiting for something from us other than such an imitation, which would be almost an obscene caricature."[40] The ethical cry is resounding, a call for humankind to emerge anew. What is new will emerge with violence. Lewis R. Gordon notes, "Without the possibility of innocence, the blackened lives the disaster of appearance where there is no room to appear nonviolently. Acceptable being is nonexistence, nonappearance, or submergence."[41] The violence is inevitable as it illuminates the passing of the old with new tropes, images, and symbols. The violence is largely metaphorical, as the history of African Americans in the modern West has been overwhelmingly nonviolent. And yet their stark cry for freedom invokes violence from state and nonstate actors alike. The presence of the Black in previously segregated contexts symbolizes violence and beckons violence from whites.

WOMANISM AND SACRED SUBJECTIVITY

The new humanism expressed in Fanon shows up in Womanist thought and theology. The insistence on self-invention, self-repair, and self-transformation as an extension of the group is symbolic of the ethical turn involved in humanistic nationalism. The move gained significant traction nearly two decades after the end of Black Power within Womanist theology. Unlike Black theology of liberation and the Black liberalism of the civil rights movement, Womanism[42] explores the wholeness of Black life by turning to literature and folk traditions to uncover the motivating religious and political principles driving Black women. Interestingly enough, Womanists, similar to American pragmatists such as Jeffrey Stout, raise serious questions concerning the nature of authority and tradition in light of increasing questions facing religion and its role in public life. Unlike Stout's account of these concerns in *The Flight from Authority*, which examines how rational autonomy replaced traditional authority, Black Power and subsequently Womanism take a slightly different approach to the problem of authority and tradition. In their accounts, freedom in community, rather than individual autonomy, is the answer to growing criticisms of white Christianity's morally repugnant response to Black subjugation, racism, sexism, and classism.

While James Cone and other scholars of liberation theology turn primarily to scripture and the Black "experience" to reimagine new pathways to emancipation, many Womanists and Black feminists focus on embodiment and Black women's "experience" as the primary sources for responding to sexism, classism, and racism. Within this epistemic framework, Womanists shy away from thick commitments to liberation and focus instead on recovering the lived experience of Black women to determine how a subjugated people unfold what in *The Souls of Black Folk* Du Bois called "human passion" in the context of unmerited terror and injustice.

Whether or not God is present in the lives of Black women, say Womanists such as Delores Williams and Katie Cannon, is not of critical concern. At issue is the display among Black women of dogged resilience both in times of joy and pain. The uncanny willingness to act, to express one's agency in spite of the reigning circumstances, serves as a starting point for understanding knowledge production within and among communities long ignored by scholars. "Womanism requires that we stress the urgency of the African American women's movement from death to life."[43] Liberation theology, therefore, was not at the center of Womanism; rather, survival and existence within the wilderness, as characterized by Delores Williams, guided adherents' emancipatory visions.

Three points are worth noting in *Black Womanist Ethics*. First, Cannon frames ethical behavior as emanating from Black women's moral wisdom traditions. By moral wisdom Cannon means the rituals through which "Blacks purge themselves of self-hate, thus asserting their own validity."[44] Moral wisdom does not appeal to "fixed rules" or explicitly normative commitments; rather, moral wisdom traditions are entangled in the lived reality of Black women's encounters with scripture, sexism in politics, and misogyny within the workplace. Cannon turns to Black literary traditions to lay out the conceptual framework of moral wisdom traditions. Second, Cannon examines African American oral traditions to explore how Black women "deal with our perennial quest for liberation" as well as to shed light on how they invented and maintained freedom within a context of racial domination. "Canon formation is a way of establishing new and larger contexts of experience within which African American women can attend to the disparity between sources of oppression and sources for liberation."[45] Third, Cannon shows how the question for liberation surfaces within Black women's refusal to die in suffering. She calls this "unctuousness [a] virtue." As she frames it, liberation is entangled in Black women's response to dehumanizing sexism and domination, and it surfaces as a virtue when Black women actively push against oppression and white supremacy. Virtue, both as faith and action, symbolizes "the quality of steadfastness, akin to fortitude, in the face of formidable oppression that serves as the most conspicuous feature in the construction of Black women's ethics."[46] And yet, Cannon is clear: unctuousness as virtue will not "save" or "liberate" Black women without the sustained support of the entire African American community. This virtue must surface in the flesh of community values, habits, and beliefs.

As Womanists examine the limits of invoking liberation theology to ameliorate injustice, Black feminists, Patricia Williams among them, are retrieving slavery and anti-Black racism to expose the deep flaws of liberalism. In both instances, Womanists and Black feminists alike move from liberation and ideal philosophies to ethics as a way to examine long-standing concerns facing democracy and democratic practices. To this end, ethics and the ethical turn take on a more profound, though dubiously latent, role in formulating responses to politics and moral disagreements. The ethical turn does not involve a particular telos or set of duties and responsibilities; instead, it reflects the behavior, ethos, and guiding assumptions that underscore the religious nature and political strivings of Black radicalism's unflinching desire to shape and sustain human flourishing.[47]

It is commonplace to think of ethics as virtue, normative, prescriptive. At least for Black women in and after Black Power, the decisions to engage in political life, sometimes at the risk of so much loss, were guided in the loose sense by ethics, and more specifically by sacred subjectivity—this ongoing critical engagement of self and community that guided their sense of political obligations and longing. Why is this important? It provides a different perspective on Black radical politics. It is not simply secular, anti-establishment, and devoid of individual examination. A great deal of attention is focused on agency, intentionality, and regulation. There seemed to be awareness both of the limits of authority and the limitless bounds of individual agency within the group. The radicalism imagined by many Womanists involved inventing and imagining the political import of sacred subjectivity.

SACRED SUBJECTIVITY

Cannon builds her Womanist ethics in and through the Black woman's body, both as lived experience and as text.[48] Using the body as rupturing, disrupting, and rebuilding is promising. For, as Ella Myers argues in *Worldly Ethics: Democratic Politics and Care for the World*, "an ethics defined in terms of arts of the self emphasizes the individual's capacity to consciously shape or reshape herself and acquire an admirable style of existence largely detached from the enforcement of a general moral code."[49] Herein lies what I want to pursue or develop: there is a long-standing tradition of ethics within the Black radical tradition. Within this context, ethics is best understood as sacred subjectivity. Ethics from behind the veil of Blackness plays a significant role in defining the framework in and through which Black radical traditions interrogate politics, culture, and the law. This is not ethics as a way to regulate individual behavior, or a proposal on how we should act, but an illumination of the critical impulses that one obtains or interrogates when one chooses to challenge authority.

More so than among other African American writers, Black feminists remind us that radical movements within the Black community have more often than not been led by Black women, and specifically working- and middle-class women who were without prominent official leadership roles. What guided these women was an insistence on identifying the individual as necessary, unique, and linked to community. In doing so, they turned their attention to an aspect of human nature that we have rarely discussed in relation to radical politics: sacred subjectivity.

Sacred subjectivity is a discourse by which political actors interrogate and negotiate the social narratives that govern their community and political alliances. It is a not a system or methodology but a hermeneutic (interpretive) and explanatory language by which political actors come to understand themselves, their actions, and their commitments. Sacred subjectivity rests on the knowledge that God is only alive and present when humans act justly. This form of action does not prescribe a particular set of doctrines or guidelines to follow. Instead, acting justly means questioning, challenging, resisting, and confirming narratives that allow moral actors to create, love, and act without fear of political retribution. From this foundation, sacred subjectivity acts as a way of radically emancipating the self from white supremacy and unleashing, freeing, and empowering the creative *spirit* of a political actor.

Such sacred subjectivity involves first rupturing, repairing and resisting. One ruptures one's relationship with one's social narratives by challenging and questioning the familiar rules and guidelines within the social narrative. Second, some level of repair ought to happen after the rupturing. One is always constituted by community, and so one has to come to terms with problems one finds with community. Third, as one repairs the relationship, one must resist returning to the status quo.

Sacred subjectivity accomplishes three important points: first, it sheds light on the necessary role of ethics within the Black radical tradition; second, it opens the door to examining how political actors are not defined by intertextuality; and third, it serves as a resource for understanding the moral decision-making behind radical theories of liberation, democracy and human flourishing.[50]

* * *

My grandmother's depiction of Top Hat reflects the explicit, and at time veiled, forms of code-switching she expressed as she described her religious convictions. While she articulated a rudimentary descriptive account of her faith, one rooted in scripture and embodied in outward expressions of Christian kindness and dutiful obligations to children, the poor, and the homeless, what was most striking was the degree to which Africanisms not only circumscribed her ordinary habits but also the ways they informed and established a coexisting spirituality rooted in the divine presence of ancestors and spiritual symbols. For example, in my grandmother's house, the death of loved ones was always characterized as "passing on." No one was ever dead but always moving on and ever present. Strangely enough, she would locate the person in heaven, and in the same sentence the person appeared to be in transition to another life. A case in point: "My sister Pearl has passed on. She's in heaven now." But we could never speak ill of Aunt Pearl, or mention the wrongs committed against her by loved ones. I once attempted to ask about Aunt Pearl's abusive husband, and my grandmother stopped me midsentence. "We don't ever talk against those who have passed on." When I pushed for an explanation, she implied that the person was nearby, within reach. Such pernicious talk, she implied, would make Aunt Pearl unhappy.

In terms of my great-grandfather's conjuring, my grandmother was not ashamed of his priestly practices. In fact, whenever she was ill or needed assistance, she would ask for his help. And after reading the Bible she would pray to Jesus as a way of sealing and affirming the reading. These examples point to meaning-making and the lived expression of sacred subjectivity; they demonstrate the emergence of sacred subjectivity, a distinct religious and spiritual ethos within African American religions.

Black religion cultivated a unique or demonstrative understanding of the triangulation of spirit, body, and soul as the single most important principle for imagining, constructing, and producing religious subjectivity and the orientation or hermeneutical turn of remapping scripture onto the body and vice versa. This remapping was not necessarily aimed at liberation, or for that matter any kind of wholeness. Instead, it produced and cultivated competitive vocabularies, symbols, and signs for navigating one's way through treacherous storms, sun-filled valleys, and vacuous mountaintops. What a radical shift away from Anglo-Christianity's ongoing tryst with exceptionalism, puritanical bliss, and sacred negative theologies! Conjuring shatters these barriers, not triumphantly but rather in ways that expose the fragility of the unfolding of our humanness. Charles Long calls this kind of framework or hermeneutical turn "an-other attitude."[51]

The approach imagined America and its idealism as steel, something impenetrable by and through Black hands. It saw the world "not as plastic and flexible, amenable to the will of the human being through hard work and moral fortitude, but a reality, impenetrable, definite, subtle, and *other*—a reality so agonizing that it forced us to give our innocence while at the same time it sustained us in humor, joy, and promise."[52] Innocence also "sustained" itself through love, deferred or otherwise, music, reinventions of the self, and conjuring.

We are now charged with exploring Blackness through the lens of conjure and sacred subjectivity without establishing a *new scripture* with strict guidelines for comprehending Blackness or African American religions. Conjurers like Top Hat now call us to explore the depths of religious meaning-making and to discover new means by which to expand our knowledge of human strivings within the context of slavery and subjugation. As my late grandmother retorted, "This may not make sense to you, but it makes plenty sense to me" and to the dogged souls of Black folk.

CONCLUSION

We are involved in a struggle for liberation: liberation from the exploitative and dehumanizing system of racism, from the manipulative control of a corporate society; liberation from the constrictive norms of "mainstream" culture, from the synthetic myths that encourage us to fashion ourselves rashly from without (reaction) rather than from within (creation). What characterizes the current movement of the '60s is away from the larger society and a turning toward each other. Our art, protest, dialogue no longer spring from the impulse to entertain, or to indulge or enlighten the conscience of the enemy; white people, whiteness, or racism; men, maleness, or chauvinism: America or imperialism . . . depending on your viewpoint and your terror. Our energies now seem to be invested in and are in turn derived from a determination to touch and to unify. What typifies the current spirit is an embrace, an embrace of the community and a hardheaded attempt to get basic with each other.[1]

From Black Power to Black Lives Matter, African Americans have testified with their lives to the possibility of freedom, love, and imagination in their struggle against the enduring burden of hatred, contempt, and violence from an unjust, racist, and sexist society. Dating back to African enslavement in the Americas, noted historian Sterling Stuckey writes that Blacks routinely responded to dehumanizing political conditions through a dynamic weaving together of religion and "folklore."[2] This "crawling back," both to discover and invent traditions for understanding their human condition, established what Stuckey calls a "black ethos," the epistemic grounds for how African slaves might "endure" enslavement.[3] What Stuckey characterizes as endurance translates into elaborate and sustained conceptions, symbols, and customs birthed in the "New World," where rituals and metaphors draped in Africanisms produced the Black ethos: ways of knowing, imagining, and understanding the world. Stuckey's insightful scholarship narrates the history of slavery by retrieving through the archives the symbols, hands, eyes, and minds of *thinking* and *feeling* Black bodies that resisted, endured, and sometimes suffocated from enslavement's dehumanizing conditions. Stuckey writes, "It is one of the curiosities of American historiography that a people who were as productive esthetically as American slaves could be studied as if they had moved in a cultural cyclotron, continually bombarded by devastating, atomizing forces which denuded them in meaningful Africanisms while destroying any and all impulses toward creativity."[4]

For Stuckey, folklore in the form of Negro spirituals and oral traditions provides the reader material culture of Black life, where burial practices, for example, were informed by and produced tradition, and herbalists and diviners mirrored and cultivated complex responses to human sorrow and suffering. Whereas missionaries introduced Christianity to maintain political and economic domination over the enslaved, many African slaves envisioned within the religion a glimpse of a familiar

God, sacred stories in which they could write themselves into the narrative, and a vocabulary expansive enough to hold the wisdom traditions they inherited from their African homelands and reproduced in the New World. This hermeneutical invention, dialogical engagement with texts and scared traditions, and reflective imagination informed the depth and range of Black politics, religion, art, and literature—all of which generated the substance of Stuckey's Black ethos. "Through their folklore," and corresponding traditions Black preaching and the Blues, "black slaves affirmed their humanity and left a lasting imprint on American culture."[5] While religion is not inherent within every aspect of Black life, scholars will be hard pressed to identify an African American tradition or set of cultural practices uninformed by Black religions, religious expressions, or sacred subjectivity. "What they learned about handling misfortune was not only a major factor in their survival as a people, but many of the lessons learned and esthetic standards established would be used by future generations of Afro-Americans in coping with a hostile world."[6]

While the civil rights movement inherited Black preaching and Negro spirituals from its institutional reliance on and connection to the historic Black church, Black Lives Matter was birthed by three Black women—Alicia Garza,[7] Patrisse Cullors[8], and Opal Tometi—who are all unaffiliated with the Black church or organized religious institutions. And yet, the political movement's foundational principles of affirming Black human dignity and rituals of "summing the ancestors" emerged from the lingering fragments of Black religious expressions of mourning the dead, honoring the ancestors, self-love, and healing. In fact, Pan-African Studies scholar Melina Abdullah, cofounder of BLM Los Angeles, suggests spirituality and "spiritual power and groundedness" of BLM were always present within the

movement, even if not "recognized explicitly" as religious expressions."[9] One of the ongoing rituals at BLM events, at least in
Los Angeles, is the pouring of libation in recognition of "those
whose bodies have been stolen through state sponsored violence"
as well as of the "warrior ancestors" of African Americans. By all
estimations, the opening ceremony at BLM demonstrations
and events is a religious expression of sacred subjectivity that
Abdullah translates into "the conscious reclamation of Black
Lives Matter as a spiritual movement. We call this our sacred
duty. . . . It's what we're summoned in to do."[10]

From BLM's inception, the founders imagined their political act of honoring and fighting for the humanity of all Black
lives through the prism of sacred duty was underscored by a
dogged love of Black people. Garza's "A Love Letter to Black
People" was posted on Facebook on July 13, 2013, the day George
Zimmerman was acquitted of the murder of Black teenager
Trayvon Martin. Her appeal changed the trajectory of Black
politics and the content of public debates on race and social
justice. Garza proclaimed, "We don't deserve to be killed with
impunity. We need to love ourselves and fight for a world where
Black lives matter. Black people. I love you. I love us. We matter.
Our lives matter."[11] Garza's posting captured the imagination of
countless Black lives long before the established media and pun-
dits recognized the political scope of what would become the
movement known as Black Lives Matter.[12]

Seven years following Twitter's explosion of #BlackLives-
Matter, the nation is once again confronting its culture of
state-sponsored killings of unarmed Black men and women.
Indeed, the killings of George Floyd, Breonna Taylor, and
Ahmaud Arbery in 2020 triggered a national and international
response unlike any other since the Montgomery Bus Boycott
in 1954 set off a national movement to address Black political

disenfranchisement. In both instances, ordinary Blacks raised their voices to demand restoration from generations of systemic, and in many cases, intentional efforts to exploit, kill, and subjugate Blacks and their communities. Unlike the heralded civil rights movement, which was largely undergirded by a fundamental belief in a constitutional democracy to overcome racial prejudices, economic disparity, and gender biases, the political ideology of BLM is being steered by a *disbelief* in America and its democratic ideals. This political disbelief introduces a piercing analysis of American democracy. The system is not broken. It is functioning as it was designed. To believe otherwise, many of our protesters are screaming, is to believe in a lie and to possess "bad faith." Rapper and social critic Killer Mike described it this way at an Atlanta press conference following days of social protest: "We don't want to see Targets burning—we want to see the system that sets up for systemic racism burned to the ground."[13] Black Lives Matter cofounder Alicia Garza raised on Twitter during the 2020 protests her growing disdain for arguments that call for "tinkering" with, for instance, the criminal justice system. "Are we going to keep tinkering with the same old same old—or will we find the courage to transform?"[14] Repairing the system from within BLM's framework involves both political organizing and spiritual work. BLM cofounder Cullors noted in a 2015 interview the dire importance of the latter. "When you are working with people who have been directly impacted by state violence and heavy policing in our communities, it is really important that there is a connection to the spirit world. . . . People's resilience, I think, is tied to their will to live, our will to survive, which is deeply spiritual."[15] Cullors's philosophical commitment is deeply woven into the infrastructure of the organization she founded, Dignity and Power Now. The organization employs a director of health and wellness, a decision

Cullors calls "a political choice to try to build a new way of fight-ing."[16] By starting with the fight for human dignity, rather than articulating a call for police reform or increased gun regulation, BLM activists are expressing a new political expression that is far reaching and consequential.

From Black Power to Black Lives Matter, Black religion has played varying roles in breaking silences and testifying to the world the failures of American democracy. From African American Muslims and Quakers, to Protestants, Universalists, and Humanists, Black religion and its ethical commitments have informed and established counter-publics, where religious and political concerns of ordinary Black folk are expressed. The BLM movement emerges in conversation with Black religious expressions of mourning, grief, and grievance, and public pro-tests stand as cultural sites re-envisioning the aims and aspira-tions of Black politics and Black political thought.

The BLM movement inherits its call to "(re)build the Black Liberation movement" from the Black church's historical role in developing a public theology of liberation based on social justice. I am not suggesting the founders of BLM turned to the church for assistance as they imagined their movement. However, the vocabulary and hermeneutical moves they employ resonate with the political vocabulary and ambitions of many progressive Black churches and BLM practitioners of African-based religions such as Yoruba or Santería. For instance, BLM's political shift away from a rights-based political project to a movement based on liberation reflects a core component of the Black religions' theo-political legacy: liberation does not always translate into the immediate acquisition of political rights but it must be pursued without fear or trembling. Liberation in many Black churches was interwoven into what Albert Raboteau in "Down at the Cross: Afro-American Spirituality" calls the "perennial mystery" of Black suffering. In this context, liberation is not an event but one that tries to make sense of an anti-Black society. The political philosopher Juliet Hooker argues Anglo-American political philosophy is ill-equipped to understand and address the comprehensive nature and role of Black suffering and dehumanization within liberalism's ideal model of justice.

> The limits of liberal democracy's ability as an institution to deal with certain types of injustice, particularly systemic racial violence and terror that is (implicitly or explicitly) sanctioned by other citizens and carried out by the state, raises key questions about our expectations of black citizens. In particular, it forces us to confront the inability of dominant approaches in liberal democratic theory to accept black anger as a legitimate response to racial terror and violence.[17]

Since 2013, BLM and its supporters have been organizing, marching, and gaining influence by speaking the painful truth that the nation has not valued Black lives. BLM carries the legacy of Black religions in how it imagines ethics, self-love, and struggle in relation to freedom and liberation.

BLM's political ideology extends the categories by which Black political thought understands politics and political activism. The political philosopher Michael Hanchard highlights two overlapping concerns facing Black political thought. First, the tradition emerges from the conceptual frameworks developed to understand racial domination and, second, "racism and race-making" sit at the center of Black political thought's understanding of Western modernity.[18] BLM extends the former by inserting human dignity and claiming the social ontology of Blackness as deserving of full attention and interrogation from political theorists.

BLM's increasingly respectable status within American politics was not always the case. Many ignored the evidence presented by BLM. Some ruled police shootings of unarmed Blacks as an aberration, a reflection of a bad apple. They chose to believe in a lie. Bad faith. Eight years later, the nation is painstakingly accepting the truth. The system is broken. Tinkering with it will not work. Transformation is needed. What does this mean? It begins with speaking the truths ignored by those in power or blinded by power's intoxicating glitter. In 1977, Lorde articulated her truth of experiencing racism within the largely white women's movement in the United States to an audience at the Modern Language Association's annual conference. She used her experience as a call for others to find their courage to break their silences. "For to survive in the mouth of this dragon we call america, we have had to learn this first and most vital lesson—that we were never meant to survive. Not as human beings. And neither were most of you here today, Black or not. And that visibility which makes us most vulnerable is that which also is the source of our greatest strength."[19]

The only way to survive in America is to believe in a lie. Especially if you are Black, the world looks upon you with disgust, disdain, and even pity. Every day you deny these beliefs as outlandish, overblown, or benign. It's a part of Black survival in America. You dismiss discriminatory acts, and even deadly violence, as symptoms of bad actors in an otherwise safe and democratically aspiring country. Even when you articulate the psychic and political pain of your existence, you are quickly reminded by colleagues and the media that countless others are chanting a similar refrain of marginalization and invisibility—Asian Americans, women, Latinx communities, Native Americans, transgendered persons, etc. This is almost always followed by a reminder that anti-Blackness is un-American, a contradiction to the fundamental principles of American democracy. You walk away from the conversation justifying "bad acts" as the price of being Black. Anti-Blackness, as we have watched it unfold on social media during the height of BLM, is *American*. It is a fundamental cornerstone retrieved to build and sustain American democracy. For far too long, African Americans in particular have chosen to struggle against anti-Blackness by employing double consciousness as a strategic tool to uncover the buried *promises* of democracy. Always believing in an America that is yet to be born demands relentless faith, some might call it *bad faith*.

The philosopher Lewis R. Gordon reminds us that bad faith is the quintessential hallmark of life in a country invested in color-blind laws, equality, and equal opportunity to overcome racial prejudice and anti-Blackness. This line of thinking assumes anti-Black racism is akin to disliking a group's cultural traditions, spicy foods, or religious expressions. This is far from the case. Anti-Black racism emerges from the belief that Blacks are intellectually and morally inferior to whites. To this end, when many whites look upon them, they "see" living and breathing people who are the cause of what is wrong in America. To make America great again, the "Negro problem" must be subdued. This is bad faith. In fact, to believe the country is fundamentally just and fair is to live in a constant state of denial.

In far too many instances, Black life is an existence born from the despair and grief of ongoing economic and social factors that treat Blacks as inferior and the source of their conditions. COVID-19 exposed as much. According to the Centers for Disease Control and Prevention, health conditions such as hypertension, diabetes, and obesity are disproportionately higher among Blacks.[20]

This is due in large part to social factors including poverty and lack of access to healthy food options and adequate health care. Ta-Nehisi Coates's 2014 groundbreaking essay, "The Case for Reparations," exposed the financial death to Black families who lived through redlining and endured decades of exploitative lending practices.

In nearly every facet of life, anti-Black racism unduly determines social, economic, and educational outcomes. The survival of the race in too many instances demands that we wear the mask that "grins and lies" and hides "our cries," Paul Lawrence Dunbar famously penned in 1896. Black folks testify with their lives to the horrors of anti-Blackness each day when they leave their homes. Most will embrace the mask wholeheartedly, some try to change its contours, and others will spend a lifetime struggling to remove it. *We Testify with Our Lives* understands the religion of Black Power and Black Lives Matter as symbols, rituals, and expressions of Black people's faith in freedom, justice, and democracy. This translates into the ethical turn in Black political thought, a move away from finding solace in existing political categories of "liberal versus conservative" to claiming Black interiority as a legitimate source for understanding, measuring, and defining freedom and determining the grounds on which *all* Black lives matter. Black interiority as expressed in sacred subjectivity is the site where folklore, Negro spirituals, jazz, hip hop, Black preaching, and oral traditions have sustained Black life and served as sites for healing the wounds from generations of psychic and physical trauma against Black and Brown bodies. By pursuing the ethical turn, we testify with our lives to the ingenuity, courage, and strength of the ancestors and the spirit of African American religions to sustain, protect, and heal the lives of the dispossessed and disinherited.

NOTES

PROLOGUE

1. For a nuanced narrative of African American political ideologies during the late nineteenth and twentieth centuries, please see Michael C. Dawson's *Black Visions: The Roots of Contemporary African-American Political Ideologies* (Chicago: University of Chicago Press, 2001); August Meier's *Negro Thought in America, 1880–1915: Racial Ideologies in the Age of Booker T. Washington* (Ann Arbor: University of Michigan Press, 1988) is another good starting point for exploring the development and rise of African American political thought.

2. A number of important books have been written on Black-elected officials during and after the civil rights movement, including Leonard N. Moore, *Carl B. Stokes and the Rise of Black Political Power* (Urbana: University of Illinois Press, 2002); Jeffrey S. Adler and David R. Colburn, *African-American Mayors: Race, Politics, and the American City* (Urbana: University of Illinois Press, 2001); J. Phillip Thompson, *Double Trouble: Black Mayors, Black Communities, and the Call for a Deep Democracy* (New York: Oxford University Press, 2006).

3. Please see Matthew Delmont's *Why Busing Failed: Race, Media, and the National Resistance to School Desegregation* (Oakland: University of California Press, 2016). Delmont explores the degree to which white parents and politicians in the North resisted integration by "reframing" the debate away from desegregation to "busing" and "neighborhood schools."

4. See Gerald Frug, "The Legal Technology of Exclusion in Metropolitan America," in *The New Suburban History*, ed. M. Kruse and Thomas J.

Sugrue (Chicago: University of Chicago Press, 2006), 205–19; Colin Gordon, *Mapping Decline: St. Louis and the Fate of the American City* (Philadelphia: University of Pennsylvania Press, 2008).

5. Rhonda Y. Williams, *The Politics of Public Housing: Black Women's Struggles Against Urban Inequality* (New York: Oxford University Press, 2004).

6. Williams, *The Politics of Public Housing*, 129.

7. By social problems, I build on Lewis R. Gordon's social ontology of Blackness as *the* penultimate problem facing the nation. Gordon develops his argument in conversation with W. E. B. Du Bois's "The Study of Negro Problems" (1898). See "W. E. B. Du Bois and the Study of Social Problems," in *The Study of African American Problems : W.E.B. Du Bois's Agenda, Then and Now*, ed. Tukufu Zuberi and Elijah Anderson (Thousand Oaks, CA: Sage, 2000), 265–80.

8. Jane Anna Gordon, and Lewis R. Gordon, *Not Only the Master's Tools : African-American Studies in Theory and Practice* (Boulder, CO: Paradigm, 2006), ix.

9. In " 'Dismantling the Master's House': Freedom as Ethical Practice in Brandom and Foucault," Jason Springs understands Lorde's notion of theory as "a basis for resistance. It is a central feature of a framework of discursive exchange based upon accountability and judgment, and thus (plausibly) confrontation and agonism" (*Journal of Religious Ethics* 37, no. 3 (September 2009): 442).

10. Seyla Benhabib, *Democracy and Difference: Contesting the Boundaries of the Political* (Princeton, NJ: Princeton University Press, 1996).

11. Beverly Guy-Sheftall's "Black Feminist Studies: The Case for Anna Julia Cooper" outlines the compelling work of Black feminists in the twentieth century as they attempted to uncover the buried histories of Black women in the U.S. Guy-Sheftall's essay can be found in *African American Review* 43, no. 1 (Spring 2009): 11–15.

12. Audre Lorde, *Sister Outsider: Essays and Speeches*. Trumansburg, NY: Crossing, 1984, 25.

13. Lorde, *Sister Outsider*, 117.

14. President Barack Obama's "Let Freedom Ring" speech at the fiftieth commemoration of the March on Washington characterized voting as the fuel needed to change America as well as citizenship for all

Americans. He noted that dignity was given to everyone by God; however, the execution of voting and the struggle for freedom were the material signs, Obama implied, of human dignity. Retrieved from https://
obamawhitehouse.archives.gov/the-press-office/2013/08/28/remarks
-president-let-freedom-ring-ceremony-commemorating-50th-anniversa

15. Rudolph P. Byrd, "Create Your Own Fire: Audre Lorde and the Tra-
dition of Black Radical Thought," in *I Am Your Sister: Collected and
Unpublished Writings of Audre Lorde*, ed. Rudolph P. Byrd, Johnnetta
Betsch Cole, and Beverly Guy-Sheftall (New York: Oxford University
Press, 2009), 22.

16. Gordon Lewis R, "Du Bois's Humanistic Philosophy of Human Sciences," *Annals of the American Academy of Political and Social Science* 568
(2000): 265–80.

17. Olson, Lester C., "The Personal, the Political, and Others: Audre Lorde
Denouncing 'The Second Sex Conference,' " *Philosophy & Rhetoric* 33.3
(2000): 268.

18. Fanon, Frantz, *Black Skin, White Masks* (New York: Grove Weidenfeld,
1991), 28.

19. Fanon, *Black Skin*, 41.

20. Audre Lorde, *I Am Your Sister: Collected and Unpublished Writings of
Audre Lorde*, ed. Rudolph P. Byrd, Johnnetta Betsch Cole, and Beverly
Guy-Sheftall (New York: Oxford University Press, 2009), 40.

21. Lorde, *I Am Your Sister*, 40..

22. Saidiya Hartman, *Scenes of Subjection: Terror, Slavery, and Self-Making in
Nineteenth Century America* (New York: Oxford University Press, 1997).

23. Lorde, *I Am Your Sister*, 42.

24. Cheryl Higashida, *Black Internationalist Feminism: Women Writers of the
Black Left, 1945–1995* (Urbana: University of Illinois Press, 2011), 4.

25. Lorde, *I Am Your Sister*, 111.

26. Lorde, *I Am Your Sister*, 218.

27. Henry Louis Gates Jr.'s groundbreaking examination of the link between
African and African American epistemologies introduced to literary the-
ory the category of the "talking book" in *The Signifying Monkey: A Theory
of African-American Literary Criticism* (New York: Oxford University
Press, 1988). Scholars of religion like Allen Callahan (*The Talking Book:
African Americans and the Bible* (New Haven, CT: Yale University Press,

2008) apply the category to African American biblical hermeneutics, where Blacks write themselves into the text and engage in a dialogical exchange with scripture. The move introduces a radical tradition of biblical hermeneutics within Afro-Christianity.

28. Bishop Henry McNeal Turner of the African Methodist Episcopal Church preached a sermon in 1895 at the historic Friendship Baptist Church in Atlanta, Georgia, where he proclaimed, "I worship a Negro God. I believe God is a Negro." Andre E. Johnson examines the rhetorical use of Turner's retort. Johnson believes it signifies a deeper understanding of God-talk and hermeneutics and "contextual theology." See Johnson's "God Is a Negro: The (Rhetorical) Black Theology of Bishop McNeal Turner," *Black Theology: An International Journal* 13 (2015): 29–40. I envision the retort, God is a Negro, as providing insight into Black Power's retort, which is fundamentally dialogical and designed to dismantle W. E. B. Du Bois's Negro problem.

29. Gayraud Wilmore's *Black Religion and Black Radicalism: An Interpretation of the Religious History of African Americans* (Maryknoll, NY: Orbis, 1988) explores the emergence of Black religious radicalism in and outside of Afro-Christianity. This radicalism is informed by a belief in God's divine justice on behalf of African Americans as well as a unique understanding of God working through human hands to achieve Black freedom.

30. Lorde, *I Am Your Sister*, 216.

31. Lorde, *I Am Your Sister*, 218. Italics are my emphasis.

I. POLITICS OF HEALING

1. Toni Cade Bambara, *The Salt Eaters* (New York: Vintage, 1992), 2–5.

2. John Edgar Wideman, "The Healing of Velma Henry: Bambara Authors' Queries" (*New York Times*, June 1, 1980), 14.

3. In Wideman's *Times* review, he takes note of Bambara's melodic literary technique as one of the strengths of the novel. He writes that "its language rings the changes from scientific jargon to street slang. The gift for rendering accurate snappy allusive dialogue is as evident in Toni Cade Bambara's novel as it's been in her short fiction." "The Healing of Velma Henry," 28.

4. Bambara, *The Salt Eaters*, 147.

5. Gay Wilentz places *The Salt Eaters* within a broader tradition of healing narratives within African American literature. From Alice Walker and Paule Marshall to Gloria Naylor, Black women writers invent characters whose struggle to justice involves healing themselves individually and collectively. Please see Wilentz's *Healing Narratives: Women Writers Curing Cultural Dis-ease* (New Brunswick, NJ: Rutgers University Press, 2000).

6. Delores Williams, *Sisters in the Wilderness: The Challenge of Womanist God-Talk* (Maryknoll, NY: Orbis, 1993).

7. Beverly Guy-Sheftall, "African-American Studies: Legacies and Challenges: 'What Would Black Studies Be If We'd Listened to Toni Cade?' " *Black Scholar* 35, no. 2 (Summer 2005): 23.

8. Valerie Boyd, "She Was Just Outrageously Brilliant': Toni Morrison Remembers Toni Cade Bambara," in *Savoring the Salt: The Legacy of Toni Cade Bambara*, ed. Linda Janet Holmes and Cheryl A. Wall (Philadelphia: Temple University Press, 2008), 91.

9. Toni Cade Bambara, *Deep Sightings and Rescue Missions: Fiction, Essays, and Conversations*, ed. Toni Morrison (New York: Pantheon, 1996), x.

10. Charles A. Frye, Charlyn Harper, Linda James Myers, and Eleanor W. Traylor, "How to Think Black: A Symposium in Toni Cade Bambara's *The Salt Eaters, Journal of African and Afro-American Studies* 6 (September 8, 2008): 47.

11. Please see Michael Dawson's *Black Visions: The Roots of Contemporary African-American Political Ideologies* (Chicago: The University of Chicago Press, 2001).

12. Trudier Harris, "Christianity's Last Stand: Visions of Spirituality in Post-1970 African American Women's Literature," *Religions* 11. no. 7 (July 2020): 369.

13. Shatema Threadcraft, *Intimate Justice: The Black Female Body and the Body Politic* (New York: Oxford University Press, 2016), 29.

14. The masculinist vision of justice is not only associated with Black liberalism but was also expressed among Black nationalists such as Marcus Garvey and Stokely Carmichael.

15. Threadcraft, *Intimate Justice*, 33.

16. Threadcraft, *Intimate Justice*, 141.

17. Threadcraft, *Intimate Justice*, 141.

18. Threadcraft, *Intimate Justice*, 141.

19. Threadcraft, *Intimate Justice*, 144.

20. Threadcraft, *Intimate Justice*, 146.

21. Robin D. G. Kelley shows in powerful prose the substantive efforts among organizers for the Communist Party to solicit support for and lead many protests against illegal home and land foreclosures and join in efforts to support workers against white supremacist practices on the job. Please see Kelley's *Hammer and Hoe: Alabama Communists During the Great Depression* (Chapel Hill: University of North Carolina Press, 1990). Cheryl Gilkes's *If It Wasn't for the Women: Black Women's Experience and Womanist Culture in Church and Community* (Maryknoll, NY: Orbis) examines Black women's political and social agency within Black churches as well as in their communities. Her account provides a rich narrative of Black women's resistance to anti-Black racism and male domination.

22. Robin D. G. Kelley argues that Black tradition was not so much invented as it was discovered by those working with and studying working-class Black political movements. See his introduction to Cedric Robinson's *Black Marxism: The Making of the Black Radical Tradition* (Chapel Hill: University of North Carolina Press, 2000), xv.

23. Belinda Waller Peterson, " 'Are You Sure, Sweetheart, That You Want to Be Well?': The Politics of Mental Health and Long-Suffering in Toni Cade Bambara's *The Salt Eaters*, *Religions*, 10, no. 4 (2019): 1.

24. The now classic term in postcolonial studies denotes a subjugated people who are politically, socially, economically, and culturally marginalized from the colonial power. See Gayatri C. Spivak, "Can the Subaltern Speak?" in *Marxism and the Interpretation of Culture*, ed. Cary Nelson and Lawrence Grossberg (Urbana: University of Illinois Press, 1988), 271–313.

25. Robinson, *Black Marxism*, 310.

26. Robinson, *Black Marxism*, 310.

27. One of the best definitions of Black folk religion was given by the civil rights activist Ruby Sales during a 2016 Krista Tippet interview. She defined Black folk religion as "a religion that combined the ideals of American democracy with the theological sense of justice. It was a religion that said that people who were considered property and disposable were essential in the eyes of God and even essential in a

democracy, although we were enslaved." What underscored Black religion's sense of democracy were traditions such as conjure, divination, and hoodoo—all of which allowed the formerly enslaved to manipulate and reimagine their social contexts, https://onbeing.org/programs/ruby-sales-where-does-it-hurt/.

28. Courtney Thorsson, *Women's Work: Nationalism and Contemporary African American Women's Novels* (Charlottesville: University of Virginia Press, 2013), 33.

29. Bambara, *The Salt Eaters*, 20.

30. See Toni Morrison's *Mouth Full of Blood: Essays, Speeches, Meditations* (New York: Random House, 2019). https://www.theguardian.com/books/2019/aug/08/toni-morrison-rememory-essay

31. Toni Cade Bambara, "Preface," *The Black Woman: An Anthology* (New York: New York American Library, 1970), 7.

32. Orlando Patterson, *Slavery and Social Death: A Comparative Study* (Cambridge, MA: Harvard University Press, 1982).

33. Father Divine founded the Peace Mission in the 1930s. His followers believed he was God. Jill Watts captures the richness of his life and religious movement in *God, Harlem U.S.A.: The Father Divine Story* (Berkeley: University of California Press, 1992).

34. Charles Long, *Significations: Signs, Symbols, and Images in the Interpretation of Religion* (Philadelphia, PA: Fortress, 1986), 9.

35. Wilentz, *Healing Narratives*, 78.

36. Bambara, "On the Issues of Roles," *The Black Woman*, 105–6.

37. Bambara, "On the Issues of Roles," 105.

38. In both instances, the political philosopher Danielle Allen asserts in *Talking to Strangers: Anxieties of Citizenship Since Brown v. Board of Education* (Chicago: University of Chicago Press, 2009), the groups engaged public life through competing understandings of democracy and democratic life.

39. *The Black Woman: An Anthology* (1970) "was the first major feminist anthology featuring Nikki Giovanni, Audre Lorde, Alice Walker, Paule Marshall, and others" that in many ways responded to the invisibility of Black women in public spaces during the civil rights and women's movements. Please see Maureen Schirack and Lauren Curtright, "Toni Cade Bambara," *Voices from the Gaps* 2 (2004), https://conservancy.umn.edu/handle/11299/167858.

40. Bambara, "On the Issues of Roles," 109.

41. Kimberly W. Benston, *Performing Blackness: Enactments of African-American Modernism* (New York: Routledge, 2000), 15.

42. Bambara, "On the Issues of Roles," 109.

43. Derek Alwes, "The Burden of Liberty: Choice in Toni Morrison's *Jazz* and Toni Cade Bambara's *The Salt Eaters*," *African American Review* 30 (Autumn 1996): 354.

44. Benston, *Performing Blackness*, 14.

45. Alwes, "The Burden of Liberty," 359.

46. Lewis R. Gordon, *What Fanon Said: A Philosophical Introduction to His Life and Thought* (New York: Fordham University Press, 2015), 97.

47. Bambara, *The Salt Eaters*, 54.

48. Bambara, *The Salt Eaters*, 51.

49. Bambara, *The Salt Eaters*, 53.

50. Bambara, *Deep Sightings and Rescue Missions*, 214.

51. Bambara, *Deep Sightings and Rescue Missions*, 215.

52. Bambara, *The Salt Eaters*, 120.

53. Bambara, *Deep Sightings and Rescue Missions*, 214.

54. Bambara, *Deep Sightings and Rescue Missions*, 215.

55. Bambara, *Deep Sightings and Rescue Missions*, 160.

56. *New Revised Standard Version*. Bible Gateway, https://www.biblegateway.com/passage/?search=Matthew+5%3A13-16&version=NRSV. Matthew 5:13–16. Accessed September 6, 2020.

57. Bambara, *The Salt Eaters*, 47.

58. Bambara, *The Salt Eaters*, 53.

59. Bambara, *The Salt Eaters*, 111.

60. Bambara, *The Salt Eaters*, 295.

61. Bambara, *The Salt Eaters*, 107.

2. AWAKENING TO BLACK POWER CONSCIOUSNESS

1. Singin' wid a sword in ma han'/ Singin' wid a sword in m han', http://www.negrospirituals.com/songs/singing_wid_a_sword_in_ma_han.htm, accessed March 8, 2019.

2. Donald J. McCormack, "Stokely Carmichael and Pan-Africanism: Back to Black Power," *Journal of Politics* 35 (May 1973): 389.

3. James Meredith organized the March Against Fear in 1966. From Memphis, Tennessee, to Jackson, Mississippi, Meredith led the 220-mile march to encourage African American voter registration and to call attention to random and ubiquitous white violence against Blacks in Mississippi. Though at the time he was living in New York City and attending Columbia Law School, the march was a homecoming of sorts for Meredith, the first Black to integrate the University of Mississippi in 1962. On the second day of the march, it took an ugly turn: Meredith was shot in the back by a white man. The shooting stunned the participants. Though they had grown accustomed to violence, no one anticipated it at a march led by one of the patron saints of student nonviolence. Meredith's shooting drew national attention, and African Americans, even from clashing political and religious movements, descended upon Mississippi to support the march. Among them were members of the Student Nonviolent Coordinating Committee (SNCC), the Southern Christian Leadership Conference, and the Deacons for Defense, an armed group of African American men who often provided security to Black organizations and African American leaders in the South. The march continued without its leader.

4. Gene Roberts, "Mississippi Reduces Police Protection for Marchers," *New York Times* (June 17, 1966), 33.

5. Carmichael's election to chair the SNCC exposed the expanding ideological rifts within the organization. John Lewis was elected to the chair's position in 1966, but a Carmichael supporter challenged the constitutionality of the election. Within weeks, a new election was held, which led to Lewis's defeat. See Clayborne Carson, *In Struggle: SNCC and the Black Awakening of the 1960s* (Cambridge, MA: Harvard University Press, 1995), 202–4.

6. Roberts, "Mississippi Reduces Police Protection for Marchers," 33.

7. Gene Roberts, "Black Power Idea Long in Planning: S.N.C.C. Dissidents Wrote Document Last Winter" (*New York Times*, August 5, 1966), 1.

8. Carson, *In Struggle*, 209.

9. Carson, *In Struggle*, 210. Carson also notes that the concept of Black Power had been operative long before Carmichael's appropriation of it. Leaders, activists, and writers ranging from Adam Clayton Powell and Richard Wright to Paul Robeson invoked the term earlier (209).

10. Komozi Woodard, *A Nation Within a Nation: Amiri Baraka (Leroi Jones) and Black Power Politics* (Chapel Hill: University of North Carolina Press, 1999), 40.

11. Woodard, *A Nation Within a Nation*, 40.

12. By liberalism, I mean loosely the principles of equality, liberty, and justice as imagined in and through John Locke and later by John Rawls and Charles Mills.

13. Peniel Joseph, "The Black Power Movement: A State of the Field," *Journal of American History* 96, no. 3 (December 2009): 772.

14. Fanon Che Wilkins, "The Making of Black Internationalists: SNCC and Africa before the Launching of Black Power, 1960–1965," *Journal of African American History* 92, no. 4 (Autumn 2007): 469. Wilkins makes an important point regarding SNCC's internationalist vision: SNCC's "decentralized organizational structure" prevented the organization from developing a uniform, transnational vision but it nevertheless was as important as ending Jim Crow.

15. Hazel Carby, *Race Men: The W. E. B. Du Bois Lectures*. (Cambridge, MA: Harvard University Press, 1998), 6.

16. Ashon T. Crawley, *Blackpentecostal Breath: The Aesthetics of Possibility* (New York: Fordham University Press, 2017), 2.

17. Wilkins, "The Making of Black Internationalism," 469.

18. Wilkins, "The Making of Black Internationalists," 470.

19. Barbara Ransby, *Ella Baker and the Black Freedom Movement: A Radical Democratic Vision* (Chapel Hill: University of North Carolina Press, 2003), 242.

20. Ransby, *Ella Baker and the Black Freedom Movement*, 241–42.

21. Ransby, *Ella Baker and the Black Freedom Movement*, 244.

22. Ransby writes that in 1961 the buses carrying the Freedom Riders were firebombed and pummeled with rocks. In some instances, the riders were beaten up by segregationists. See *Ella Baker and the Black Freedom Movement*, (265.

23. Ransby, *Ella Baker and the Black Freedom Movement*, 270.

24. James Forman, James Forman Papers, *Library of Congress* (Forman Box 29, Folder 11), 63.

25. Stokely Carmichael and Michael Thelwell, *Ready for Revolution: The Life and Struggle of Stokely Carmichael (Kwame Ture)* (New York: Scribner, 2003), 529.

26. As mentioned in chapter 1, Kimberly Benston coined the category to explain the performative elements of Black literary criticisms in *Performing Blackness: Enactments of African-American Modernism* (New York: Routledge, 2000), 112. Indeed, the "meaningful response [to the historical moment] is always an intrinsic element of the artist's project of redefinition and renewal" (112). At a moment of growing frustration with the nation's snail's pace response to the demands for integration, Carmichael's speech initiated a moment of renewal in the possibility of social transformation.

27. Stokely Carmichael, speech at the University of California, Berkeley, October 29, 1966. http://americanradioworks.publicradio.org/features/sayitplain/scarmichael.html, accessed September 6, 2020.

28. Carmichael, speech at the University of California, Berkeley.

29. Carmichael, speech at the University of California, Berkeley.

30. Carmichael, speech at the University of California, Berkeley.

31. https://kinginstitute.stanford.edu/encyclopedia/black-power accessed March 8, 2019.

32. Manning Marable, *Race, Reform, and Rebellion: The Second Reconstruction and Beyond in Black* America, 1945–2006 (Jackson: University Press of Mississippi, 2007), 92.

33. It is important to note that the passage of the 1965 Voting Rights Act seemed to heighten acts of violence against Blacks attempting to register and exercise their rights, most notably in Alabama and Mississippi. The legislation seemed to suggest the limits, at least among the SNCC's leftist members, of national legislation to protect and ensure the fight of African Americans (Carson, *In Struggle*, 165–66).

34. Martin Luther King Jr., *Where Do We Go from Here: Chaos or Community?* (Boston, MA: Beacon, 2010), 35.

35. King, who borrowed the category from American philosopher Josiah Royce, discussed the Beloved Community in many of his speeches and sermons, including the 1957 speech "Birth of a New Nation" and the 1959 "Sermon on Gandhi." He defines it in terms of interracial reconciliation through nonviolence as well as the culmination of reducing poverty and violence based on internationally agreed upon norms. For additional information on King's use of the Beloved Community, see "The King Philosophy" at The King Center, https://thekingcenter.org/king-philosophy/, accessed September 6, 2020.

36. King, *Where Do We Go from Here?* 26.

37. King, *Where Do We Go from Here?* 33.

38. King, *Where Do We Go from Here?* 35–36.

39. King, *Where Do We Go from Here?* 37.

40. King, *Where Do We Go from Here?* 37.

41. King, *Where Do We Go from Here?* 37.

42. King, *Where Do We Go from Here?* 38.

43. King, *Where Do We Go from Here?* 38.

44. King, *Where Do We Go from Here?* 38–39.

45. King, *Where Do We Go from Here?* 41.

46. King, *Where Do We Go from Here?* 55.

47. King, *Where Do We Go from Here?* 56.

48. King, *Where Do We Go from Here?* 68.

49. Robert Michael Franklin, "In Pursuit of a Just Society: Martin Luther King, Jr., and John Rawls," *Journal of Religious Ethics* 18, no. 2 (1990): 59.

50. Franklin, "In Pursuit of a Just Society," 60.

51. Lewis R. Gordon frames African phenomenology as addressing these two fundamental questions in the quest toward emancipation. See *Existentia Africana: Understanding Africana Existential Thought* (New York: Routledge, 2000).

52. James Forman Papers, Box 17, Folder 23 (October 11, 1966).

53. I develop this point in chapter 4.

54. Julien Bond, "SNCC: What We Did," *Monthly Review* 17, no. 52 (October 2000), 5.

55. That being said, it is not as if Malcolm X enjoyed ubiquitous or popular approval, even among African Americans. According to Clayborne Carson, "a national survey of African-Americans by *Newsweek* in the summer of 1963 found that 88 percent had positive opinions regarding Martin, while only 15 percent thought positively about Elijah Muhammad. Malcolm was not even deemed sufficiently prominent to be listed on the survey form." http://www.columbia.edu/cu/ccbh/mxp/Souls .The_Unfinished_Dialogue.pdf accessed February 14, 2020.

3. MARTIN LUTHER KING JR.'S RELIGIOUS RADICALISM

1. Martin Luther King Jr., *Testament of Hope: Essential Writings and Speeches of Martin Luther King, Jr.* (New York: HarperCollins, 1991), 233.

2. King, *Testament of Hope*, 231.
3. King, *Testament of Hope*, 233.
4. King, *Testament of Hope*, 233.
5. Nikhil Singh, *Black Is a Country: Race and the Unfinished Struggle for Democracy* (Cambridge, MA: Harvard University Press, 2005), 4.
6. Abraham Smith, "I Saw the Book Talk: A Cultural Studies Approach to the Ethics of African American Biblical Hermeneutics," *Semeia* 77 (1997): 118.
7. "Beyond Vietnam," https://kinginstitute.stanford.edu/king-papers /documents/beyond-vietnam. accessed March 4, 2020.
8. Thomas F. Jackson, *From Civil Rights to Human Rights: Martin Luther King, Jr., and the Struggle for Economic Justice* (Philadelphia: University of Pennsylvania Press, 2009), 2.
9. Martin Luther King Jr., "The Birth of a New Age" speech, August 11, 1956, Buffalo, New York. https://kinginstitute.stanford.edu/king-papers /documents/birth-new-age-address-delivered-11-august-1956-fiftieth -anniversary-alpha-phi accessed February 15, 2020.
10. Susannah Heschel, "'A Different Kind of Theo-Politics: Abraham Joshua Heschel, the Prophets and the Civil Rights Movement," *Journal of Political Theology* 21 (2020): 35.
11. Nikhil Singh, *Black Is a Country*, 4.
12. Vincent Harding's *Martin Luther King: The Inconvenient Hero* (Maryknoll, NY: Orbis, 1996) identifies the SNCC as playing a decisive role in shaping King's radical political vision.
13. Lucile Montgomery Papers, 1963–1967, *Wisconsin Historical Society*, "Freedom Summer Digital Collection," https://content.wisconsinhistory.org /digital/collection/p15932coll2/id/35466, accessed September 12, 2020.
14. Michael Eric Dyson's noteworthy analysis of King's philosophy, *I May Not Get There with You: The True Martin Luther King Jr.* (New York: Simon & Schuster, 2000), identifies King's expanding radicalism as stemming from his engagement with urban cities in the North. "When King turned his attention North, he faced a far more brutal and complex terrain" (36).
15. Dyson, *I May Not Get There with You*, 40.
16. Orlando Patterson, *Slavery and Social Death: A Comparative Study* (Cambridge, MA: Harvard University Press, 1982), 76.
17. W. E. B. Du Bois, "Of Our Spiritual Strivings," in *The Souls of Black Folk* (New York: Oxford University Press, 2009), 9.

18. Gates, *The Signifying Monkey*, 42.

19. Gates, *The Signifying Monkey*, 186.

20. Allen Callahan, *The Talking Book: African Americans and the Bible* (New Haven, CT: Yale University Press, 2008), 243.

21. Vincent Wimbush, "The Bible and African Americans: An Outline of an Interpretive History," in *Stony the Road We Trod: African American Biblical Interpretation*, ed. Cain Hope Felder (Minneapolis: Fortress, 1991), 83.

22. Wimbush, "The Bible and African Americans," 83.

23. James Weldon Johnson, *God's Trombones: Seven Negro Sermons in Verse* (New York: Viking, 1930), 17. https://docsouth.unc.edu/southlit/johnson/johnson.html

24. Johnson, *God's Trombones*, 18

25. Gregory S. Carr, "Theatricality, Themes, and Theology in James Weldon Johnson's *God's Trombones*," *Theatre Symposium* (2013): 54.

26. Three fundamental beliefs provide clear examples of the theology that informed these rituals: that the Spirit of God would dismantle the normalcy of the worship service; that the Spirit would disclose him- or herself in the process; and that through prayer, worship, and reflection, God would create anew those who had gathered to worship. This phenomenology of Afro-Christian worship was often described as an ecstatic moment, an out-of-body moment of religious expression. It is generally imagined and studied as antithetical to reason. I want to shatter this characterization and suggest that the experiential accounts of worship shed light on the ethical terrain of Black politics.

27. Frank Wilderson III, *Red, White and Black: Cinema and the Structure of U.S. Antagonisms* (Durham, NC: Duke University Press, 2010), 2.

28. Wilderson, *Red, White and Black*, 2

29. Wilderson, *Red, White and Black*, 11.

30. Martin Luther King, Jr., "Beyond Vietnam: A Time to Break Silence," *A Testament of Hope: Essential Writings and Speeches of Martin Luther King, Jr.* (New York: HarperCollins, 1991), 233.

31. This move challenges the usefulness of "nation" within Black Power. Even though the SNCC changed its name in 1969 to the Student National Coordinating Committee, I believe the move was designed to symbolize national unity that did not undermine its global interest.

32. Boston Friends of the Student Nonviolent Coordinating Committee, March 3, 1967 newsletter.

33. Martin Luther King Jr., "Martin Luther King Defines Black Power," *New York Times Magazine,* June 11, 1967.

34. King, "Beyond Vietnam," https://kinginstitute.stanford.edu/king-papers /documents/beyond-vietnam

35. Peniel Joseph, "The New Black Power History: A *Souls* Special Issue." *Souls* 9.4 (2007): 278.

36. Clayborne Carson, *In Struggle: SNCC and the Black Awakening of the 1960s.* (Cambridge, MA: Harvard University Press, 1995), 208–10.

37. The editorial is representative of a knee-jerk response to King's speech and the race problem. Far truer is that in following in the tradition of Du Bois and Cooper, King envisions the race problem as emblematic of the latent problems of American hegemony. Niebuhr also linked the nation's hubris to its international problem. There's a discourse that binds King and the SNCC and pushes them beyond the rhetoric of the jeremiad.

38. Charles Mills, *Blackness Visible: Essays on Philosophy and Race* (Ithaca, NY: Cornell University Press, 1998).

39. Hak Joon Lee, "Toward the Great World House: Hans Küng and Martin Luther King, Jr. on Global Ethics," *Journal of the Society of Christian Ethics,* 29, no. 2 (2009): 97–98.

40. Evelyn Brooks Higginbotham, *Righteous Discontent: The Women's Movement in the Black Baptist Church, 1880–1920* (Cambridge, MA: Harvard University Press, 1993), 186.

41. Higginbotham, *Righteous Discontent,* 186–87.

42. Higginbotham, *Righteous Discontent,* 187.

43. Dyson, *I May Not Get There with You,* 127.

44. King, "A Time to Break Silence," 242.

4. MALCOLM X AND THE SPIRIT OF HUMANISTIC ACTIVISM

This chapter is largely taken from my previously published essay, "Religious Heretic, Political Prophet: Malcolm X, Democracy, and Abolition Ethics," *Journal of Africana Religions* 3, no. 1 (2015): 62–82. I have revised and modified my argument since its publication.

1. Donna Tressler, "Cory United Methodist Church," Cleveland Historical Society, http://clevelandhistorical.org/items/show/643

2. Malcolm X and George Breitman, *Malcolm X Speaks: Selected Speeches and Statements*, (New York: Grove Weidenfeld, 1990), 31.

3. Malcolm X, *Malcolm X Speaks*, 30.

4. Malcolm X, *Malcolm X Speaks*, 28.

5. Malcolm X, *Malcolm X Speaks*, 35.

6. Malcolm X, *Malcolm X* Speaks, 38.

7. Frederick C. Harris, *The Price of the Ticket: Barack Obama and the Rise and Decline of Black Politics* (New York: Oxford University Press, 2014), 5.

8. In my book, *Tragic Soul-Life: W. E. B. Du Bois and the Moral Crisis Facing American Democracy* (Oxford: Oxford University Press, 2012), I discuss at length how Du Bois's understanding of the "Negro problem" emerged from what I call white contempt of Blackness—cultural and religious beliefs among whites in the innate moral and intellectual inferiority of Blacks. The moral problem of Blackness, hence, emerges as a hermeneutic lens that informs how non-Blacks conceptualize the "Black."

9. I am indebted to Du Bois's construction of "humanistic democracy" as a model for developing my own understanding of humanistic democracy. Du Bois used the term in *Black Reconstruction* to denote how race and class inform democracy and democratic traditions.

10. Anthony Pinn, "The End: Thoughts on Humanism and Death," *Dialog: A Journal of Theology* 54, no. 4 (2015): 347.

11. Lewis R. Gordon, *What Fanon Said: A Philosophical Introduction to His Life and Thought*, (New York: Fordham University Press, 2015), 3.

12. Gordon, *What Fanon Said*, 48.

13. Gordon, *What Fanon Said*, 48.

14. Gordon, *What Fanon Said*, 48.

15. Gordon, *What Fanon Said*, 20.

16. Gordon, *What Fanon Said*, 21.

17. Gordon, *What Fanon Said*, 22.

18. Gordon, *What Fanon Said*, 33.

19. Gordon, *What Fanon Said*, 35.

20. Gordon, *What Fanon Said*, 97.

21. Gordon, *What Fanon Said*, 119.

22. Gordon, *What Fanon Said*, 69.

23. Gordon, *What Fanon Said*, 130.

24. Joy James, "Ella Baker, 'Black Women's Work' and Activist Intellectuals," *The Black Scholar* 24, no. 4 (1994): 8.

25. K. Tutashinda, "The Grassroots Political Philosophy of Ella Baker: Oakland, California Applicability," *The Journal of Pan African Studies* 3, no. 9 (2010): 27–28.

26. Malcolm X, *Malcolm X Speaks*, 141.

27. Dean E. Robinson, *Black Nationalism in American Politics and Thought* (New York: Cambridge University Press, 2001), 8–9.

28. Barbara Ransby, in *Ella Baker and the Black Freedom Movement*, writes, according to Baker, "the Negro must quit looking for a savior, and work to save himself" (Ransby, 147).

29. Wilson Jeremiah Moses, *Black Messiahs and Uncle Toms: Social and Literary Manipulations of a Religious Myth* (University Park: Pennsylvania State University Press, 1993), 231.

30. Moses, *Black Messiahs and Uncle Toms*, 231–32.

31. Malcolm X, *The Speeches of Malcolm X at Harvard*, ed. Archie Epps (New York: Paragon, 1991), 128.

32. Erik S. McDuffie and Komozi Woodard, "'If You're in a Country That's Progressive, the Woman Is Progressive': Black Women Radicals and the Making of the Politics and Legacy of Malcolm X," *Biography* 36, no. 3 (2013): 513.

33. Barbara Ransby and Tracye Matthews, "Black Popular Culture and the Transcendence of Patriarchal Illusions," in *Words of Fire: An Anthology of African-American Feminist Thought*, ed. Beverly Guy-Sheftall (New York: New Press, 1995), 529.

34. McDuffie and Woodard, "If You're in a Country That's Progressive," 511–12.

35. McDuffie and Woodard, "If You're in a Country That's Progressive," 518. For instance, Garvin reinforced three important points that proved beneficial for Malcolm X's organizing: religious institutions as critical sites for organizing, the working class as a viable political force, and independent media as a necessary tool for disseminating information.

36. McDuffie and Woodard, "If You're in a Country That's Progressive," 527.

37. William W. Sales Jr., *From Civil Rights to Black Liberation: Malcolm X and the Organization of Afro-American Unity* (Boston: South End, 1994), 60–61.

38. Malcolm X, http://www.malcolm-x.org/speeches/spc_12, accessed February 6, 2021.

39. Robinson, *Black Nationalism in American Politics and Thought*, 38.

40. I've slightly revised this sentence, since the quote doesn't suggest the nation can be saved—it seems to suggest that the Western world is doomed and that Blacks can only be saved by cutting themselves off from the white world.

41. Harlem Freedom Rally, http://malcolmxfiles.blogspot.ca/2013/05/harlem -freedom-rally-1960.html, accessed September 25, 2020.

42. Malcolm X, *The Speeches of Malcolm X at Harvard Law School*, 116.

43. Malcolm X, *The Speeches of Malcolm X at Harvard Law School*, 118.

44. Malcolm X, *The Speeches of Malcolm X at Harvard Law School*, 119.

45. Malcolm X, *The Speeches of Malcolm X at Harvard Law School*, 120.

46. Malcolm X, *The Speeches of Malcolm X at Harvard Law School*, 120; *Malcolm X Speaks*, 10.

47. Edward E. Curtis IV, "Why Malcolm X Never Developed an Islamic Approach to Civil Rights," *Religion* 32 (2002): 229.

48. Curtis, "Why Malcolm X Never Developed an Islamic Approach to Civil Rights," 228.

49. Rod Bush, *We Are Not What We Seem: Black Nationalism and Class Struggle in the American Century* (New York: New York University Press, 1999), 184.

50. McDuffie and Woodard's "If You're in a Country That's Progressive" provides a great deal of primary research in this area.

51. Patricia Hill Collins, "Learning to Think for Ourselves: Malcolm X's Black Nationalism Reconsidered," in *Malcolm in Our Own Image*, ed. Joe Wood (New York: St. Martin's, 1992), 74.

52. Collins, "Learning to Think for Ourselves," 78.

53. Ransby and Matthews, "Black Popular Culture and the Transcendence of Patriarchal Illusions," 530.

54. Michelle Ann Stephens, *Black Empire: The Masculine Global Imaginary of Caribbean Intellectuals in the United States, 1914–1962* (Durham, NC: Duke University Press, 2005), 40.

55. Robinson, *Black Nationalism in American Politics and Thought*, 35.

56. Malcolm X, *Malcolm X Speaks*, 26.

57. Malcolm X, *Malcolm X Speaks*, 39.

58. Harlem Freedom Rally, http://malcolmxfiles.blogspot.ca/2013/05/harlem -freedom-rally-1960.html, accessed February 6, 2021.

59. James Cone, *Martin & Malcolm & America* (Maryknoll, NY: Orbis, 1992), 193.

60. Bush, *We Are Not What We Seem*, 187–88.

61. Saladin Ambar, *Malcolm X at Oxford Union: Racial Politics in a Global Era* (New York: Oxford University Press, 2014), 169.

62. Ambar, *Malcolm X at Oxford Union*, 178.

63. Ambar, *Malcolm X at Oxford Union*, 172.

64. Kevin Gaines, "Malcolm X in Global Perspective," *The Cambridge Companion to Malcolm X*, ed. Robert E. Terrill (New York: Cambridge University Press, 2010), 167.

65. Ambar, *Malcolm X at Oxford Union*, 49.

66. Ambar, *Malcolm X at Oxford Union*, 84.

67. Gaines, "Malcolm X in Global Perspective," 168.

68. Malcolm X with Alex Haley, *The Autobiography of Malcolm X* (New York: Random House, 1992), 419.

69. Malcolm X with Haley, 420.

5. HUMANISTIC NATIONALISM AND THE ETHICAL TURN

1. Ashley Farmer, *Remaking Black Power: How Black Women Transformed an Era* (Chapel Hill: University of North Carolina Press, 2017), 163.

2. Farmer, *Remaking Black Power*, 162.

3. A number of scholarly articles and books discuss the ethical turn in relationship to Michel Foucault's late lectures at the College de France on ethics, self-governance, and ethical engagement in politics as an indication of Foucault's ethical turn or ethical imagination. Such works include Timothy O'Leary's *Foucault and the Art of Ethics* (New York: Continuum, 2006), Cressida J. Heyes's *Self-Transformations: Foucault, Ethics, and Normalized Bodies* (New York: Oxford University Press, 2007), and Nany Luxon's "Ethics and Subjectivity: Practices of Self-Governance in the Late Lectures of Michel Foucault," *Political Theory* 36 (June 1, 2008): 377–402. My focus is on exploring "ethics" and the "ethical turn" as categories for understanding Black political thought in conversation with SNCC activists and scholars and Womanist ethicists such as Katie Cannon.

4. James Forman Papers, Library of Congress, Box 29, Folder 11, 47.

5. Peniel E. Joseph, "Black Power Studies: A New Scholarship," *The Black Scholar*. 31.3-4, (2001), 2.

6. Ethel Minor is a little-known figure in the Black Power movement. However, she played a significant role in shaping the chief architects of the movement: Malcolm X and Stokely Carmichael. See Ethel Minor, "An African American Tells Why She Followed Malcolm X," in *Oh Freedom! Kids Talk about the Civil Rights Movement with the People Who Made It Happen*, ed., Casey King and Linda Barrett Osborne (New York: Random House, 1997), 94–96. Accessed April 17, 2020, http://herb.ashp.cuny.edu/items/show/963

7. For a more detailed account of empire as it relates to African American communities, see Robert Allen's *Black Awakening in Capitalist America* (New York: Doubleday, 1969).

8. Lucius Outlaw, chapter 2 in *On Race and Philosophy* (New York: Routledge, 1996).

9. Congress of Racial Equality. Mississippi 4th Congressional District records, Historical Society Library, Micro 793, Reel 3, Segment 4. https://content.wisconsinhistory.org/digital/collection/p15932coll2/id/42319, accessed September 2, 2020.

10. Martin Buber, *On Zion: The History of an Idea* (New York: Schocken, 1973), 137. https://archive.org/details/onzionhistoryofioooobube_c7r8/page/n7/mode/2up, accessed September 2, 2020.

11. Paula Span, "The Undying Revolutionary: As Stokely Carmichael, He Fought for Black Power. Now Kwame Ture's Fighting for His Life," *Washington Post* (April 8, 1998), 1.

12. In conversation with Alex Zamalin's *Struggle on their Minds: The Political Thought of African American Resistance* (New York: Columbia University Press, 2017), humanistic nationalism is both an ideology as well as a symbol of a "resistance movement," political acts and ways of thinking that do not always correspond to Anglo-American political philosophy. For instance, the notion of developing and articulating a theory of existence based on justifying Black humanity will likely seem foreign to theorists focusing on ideal theory, sovereignty, or justice.

13. Lewis R. Gordon and LaRose T. Perry, "Frantz Fanon's Psychology of Black Consciousness," in *Global Psychologies*, ed. S. Fernando and R. Moodley (London: Palgrave Macmillan, 2018), 225.

14. Stokely Carmichael, "Black Power," *The Will of a People: A Critical Anthology of Great African American Speeches*, ed. Richard W. Leeman and Bernard K. Duffy (Carbondale: Southern Illinois University Press, 2012), 310.

15. Gordon and Perry, "Frantz Fanon's Psychology of Black Consciousness," 226.

16. Alasdair MacIntyre's well-regarded *After Virtue: A Study in Moral Theory* (Notre Dame, IN: University of Notre Dame Press, 1984) frames the human good and flourishing as tied to the fulfillment of virtue. He writes, "The virtues are precisely those qualities the possession of which will enable an individual to achieve eudaimonia and the lack of which will frustrate his movement toward that telos" (148). Human flourishing as I develop the category emerges in conversation with Frantz Fanon's new humanism and the ends of W. E. B. Du Bois's double consciousness, which I address in *Tragic Soul-Life: W. E. B. Du Bois and the Moral Crisis Facing Democracy* (New York: Oxford University Press, 2012). That is, human flourishing emanates from Du Bois's striving to achieve "a truer" self and Fanon's insistence in *Les damnés de la terre* for the colonized to rebel against colonialism. The fight against colonialism created the conditions for a new humanism.

17. Charles Mills, "Dark Ontologies: Blacks, Jews, and White Supremacy," in *Blackness Visible: Essays on Philosophy and Race* (Ithaca, NY: Cornell University Press, 1998), 70.

18. Mills, "Dark Ontologies," 71.

19. Stokely Carmichael and Charles V. Hamilton, *Black Power: The Politics of Liberation in America* (New York: Vintage, 1992), 34–35.

20. Stokely Carmichael, "Toward Black Liberation," *The Massachusetts Review* (Autumn 1966), 642.

21. Stokely Carmichael, *Stokely Speaks: Black Power to Pan-Africanism* (New York: Random House, 1971), 145.

22. Carmichael, *Stokely Speaks*, 146.

23. Carmichael, *Stokely Speaks*, 154.

24. Carmichael, *Stokely Speaks*, 157–59. Carmichael distinguishes revolutionary violence from counterrevolutionary violence. The latter seeks to dismantle a government to maintain power for a minority of the people in society. He labels America's involvement in Vietnam as counterrevolutionary. Carmichael rejects this form of violence.

25. Carmichael, *Stokely Speaks*, 150–51.

26. Tommie Shelby, *We Who Are dark: The Philosophical Foundations of Black Solidarity* (Cambridge, MA: Harvard University Press, 2009), 107.

27. Toni Cade, "On the Issue of Roles" in *The Black Woman: An Anthology* New York: New American Library, 1970, 101.

28. Cade, "On the Issues of Roles," 103.

29. Cade, "On the Issues of Roles, 103.

30. Cade, "On the Issues of Roles," 108.

31. Cade, "On the Issues of Roles," 109.

32. Anthony Bogues, *Empire of Liberty: Power, Desire, and Freedom* (Hanover, NH: Dartmouth College Press, 2010), 6.

33. Toni Morrison, "A Slow Walk of Trees," in *What Moves at the Margin: Selected Nonfiction*, ed. Carolyn C. Denard (Jackson: University of Mississippi Press, 2008), 8.

34. Daniel Boyarin, *Intertextuality and the Reading of Midrash* (Bloomington: Indiana University Press, 1990), 12.

6. SNCC'S PALESTINIAN PROBLEM

1. Lawrence Geller Israel is Defended by Negro Groups After SNCC Attack, *Philadelphia Tribune* (August 19, 1967), 1.

2. Ethel Minor, "Editorial," *Aframerican: News for You* II (November 12, 1966): A-1.

3. What Black Power advocates called the "Israel/Palestine" problem opens the door to exploring the tension between ideal and nonideal theory—how normative commitments and the lived experience of political ideas coexist, coalesce, or remain detached and in opposition to one another.

4. Russell Rickford, "'To Build a New World': Black American Internationalism and Palestine Solidarity," *Journal of Palestine Studies* 48 (2019): 54.

5. For additional insight on Zionism in Black political thought, see Harold Brackman's "Zionism in Black and White: Part I:1, 1898–1948 (Report), *Midstream*, January 1, 2010.

6. W. E. B. Du Bois, *The Crisis*, 17, no. 4 (February, 1919), 166.

7. The draft of this 1950 speech was written for the Jewish People's Fraternal Order. The essay was found in the W. E. B. Du Bois Papers at the University of Massachusetts at Amherst. It was accessed on October 10, 2019.

https://credo.library.umass.edu/cgi-bin/pdf.cgi?id=scua:mums312
-b201-i022

8. Harold Brackman, "Zionism in Black and White: Part I:1, 1898–1948 (Report)," *Midstream* (January 1, 2010), 19.

9. Brackman, "Zionism in Black and White," 21.

10. Stokely Carmichael and Michael Thelwell, *Ready for Revolution: The Life and Struggles of Stokely Carmichael (Kwame Ture)* (New York: Scribner, 2003), 557

11. SNCC's turn to Black Power set the stage for a robust Zionist movement in the United States, according to Marc Dollinger. Indeed, Dollinger suggests that Black Power fueled American Zionism by advancing ethnic nationalism as a response to oppression. "Black Power gifted American Jews a new appreciation and enthusiasm for Jewish nationalism, redefining the very meaning of what it meant to be an ethnic American and helping inspire an unprecedented growth in American Zionism. If African Americans could advocate for black nationalism, so too could Jews press for their version of sovereignty" (Dollinger, *Black Power, Jewish Politics: Reinventing the Alliance of the 1960s*, 151).

12. Ethel Minor, "Black Voices: What Is Stokely Doing?" *Afro-American* (1893–1988) (October 4, 1969), 5.

13. Ethel Minor, "An African American Tells Why She Followed Malcolm X,", 94–96. Accessed April 17, 2020, http://herb.ashp.cuny.edu/items /show/963.

14. *The Hilltop* (Washington, DC: Howard University, 1972), 4.

15. Minor, "An African American Tells Why She Followed Malcolm X," 94.

16. "The Nation of Islam and the Politics of Black Nationalism, 1930–1975." Garrett A. Felber, PhD dissertation, 2017, 321.

17. *The Hilltop*, 1972, 4.

18. Brenda Gayle Plummer, "African Americans in the International Imaginary: Gerald Horne's Progressive Vision," *Journal of African American History* 96, no. 2 (2011): 222.

19. Fanon Wilkins, "The Making of Black Internationalists: SNCC and Africa Before the Launching of Black Power, 1960–1965," *The Journal of African American History* 92.4 (2007): 469.

20. Carmichael and Thelwell, *Ready for Revolution*, 559.

21. Keith P. Feldman, "Representing Permanent War: Black Power's Palestine and the End(s) of Civil Rights," *The New Centennial Review* 8.2 (2008): 194.

22. Feldman, "Representing Permanent War," 194.

23. Feldman, "Representing Permanent War," 197.

24. Marc Dollinger, *Black Power, Jewish Politics: Reinventing the Alliance of the 1960s* (Waltham, Mass.: Brandeis University Press, 2018, 151.

25. Clayborne Carson, "Black-Jewish Universalism in the Era of Identity Politics," in *Struggles in the Promised Land: Towards A History of Black-Jewish Relations in the United States* (New York: Oxford University Press, 1997), 177.

26. Carson, "Black-Jewish Universalism in the Era of Identity Politics," 177.

27. Carson, "Black-Jewish Universalism in the Era of Identity Politics," 183.

28. Carson, "Black-Jewish Universalism in the Era of Identity Politics," 178.

29. Dollinger, *Black Power, Jewish Politics*, 156.

30. Dollinger, *Black Power, Jewish Politics*, 158.

31. Nelson Maldonaldo-Torres, "On the Coloniality of Being: Contributions to the Development of a Concept," *Cultural Studies* 21, nos. 2–3 (2007): 260.

32. Maldonaldo-Torres, "On the Coloniality of Being," 243.

33. Maldonaldo-Torres, "On the Coloniality of Being," 260.

34. Maldonaldo-Torres, "On the Coloniality of Being," 243.

35. Maldonaldo-Torres, "On the Coloniality of Being," 259.

36. Maldonaldo-Torres, "On the Coloniality of Being," 242.

37. Maldonado-Torres, "On the Coloniality of Being," 255.

38. Carmichael and Thelwell, *Ready for Revolution*, 523.

39. W. E. B. Du Bois, *Black Reconstruction* (New York: Free Press, 1998), 3.

40. Stokely Carmichael, *Stokely Speaks: Black Power to Pan-Africanism* (New York: Random House, 1971), 132.

41. Carmichael, *Stokely Speaks*, 143.

7. THE RELIGION OF BLACK POWER

1. Yvonne Chireau, *Black Magic: Religion and the African American Conjuring Tradition* (Berkeley: University of California Press, 2006), 3–4.

2. Callahan, *The Talking Book*, xi.

3. Callahan, *The Talking Book*, 12.

4. Theophus Smith, *Conjuring Culture: Biblical Formations of Black America* (New York: Oxford University Press, 2006), 18.
5. Lewis R. Gordon, et al., "Afro Pessimism," *Contemporary Political Theory* 17, no. 1 (2018): 106.
6. Gordon, "Afro Pessimism," 106–7.
7. Frank B. Wilderson III. *Afropessimism* (New York: Liveright, 2020), 42.
8. Lewis R. Gordon, *Bad Faith and Antiblack Racism* (Atlantic Highlands, NJ: Humanities, 1995), 143.
9. Anthony Pinn, *The End of God-Talk: An African American Humanist Theology* (New York: Oxford University Press, 2012), 10.
10. Albert J. Raboteau, *Slave Religion: The "Invisible Institution" in the Antebellum South* (New York: Oxford University Press, 1980), 42.
11. Raboteau, *Slave Religion*, 288.
12. Raboteau, *Slave Religion*, 318.
13. Chireau, *Black Magic*, 151.
14. Dianne M. Stewart Diakité and Tracey Hucks, "Africana Religious Studies: Toward a Transdisciplinary Agenda in an Emerging Field," *Journal of Africana Religions* 1, no.1 (2013): 38.
15. Stephanie Smallwood, *Saltwater Slavery: A Middle Passage from Africa to American Diaspora* (Cambridge, MA: Harvard University Press), 6.
16. James Cone, *Black Theology and Black Power* (New York: Seabury, 1969), 2.
17. Cone, *Black Theology and Black Power*, 1.
18. Cone, *Black Theology and Black Power*, 39.
19. Cone, *Black Theology and Black Power*, 39.
20. Cone, *Black Theology and Black Power*, 39.
21. Cone, *Black Theology and Black Power*, 43.
22. Cone, *Black Theology and Black Power*, 44.
23. Cone, *Black Theology and Black Power*, 46.
24. Cone, *Black Theology and Black Power*, 27.
25. Cone, *Black Theology and Black Power*, 43.
26. In my book, *Tragic Soul-Life: W. E. B. Du Bois and the Moral Crisis Facing Democracy* (New York: Oxford University Press, 2012).
27. Howard Thurman, *Deep River and the Negro Spiritual Speaks of Life and Death* (Richmond, IN: Friends United, 1975), 18.
28. Thurman, *Deep River and the Negro Spiritual*, 40.
29. Thurman, *Deep River and the Negro Spiritual*, 22.
30. Thurman, *Deep River and the Negro Spiritual*, 42–43.

31. J. Kameron Carter, *Race: A Theological Account* (New York: Oxford University Press, 2008), 158.

32. Toni Morrison, "Rootedness: The Ancestor as Foundation" In *What Moves at the Margin: Selected Nonfiction* (Jackson: University Press of Mississippi, 2008), 56.

33. Morrison, "Rootedness: The Ancestor as Foundation," 56–57.

34. See Frederick Harris's *Something Within: Religion in African-American Political Activism* (New York: Oxford University Press, 1999).

35. Cone, *Black Theology and Black Power*, 18.

36. Benston, *Performing Blackness*, 31.

37. Fanon, *Black Skin, White Masks*, 139.

38. Fanon, *Black Skin, White Masks*, 140.

39. Fanon, *The Damned of the Earth*, 314.

40. Fanon, *The Damned of the Earth*, 315.

41. Lewis Gordon, "Through the Hellish Zone of Nonbeing: Thinking through Fanon, Disaster, and the Damned of the Earth." *Human Architecture* 5 (2007), 11.

42. As Cannon notes, Alice Walker coined the term Womanism in her 1983 collection of essays and poems, *In Search of Our Mothers' Garden: Womanist Prose.* Womanist derives from Walker's notion of "womanish," a characterization of a young girl behaving like a "grown-up." The term also denotes "a woman who loves other women, sexually and/or nonsexually." See *Katie's Canon: Womanism and the Soul of the Black Community* (New York: Continuum, 1995), 23.

43. Cannon, *Katie's Canon*, 24.

44. Cannon, *Katie's Canon*, 59.

45. Cannon, *Katie's Canon*, 76.

46. Cannon, *Katie's Canon*, 92.

47. In conversations with Dianne Stewart, she introduced me to a category she calls Black protest religions. Stewart's characterization of African American religions that opposed mainline integrationist ideologies, sets the stage for understanding the political shifts within Black radical political traditions. Black protest religions, such as the Nation of Islam and the Moorish Science Temple, Stewart argues, shift away from inchoate stark racial categories and racialized identities by turning to ethnicity and ethnocentric ideologies for imagining Black cultural

identity. The latter point regarding ethnicity and ethnocentric ideologies is more fully developed by Sylvester Johnson in "The Rise of Black Ethnics: The Ethnic Turn in African American Religions, 1916–1945" in *Religion and American Culture: A Journal of Interpretation* (2010).

48. Cannon, *Katie's Canon*, 74. Here, Cannon turns to Toni Morrison's *Beloved* to explore the "memories of the body" and these conceptions inform freedom and liberation within Black women's literature.

49. Ella Myers, *Worldly Ethics: Democratic Politics and Care for the World* (Durham, NC: Duke University Press, 2013), 23.

50. Sacred subjectivity is critical to understanding African American religions insofar as it serves as a resource for understanding multiple languages and epistemic resources that frame Black religions. Put more succinctly, it shows that Blacks use sacred subjectivity and are multidoctrinal when it comes to religion. Indeed, individual and group reliance on Christianity did not foreclose the retrieval of non-Christian resources to adjudicate political and social concerns.

51. Long, *Significations*, 139.

52. Long, *Significations*, 139.

CONCLUSION

1. Toni Cade Bambara, "Preface," *The Black Woman: An Anthology*, 7.

2. Sterling Stuckey, "Through the Prism of Folklore: The Black Ethos in Slavery," *Massachusetts Review* 9 (Summer 1968): 418. Stuckey characterizes folklore as a set of "songs and tales" that incorporate "Africanisms and New World elements."

3. Sterling Stuckey, "Through the Prism of Folklore," 418.

4. Stuckey, "Through the Prism of Folklore," 435–36.

5. Stuckey, "Through the Prism of Folklore," 436.

6. Stuckey, "Through the Prism of Folklore," 437.

7. Alicia Garza is Jewish. https://www.newyorker.com/magazine/2016/03/14/where-is-black-lives-matter-headed, accessed June 6, 2020.

8. Patrisse Marie Cullors is a practitioner of Ifà religious tradition from Nigeria and incorporates Buddhist meditation into her spiritual exercises and political strategies. Please see Hebah H. Farrag, "The Role of the Spirit in #BlackLivesMatter Movement," *Religious Dispatches*, June 24, 2015.

https://religiondispatches.org/the-role-of-spirit-in-the-blacklivesmatter
-movement-a-conversation-with-activist-and-artist-patrisse-cullors/
accessed June 4, 2020.

9. Jonathan Bastian, "The Role of Spirituality and Prayer in the Black Lives Matter Movement," *KCRW*, July 25, 2020. https://www.kcrw.com /culture/shows/life-examined/religion-slavery-black-lives-matter/black -lives-matter-blm-melina-abdullah-hebab-ferrag-interview

10. Jonathan Bastian, "The Role of Spirituality and Prayer in the Black Lives Matter Movement."

11. Daniel Taylor, "Morning Start: #BlackLivesMatter Started with a Love Letter." *Vernon Morning Star News* (June 2, 2020). https://www .vernonmorningstar.com/trending-now/morning-start-blacklivesmatter -started-with-a-love-letter/

12. In Christopher Lebron's *The Making of Black Lives Matter: A Brief History of an Idea* (New York: Oxford University Press, 2017), he poignantly makes the case for understanding BLM as fundamentally engaged in the battle to achieve respect and human dignity for all African Americans.

13. Daniel Kreps, "Killer Mike Delivers Emotional Speech to Atlanta Protestors at Mayor's Press Conference," *Rolling Stone* (May 30, 2020). https:// www.rollingstone.com/music/music-news/killer-mike-speech-atlanta -protestors-press-conference-1007816/, accessed June 4, 2020.

14. Alicia Garza, Twitter, June 3, 2020. https://twitter.com/sanasaleem/status /1268561495077482496, accessed June, 4, 2020.

15. Farrag, "The Role of Spirit in the #BlackLivesMatter Movement."

16. Farrag, "The Role of Spirit in the #BlackLivesMatter Movement."

17. Juliet Hooker, "Black Lives Matter and the Paradoxes of U.S. Black Politics: From Democratic Sacrifices to Democratic Repair," *Political Theory* 44 (August 2016), 450–51.

18. Michael Hanchard, "Contours of Black Political Thought: An Introduction and Perspective," *Political Theory* 38, no. 4 (August 2014): 512.

19. Audre Lorde, *Sister Outsider* (Freedom, CA: The Crossing Press, 1984), 42.

20. Centers for Disease Control and Prevention, "African American Health: Creating Equal Opportunities for Health," https://www.cdc.gov/media /dpk/healthy-living/african-american-health/index.html., accessed January 28, 2020.

BIBLIOGRAPHY

Adler, Jeffrey S., and David R. Colburn. *African-American Mayors: Race, Politics, and the American City.* Urbana: University of Illinois Press, 2001.

Allen, Danielle S. *Talking to Strangers: Anxieties of Citizenship Since Brown v. Board of Education* Chicago: University of Chicago Press, 2009.

Allen, Robert. *Black Awakening in Capitalist America.* New York: Doubleday, 1969.

Alwes, Derek. "The Burden of Liberty: Choice in Toni Morrison's *Jazz* and Toni Cade Bambara's *The Salt Eaters.*" *African American Review* 30 (Autumn 1996): 354.

Ambar, Saladin. *Malcolm X at Oxford Union: Racial Politics in a Global Era.* New York: Oxford University Press, 2014.

Bambara, Toni Cade. *The Black Woman: An Anthology.* New York: Washington Square, 2005.

——. *Deep Sightings and Rescue Missions: Fiction, Essays, and Conversations.* Ed. Toni Morrison. New York: Pantheon, 1996.

——. "On the Issue of Roles." In *The Black Woman: An Anthology*, 101. New York: New American Library, 1970.

——. *The Salt Eaters.* New York: Vintage, 1992.

Bastian, Jonathan. "The Role of Spirituality and Prayer in the Black Lives Matter Movement." *KCRW*, July 25, 2020. https://www.kcrw.com/culture/shows/life-examined/religion-slavery-black-lives-matter/black-lives-matter-blm-melina-abdullah-hebab-ferrag-interview

Benhabib, Seyla. *Democracy and Difference: Contesting the Boundaries of the Political.* Princeton, NJ: Princeton University Press, 1996.

Benston, Kimberly W. *Performing Blackness: Enactments of African-American Modernism.* New York: Routledge, 2000.

Bible, New Revised Standard Version. Bible Gateway, https://www.biblegateway .com/passage/?search=Matthew+5%3A13-16&version=NRSV. Matthew 5:13–16.

Bogues, Anthony. *Empire of Liberty: Power, Desire, and Freedom.* Hanover, NH: Dartmouth College Press, 2010.

Bond, Julien. "SNCC: What We Did." *Monthly Review* 17, no. 52 (October 2000): 5.

Boston Friends of the Student Nonviolent Coordinating Committee, March 3, 1967, newsletter.

Boyarin, Daniel. *Intertextuality and the Reading of Midrash.* Bloomington: Indiana University Press, 1990.

Boyd, Valerie. "'She Was Just Outrageously Brilliant': Toni Morrison Remembers Toni Cade Bambara." In *Savoring the Salt: The Legacy of Toni Cade Bambara*, ed. Linda Janet Holmes and Cheryl A. Wall, 91. Philadelphia: Temple University Press, 2008.

Brackman, Harold. "Zionism in Black and White: Part I: 1898–1948 (Report)." *Midstream.* January 1, 2010.

Buber, Martin. *On Zion: The History of an Idea.* New York: Schocken, 1973.

Bush, Rod. *We Are Not What We Seem: Black Nationalism and Class Struggle in the American Century.* New York: New York University Press, 1999.

Byrd, Rudolph P. "Create Your Own Fire: Audre Lorde and the Tradition of Black Radical Thought." In *I Am Your Sister: Collected and Unpublished Writings of Audre Lorde*, ed. Rudolph P. Byrd, Johnnetta Betsch Cole, and Beverly Guy-Sheftall, 22. New York: Oxford University Press, 2009.

Callahan, Allen. *The Talking Book: African Americans and the Bible.* New Haven, CT: Yale University Press, 2008.

Cannon, Katie. *Katie's Canon: Womanism and the Soul of the Black Community.* New York: Continuum, 1995.

Carby, Hazel. *Race Men: The W. E. B. Du Bois Lectures.* Cambridge, MA: Harvard University Press, 1998.

Carmichael, Stokely. "Black Power." *The Will of a People: A Critical Anthology of Great African American Speeches*, ed. Richard W. Leeman and Bernard K. Duffy, 310. Carbondale and Edwardsville: Southern Illinois University Press, 2012

——. *Stokely Speaks: Black Power to Pan-Africanism.* New York: Random House, 1971.

——. "Toward Black Liberation." *The Massachusetts Review* (Autumn 1966).

—— and Charles V. Hamilton, *Black Power: The Politics of Liberation.* New York: Vintage, 1992.

—— and Michael Thelwell. *Ready for Revolution: The Life and Struggle of Stokely Carmichael (Kwame Ture).* New York: Scribner, 2003.

Carr, Gregory S. "Theatricality, Themes, and Theology in James Weldon Johnson's *God's Trombones," Theatre Symposium* (2013): 54.

Carson, Clayborne. "Black-Jewish Universalism in the Era of Identity Politics." In *Struggles in the Promised Land: Towards A History of Black-Jewish Relations in the United States.* New York: Oxford University Press, 1997.

——. *In Struggle: SNCC and the Black Awakening of the 1960s.* Cambridge, MA: Harvard University Press, 1995.

Carter, J. Kameron. *Race: A Theological Account.* Oxford: Oxford University Press, 2008.

Chireau, Yvonne. *Black Magic: Religion and the African American Conjuring Tradition.* Berkeley: University of California Press, 2003.

Coates, Ta-Nehisi. "The Case for Reparations." *Atlantic,* June 2014. https://www.theatlantic.com/magazine/archive/2014/06/the-case-for-reparations/361631

Cohen, Cathy J. *Democracy Remixed.* Oxford: Oxford University Press, 2010.

Colbert, Soyica Diggs, Robert J. Patterson, and Aida Levy-Hussen. *The Psychic Hold of Slavery : Legacies in American Expressive Culture.* New Brunswick, NJ: Rutgers University Press, 2016.

Collins, Patricia Hill. "Learning to Think for Ourselves: Malcolm X's Black Nationalism Reconsidered," in *Malcolm in Our Own Image,* ed. Joe Wood, 74. New York: St. Martin's, 1992.

Cone, James. *Black Theology and Black Power.* New York: Seabury, 1969.

Congress of Racial Equality. Mississippi 4th Congressional District records, Historical Society Library, Micro 793, Reel 3; Segment 4. https://content.wisconsinhistory.org/digital/collection/p15932coll2/id/42319

Crawley, Ashon T. *Blackpentecostal Breath: The Aesthetics of Possibility.* New York: Fordham University Press, 2017.

Curtis, Edward E., IV. "Why Malcolm X Never Developed an Islamic Approach to Civil Rights," *Religion* 32 (2002): 229.

Dawson, Michael C. *Black Visions: The Roots of Contemporary African-American Political Ideologies*. Chicago: University of Chicago Press, 2001.

Delmont, Matthew. *Why Busing Failed: Race, Media, and the National Resistance to School Desegregation*. Oakland: University of California Press, 2016.

Diakité, Dianne M. Stewart, and Tracey E. Hucks. "Africana Religious Studies: Toward a Transdisciplinary Agenda in an Emerging Field." *Journal of Africana Religions* 1, no. 1 (2013): 38.

Dollinger, Marc. *Black Power, Jewish Politics: Reinventing the Alliance of the 1960s*. Waltham, MA: Brandeis University Press, 2018.

Douglass, Frederick Douglass. "The Constitution of the United States: Is It Pro-Slavery or Anti-Slavery?" (1860) https://www.blackpast.org /global-african-history/1860-frederick-douglass-constitution-united -states-it-pro-slavery-or-anti-slavery/.

Du Bois, W. E. B. *Black Reconstruction*. New York: Free Press, 1998.

——. *The Souls of Black Folk*. New York: Oxford University Press, 2009.

Dyson, Michael Eric. *I May Not Get There with You: The True Martin Luther King Jr*. New York: Simon & Schuster, 2000.

Fanon, Frantz. *Black Skin, White Masks*. New York: Grove Weidenfeld, 1991.

——. *The Wretched of the Earth*. New York: Grove Weidenfeld, 1992.

Farmer, Ashley. *Remaking Black Power: How Black Women Transformed an Era*. Chapel Hill: University of North Carolina Press, 2017.

Farrag, Hebah H. "The Role of the Spirit in #BlackLivesMatter Movement." *Religious Dispatches*, June 24, 2015. https://religiondispatches.org/the-role -of-spirit-in-the-blacklivesmatter-movement-a-conversation-with -activist-and-artist-patrisse-cullors/

Feldman, Keith P. "Representing Permanent War: Black Power's Palestine and the End(s) of Civil Rights." *The New Centennial Review* 8.2 (2008): 193–231.

——. *A Shadow Over Palestine : The Imperial Life of Race in America*. Minneapolis: University of Minnesota Press, 2016.

Felber, Garrett A. "The Nation of Islam and the Politics of Black Nationalism, 1930–1975." Garrett A. Felber, PhD dissertation, 2017.

Foucault, Michel, Paul Rabinow, and Robert J Hurley. *Ethics: Subjectivity and Truth*. New York: New Press, 1997.

Franklin, Robert Michael. "In Pursuit of a Just Society: Martin Luther King, Jr., and John Rawls," *Journal of Religious Ethics* 18, no. 2 (1990): 59.

Frye, Charles A. Frye, Charlyn Harper, Linda James Myers, and Eleanor W. Traylor. "How to Think Black: A Symposium in Toni Cade Bambara's *The Salt Eaters. Journal of African and Afro-American Studies* 6 (September 8, 2008).

Frug, Gerald. "The Legal Technology of Exclusion in Metropolitan America." In *The New Suburban History*, ed. M. Kruse and Thomas J. Sugrue, 205–19. Chicago: University of Chicago Press, 2006.

Gaines, Kevin. "Malcolm X in Global Perspective." In *The Cambridge Companion to Malcolm X*, ed. Robert E. Terrill, 167. New York: Cambridge University Press, 2010.

Garza, Alicia. Twitter, June 3, 2020. https://twitter.com/sanasaleem/status /1268561495077482496

Gates, Henry Louis Gates, Jr. *The Signifying Monkey: A Theory of African-American Literary Criticism*. New York: Oxford University Press, 1988.

Geller, Lawrence Israel is Defended by Negro Groups after SNCC Attack. *Philadelphia Tribune*. August 19, 1967, 1.

Gilkes, Cheryl. *If It Wasn't for the Women: Black Women's Experience and Womanist Culture in Church and Community*. Maryknoll, NY: Orbis, 2001.

Glaude, Eddie S. *Exodus!: Religion, Race, and Nation in Early Nineteenth-Century Black America*. Chicago: University of Chicago Press, 2000.

——. *Is It Nation Time?: Contemporary Essays on Black Power and Black Nationalism*. Chicago: University of Chicago Press, 2002.

Gordon, Colin. *Mapping Decline: St. Louis and the Fate of the American City*. Philadelphia: University of Pennsylvania Press, 2008.

Gordon, Lewis R. *Bad Faith and Antiblack Racism*. Atlantic Highlands, NJ: Humanities, 1995.

——. "Du Bois's Humanistic Philosophy of Human Sciences." *Annals of the American Academy of Political and Social Science* 568 (2000): 265–80.

——. *Existentia Africana: Understanding Africana Existential Thought*. New York: Routledge, 2000.

——. *Fanon and the Crisis of European Man: An Essay on Philosophy and the Human Sciences*. New York: Routledge, 1995.

——. *An Introduction to Africana Philosophy*. Cambridge: Cambridge University Press, 2008.

——. "Rarely Kosher: Studying Jews of Color in North America." *American Jewish History* 100, no. 1 (2016): 105–16.

——. "Through the Hellish Zone of Nonbeing: Thinking through Fanon, Disaster, and the Damned of the Earth." *Human Architecture* 5 (2007): 5-11.

——. *What Fanon Said: A Philosophical Introduction to His Life and Thought.* New York: Fordham University Press, 2015.

—— and LaRose T. Perry. "Frantz Fanon's Psychology of Black Consciousness." In *Global Psychologies*, ed. S. Fernando and R. Moodley, 225. London: Palgrave Macmillan, 2018.

—— et al. "Afro Pessimism." *Contemporary Political Theory* 17, no. 1 (2018): 105-37.

Guy-Sheftall, Beverly. "African-American Studies: Legacies & Challenges: 'What Would Black Studies Be If We'd Listened to Toni Cade?'" *Black Scholar* 35, no. 2 (Summer 2005): 23.

——. "Black Feminist Studies: The Case for Anna Julia Cooper." *African American Review* 43, no. 1 (Spring 2009): 11-15.

Hanchard, Michael. "Contours of Black Political Thought: An Introduction and Perspective." *Political Theory* 38, no. 4 (August 2014): 512.

Harding, Vincent. *Martin Luther King: The Inconvenient Hero* Maryknoll, NY: Orbis, 1996.

Harris, Frederick C. *The Price of the Ticket: Barack Obama and the Rise and Decline of Black Politics.* New York: Oxford University Press, 2014.

——. *Something Within: Religion in African-American Political Activism.* New York: Oxford University Press, 1999.

Harris, Trudier. "Christianity's Last Stand: Visions of Spirituality in Post-1970 African American Women's Literature." *Religions* 11, no. 7 (July 2020): 369.

Hart, William David. *Edward Said and the Religious Effects of Culture.* Cambridge: Cambridge University Press, 2000.

Hartman, Saidiya. *Scenes of Subjection: Terror, Slavery, and Self-Making in Nineteenth-Century America.* New York: Oxford University Press, 1997.

Hebah H. Farrag. "The Role of the Spirit in #BlackLivesMatter Movement." *Religious Dispatches*, June 24, 2015. https://religiondispatches.org/the-role-of-spirit-in-the-blacklivesmatter-movement-a-conversation-with-activist-and-artist-patrisse-cullors/

Heschel, Susannah. "'A Different Kind of Theo-Politics: Abraham Joshua Heschel, the Prophets and the Civil Rights Movement." *Journal of Political Theology* 21 (2020): 35.

Heyes, Cressida J. *Self-Transformations: Foucault, Ethics, and Normalized Bodies.* New York: Oxford University Press, 2007.

Higashida, Cheryl. *Black Internationalist Feminism: Women Writers of the Black Left, 1945–1995*. Urbana: University of Illinois Press, 2011.

Higginbotham, Evelyn Brooks. *Righteous Discontent: The Women's Movement in the Black Baptist Church, 1880–1920*. Cambridge, MA: Harvard University Press, 1993.

Hilltop, The. Washington, DC: Howard University, 1972.

Hooker, Juliet. "Black Lives Matter and the Paradoxes of U.S. Black Politics: From Democratic Sacrifices to Democratic Repair." *Political Theory* 44 (August 2016): 450–51.

House, Gloria. "The Road to Internationalism: A SNCC Movement Worker Reflects." *Against the Current* 27.6 (2013).

Jackson, Thomas F. *From Civil Rights to Human Rights: Martin Luther King, Jr., and the Struggle for Economic Justice*. Philadelphia: University of Pennsylvania Press, 2009.

James, Joy. "Ella Baker, 'Black Women's Work' and Activist Intellectuals," *The Black Scholar*, 24.4 (1994): 8–15.

Johnson, Andre. "God Is a Negro: The (Rhetorical) Black Theology of Bishop McNeal Turner." *Black Theology: An International Journal* 13 (2015): 29–40.

Johnson, James Weldon. *God's Trombones: Seven Negro Sermons in Verse*. New York: Viking, 1930. https://docsouth.unc.edu/southlit/johnson/johnson.html

Johnson, Terrence L. "Religious Heretic, Political Prophet: Malcolm X, Democracy, and Abolition Ethics." *Journal of Africana Religions* 3, no. 1 (2015): 62–82.

——. *Tragic Soul-Life: W. E. B. Du Bois and the Moral Crisis Facing American Democracy*. New York: Oxford University Press, 2012.

Johnson, Sylvester A. "The Rise of Black Ethnics: The Ethnic Turn in African American Religions, 1916–1945." *Religion and American Culture* 20.2 (2010): 125–163.

Joseph, Peniel E. "The Black Power Movement: A State of the Field." *Journal of American History* 96, no. 3 (December 2009): 772.

——. *The Black Power Movement: Rethinking the Civil Rights-Black Power Era*. London: Routledge, 2006.

——. "Black Power Studies: A New Scholarship," *The Black Scholar*. 31, nos. 3–4, (2001): 2.

——. "The New Black Power History: A *Souls* Special Issue." *Souls* 9.4 (2007): 278.

——.*Waiting 'Til the Midnight Hour : A Narrative History of Black Power in America.* New York: Holt, 2006.

Kelley, Robin D. G. *Hammer and Hoe: Alabama Communists During the Great Depression.* Chapel Hill: University of North Carolina Press, 1990.

King, Martin Luther, Jr. "Beyond Vietnam" speech, April 4, 1967. https:// kinginstitute.stanford.edu/king-papers/documents/beyond-vietnam.

——. *Where Do We Go from Here: Chaos or Community?* Boston, MA: Beacon, 2010.

——. "The Birth of a New Age" speech, August 11, 1956, Buffalo, New York. https://kinginstitute.stanford.edu/king-papers/documents/birth-new -age-address-delivered-11-august-1956-fiftieth-anniversary-alpha-phi

——. "Birth of a New Nation" speech, April 7, 1957.

——. "Martin Luther King Defines Black Power." *New York Times Magazine.* June, 11, 1967.

——. "Sermon on Gandhi" speech, March 22, 1959. "The King Philosophy," at The King Center. https://thekingcenter.org/king-philosophy/, accessed September 6, 2020.

——. *Testament of Hope: Essential Writings and Speeches of Martin Luther King, Jr.* New York: HarperCollins, 1991, 233.

Kreps, Daniel. "Killer Mike Delivers Emotional Speech to Atlanta Protestors at Mayor's Press Conference," *RollingStone* (May 30, 2020). https:// www.rollingstone.com/music/music-news/killer-mike-speech-atlanta -protestors-press-conference-1007816.

Lebron, Christopher. *The Making of Black Lives Matter: A Brief History of an Idea.* New York: Oxford University Press, 2017.

Lee, Hak Joon. "Toward the Great World House: Hans Küng and Martin Luther King, Jr. on Global Ethics." *Journal of the Society of Christian Ethics* 29, no. 2 (2009): 97–98.

Long, Charles. *Significations: Signs, Symbols, and Images in the Interpretation of Religion.* Philadelphia, PA: Fortress, 1986.

Lorde, Audre. *Sister Outsider: Essays and Speeches.* Trumansburg, NY: Crossing. 1984.

——. *I Am Your Sister: Collected and Uncollected Writings of Audre Lorde.* Ed. Rudolph P. Byrd, Johnnetta Betsch Cole, and Beverly Guy-Sheftall, 40. New York: Oxford University Press, 2009.Lucile Montgomery Papers, 1963–1967, *Wisconsin Historical Society*, "Freedom Summer Digital Collection."

https://content.wisconsinhistory.org/digital/collection/p15932coll2/id/35466

Luxon, Nany. "Ethics and Subjectivity: Practices of Self-Governance in the Late Lectures of Michel Foucault." *Political Theory* 36 (June 1, 2008): 377–402.

Marable, Manning. *Race, Reform, and Rebellion: The Second Reconstruction and Beyond in Black America, 1945–2006.* Jackson: University Press of Mississippi, 2007.

MacIntyre, Alasdair. *After Virtue: A Study in Moral Theory.* Notre Dame, IN: University of Notre Dame Press, 1984.

Maldonaldo-Torres, Nelson. "On the Coloniality of Being: Contributions to the Development of a Concept." *Cultural Studies* (London, England) 21.2–3 (2007): 240–70.

McCormack, Donald J. "Stokely Carmichael and Pan-Africanism: Back to Black Power." *Journal of Politics* 35 (May 1973): 389.

Myers, Ella. *Worldly Ethics: Democratic Politics and Care for the World.* Durham, NC: Duke University Press, 2013.

Minor, Ethel. "Editorial." *Aframerican: News for You* II (November 12, 1966): A-1.

——. "Black Voices: What Is Stokely Doing?" *Afro-American* (1893–1988). October 4, 1969, 5.

——. "An African American Tells Why She Followed Malcolm X," in *Oh Freedom! Kids Talk about the Civil Rights Movement with the People Who Made It Happen*, ed., Casey King and Linda Barrett Osborne, 94–96. New York: Random House, 1997.

McDuffie, Erik S. and Komozi Woodard. "'If You're in a Country That's Progressive, the Woman Is Progressive': Black Women Radicals and the Making of the Politics and Legacy of Malcolm X." *Biography* 36, no. 3 (2013): 513.

Meier, August. *Negro Thought in America, 1880–1915: Racial Ideologies in the Age of Booker T. Washington.* Ann Arbor: University of Michigan Press, 1988.

Mills, Charles Mills. *Blackness Visible: Essays on Philosophy and Race.* Ithaca, NY: Cornell University Press, 1998.

——. "Dark Ontologies: Blacks, Jews, and White Supremacy." In *Blackness Visible: Essays on Philosophy and Race*, 70. Ithaca, NY: Cornell University Press, 1998.

Moore, Leonard N. *Carl B. Stokes and the Rise of Black Political Power*. Urbana: University of Illinois Press, 2002.

Morrison, Toni. "A Slow Walk of Trees." In *What Moves at the Margin: Selected Nonfiction*, ed. Carolyn C. Denard, 8. Jackson: University of Mississippi Press, 2008.

Morrison, Toni. *Mouth Full of Blood: Essays, Speeches, Meditations*. New York: Random House, 2019.

——. "Rootedness: The Ancestor as Foundation" In *What Moves at the Margin: Selected Nonfiction*. Jackson: University Press of Mississippi, 2008.

Moses, Wilson Jeremiah. *Black Messiahs and Uncle Toms : Social and Literary Manipulations of a Religious Myth*. University Park: Pennsylvania State University Press, 1993.

Obama, Barack. "Let Freedom Ring" August 8, 2013. https://obamawhitehouse .archives.gov/the-press-office/2013/08/28/remarks-president-let-freedom -ring-ceremony-commemorating-50th-anniversa

O'Leary, Timothy. *Foucault and the Art of Ethics*. New York: Continuum, 2006.

Olson, Lester C. "The Personal, the Political, and Others: Audre Lorde Denouncing 'The Second Sex Conference.' " *Philosophy & Rhetoric* 33.3 (2000): 268.

Outlaw, Lucius. *On Race and Philosophy*. New York: Routledge, 1996.

Patterson, Orlando. *Slavery and Social Death: A Comparative Study*. Cambridge, MA: Harvard University Press, 1982.

Peterson, Belinda Waller. " 'Are You Sure, Sweetheart, That You Want to Be Well?': The Politics of Mental Health and Long-Suffering in Toni Cade Bambara's *The Salt Eaters*. *Religions* 10, no. 4 (2019): 1.

Pinn, Anthony B. *The End of God-Talk: An African American Humanist Theology*. New York: Oxford University Press, 2012.

—— "The End: Thoughts on Humanism and Death." *Dialog: A Journal of Theology* 54, no. 4 (2015): 347–354.

——. *Varieties of African American Religious Experience: Toward a Comparative Black Theology*. Twentieth anniversary edition. Minneapolis: Fortress, 2017.

Plummer, Brenda Gayle. "African Americans in the International Imaginary: Gerald Horne's Progressive Vision." *Journal of African American History* 96, no. 2 (2011): 222.

Raboteau, Albert J.. *Slave Religion: The "Invisible Institution" in the Antebellum South*. New York: Oxford University Press, 1980.

Ransby, Barbara. *Ella Baker and the Black Freedom Movement: A Radical Democratic Vision*. Chapel Hill: University of North Carolina Press, 2003.

—— and Tracye Matthews. "Black Popular Culture and the Transcendence of Patriarchal Illusions." In *Words of Fire: An Anthology of African-American Feminist Thought*, ed. Beverly Guy-Sheftall, 529. New York: New Press, 1995.

Rawls, John. *A Theory of Justice*. Cambridge, MA: Belknap, 1971.

——. *Political Liberalism*. New York: Columbia University Press, 2005.

Reed, Adolph. "Tokens of the White Left (Class Notes) (Column)." *The Progressive* 57.12 (1993).

Rickford, Russell. " 'To Build a New World': Black American Internationalism and Palestine Solidarity." *Journal of Palestine Studies* 48 (2019): 54.

Roberts, Gene. "Mississippi Reduces Police Protection for Marchers." *New York Times*. June 17, 1966, 33.

——. "Black Power Idea Long in Planning: S.N.C.C. Dissidents Wrote Document Last Winter." *New York Times*, August 5, 1966, 1.

Roberts, Neil. *Freedom as Marronage*. Chicago: University of Chicago Press, 2015.

Robinson, Cedric. *Black Marxism: The Making of the Black Radical Tradition*. Chapel Hill: University of North Carolina Press, 2000.

Robinson, Dean E. *Black Nationalism in American Politics and Thought*. New York: Cambridge University Press, 2001.

Rustin, Bayard. "From Protest to Politics: The Future of the Civil Rights Movement." *1964*. In *Time on Two Crosses: The Collected Writings of Bayard Rustin*, ed. Devon Carbado and Don Weise, 116–129. San Francisco: Cleis, 2004.

Sales, William W. Jr. *From Civil Rights to Black Liberation: Malcolm X and the Organization of Afro-American Unity*. Boston: South End, 1994.

Schirack, Maureen and Lauren Curtright. "Toni Cade Bambara." *Voices from the Gaps* 2 (2004). https://conservancy.umn.edu/handle/11299/167858.

Sexton, Jared Afro-Pessimism: The Unclear World, *Rhizomes: Cultural Studies in Emerging Knowledge* 29 (2016).

Shelby, Tommie. *We Who Are Dark: The Philosophical Foundations of Black Solidarity*. Cambridge, MA: Harvard University Press, 2009.

Singh, Nikhil. *Black Is a Country: Race and the Unfinished Struggle for Democracy*. Cambridge, MA: Harvard University Press, 2005.

Smallwood, Stephanie. *Saltwater Slavery: A Middle Passage from Africa to American Diaspora*. Cambridge, MA: Harvard University Press, 2007.

Smith, Abraham. "I Saw the Book Talk: A Cultural Studies Approach to the Ethics of African American Biblical Hermeneutics." *Semeia* 77 (1997): 118.

Smith, Theophus. *Conjuring Culture: Biblical Formations of Black America*. New York: Oxford University Press, 2006.

Span, Paula. "The Undying Revolutionary: As Stokely Carmichael, He Fought for Black Power. Now Kwame Ture's Fighting for His Life." *Washington Post* (April 8, 1998), 1.

Spivak, Gayatri C. "Can the Subaltern Speak?" In *Marxism and the Interpretation of Culture*, ed. Cary Nelson and Lawrence Grossberg. Urbana: University of Illinois Press, 1988.

Springs, Jason. "'Dismantling the Master's House': Freedom as Ethical Practice in Brandom and Foucault." *Journal of Religious Ethics* 37, no. 3 (September 2009).

Stephens, Michelle Ann. *Black Empire: The Masculine Global Imaginary of Caribbean Intellectuals in the United States, 1914–1962*. Durham, NC: Duke University Press, 2005.

Stewart, Maria. " 'Religion and the Pure Principles of Morality: The Sure Foundation on Which We Must Build' (1831)." Oxford University Press, n.d. https://doi.org/10.1093/acref/9780195301731.013.33531.

Stuckey, Sterling. "Through the Prism of Folklore: The Black Ethos in Slavery." *Massachusetts Review* 9 (Summer 1968): 418.

——. *The Ideological Origins of Black Nationalism* Boston: Beacon, 1972.

Taylor, Daniel. "Morning Start: #BlackLivesMatter Started with a Love Letter." *Vernon Morning Star News* (June 2, 2020). https://www.vernonmorningstar.com/trending-now/morning-start-blacklivesmatter-started-with-a-love-letter/

Taylor, Keeanga-Yamahtta. *From #BlackLivesMatter to Black Liberation*. Chicago, Illinois: Haymarket, 2017.

Tippet, Krista. https://onbeing.org/programs/ruby-sales-where-does-it-hurt/

Thompson, J. Phillip. *Double Trouble: Black Mayors, Black Communities, and the Call for a Deep Democracy*. New York: Oxford University Press, 2006.

Thorsson, Courtney. *Women's Work: Nationalism and Contemporary African American Women's Novels*. Charlottesville: University of Virginia Press, 2013.

Threadcraft, Shatema. *Intimate Justice: The Black Female Body and the Body Politic*. New York: Oxford University Press, 2016.

Thurman, Howard. *Deep River and the Negro Spiritual Speaks of Life and Death*. Richmond, IN: Friends United, 1975.

Tressler, Donna. "Cory United Methodist Church." *Cleveland Historical Society*, http://clevelandhistorical.org/items/show/643

Tutashinda, K. "The Grassroots Political Philosophy of Ella Baker: Oakland, California Applicability," *The Journal of Pan African Studies* 3, no. 9 (2010): 25–42.

Van Deburg, William L. *New Day in Babylon : the Black Power Movement and American Culture, 1965–1975*. Chicago: University of Chicago Press, 1992.

Walker, Alice. *In Search of Our Mothers' Gardens: Womanist Prose*. New York: Open Road Media, 2011.

Wideman, John Edgar. "The Healing of Velma Henry: Bambara Authors' Queries." *New York Times*. June 1, 1980, 14.

Wilentz, Gay. *Healing Narratives: Women Writers Curing Cultural Dis-ease*. New Brunswick, NJ: Rutgers University Press, 2000.

Wilderson, Frank, III. *Red, White and Black: Cinema and the Structure of U.S. Antagonisms*. Durham, NC: Duke University Press, 2010.

——. *Afropessimism*. New York: Liveright, 2020.

Wilkins, Fanon Che. "The Making of Black Internationalists: SNCC and Africa Before the Launching of Black Power, 1960–1965." *Journal of African American History* 92, no. 4 (Autumn 2007): 469.

Wilmore, Gayraud. *Black Religion and Black Radicalism: An Interpretation of the Religious History of African Americans*. Maryknoll, NY: Orbis, 1988.

Williams, Delores. *Sisters in the Wilderness: The Challenge of Womanist God-Talk*. Maryknoll, NY: Orbis, 1993.

Williams, Rhonda Y. *The Politics of Public Housing: Black Women's Struggles Against Urban Inequality*. New York: Oxford University Press. 2004.

Wimbush, Vincent. "The Bible and African Americans: An Outline of an Interpretive History." In *Stony the Road We Trod: African American Biblical Interpretation*, ed. Cain Hope Felder, 83. Minneapolis: Fortress, 1991.

Woodard, Komozi. *A Nation Within a Nation: Amiri Baraka (Leroi Jones) and Black Power Politics*. Chapel Hill: University of North Carolina Press, 1999.

Wright, Richard. *Black Power: A Record of Reactions in a Land of Pathos*. New York: HarperPerennial, 1996.

——. *Uncle Tom's Children*. New York: HarperPerennial, 2004.

X, Malcolm. *The Autobiography of Malcolm X*. New York: Random House, 1992.

—— "Harlem Freedom Rally," Speech, 1960 http://malcolmxfiles.blogspot
.com/2013/05/harlem-freedom-rally-1960.html. Accessed March 7, 2021.

——. "Message to the Grassroots" (1963). *African American Political Thought,
vol. 2: Confrontation vs. Compromise: 1945 to the Present*, ed. Marcus D.
Pohlmann, 115–130. New York: Routledge, 2003.

——. *The Speeches of Malcolm X at Harvard*, ed. Archie Epps, 128. New York:
Paragon, 1991.

—— and George Breitman. *Malcolm X Speaks: Selected Speeches and Statements*. New York: Grove Weidenfeld, 1990.

Young, Iris Marion. *Inclusion and Democracy*. New York: Oxford University
Press, 2000.

Zack, Naomi. *Philosophy of Science and Race*. New York: Routledge, 2002.

Zamalin, Alex. *African American Political Thought and American Culture: The
Nation's Struggle for Racial Justice*. New York: Palgrave Macmillan, 2015.

——. *Struggle on their Minds: The Political Thought of African American Resistance*. New York: Columbia University Press, 2017.

INDEX

Abdullah, Melina, 237
Absolute Spirit, 223
"Africa for Africans" (Du Bois, W.),
    173
African Americans: becoming
    human beings, 153–54; Bible
    interpretations by, 16–17;
    biblical hermeneutics of, 83–84,
    93; biblical narratives for,
    203–4; Black-Jewish relations
    decline and, 187–88; Christian
    transformative experience of,
    208; as colonized people, 156; as
    democracy victims, 134, 140–41;
    discriminatory laws against,
    82–83, 121; field Negro as, 130,
    138–39; forces defining, 155–56;
    freedom struggle of, 168–69;
    Gospel of Matthew for, 47–48;
    as human beings, 162–63; human
    dignity of, 103, 106–7; humanistic
    nationalism of, 75, 157; humanity
    denied of, 58; human rights
    problem of, 135–36, 139–40;
    M. King strategies against
    hatred of, 77; Malcolm X

on brainwashing of, 140–41;
    Malcolm X's solidarity with, 79,
    123; Negro-Jewish struggle of,
    174, 176; Negro leadership of, 111;
    Negro spirituals of, 108, 215–16,
    236–37; oral traditions of, 229;
    political strategies for, 2; political
    struggles of, 144, 214; power
    problem of, 70–71; preacher,
    49–50; racism against, 166,
    225–26; self-determination of,
    79; social justice for, 81; Speaker's
    Corner for, 45; spiritual pain of,
    5; violence against, 121; war on
    families of, 185; warrior ancestors
    of, 238; white supremacy
    independence for, 216. *See also*
    Black people
"Africana Religious Studies"
    essay, 202
African diaspora, 226
"African Religious Studies" essay
    (Stewart, D., and Hucks), 210
Africans, 32; Christianity and, 206; in
    slavery, 4–5, 88; slavery with culture
    of, 211–12; social death of, 15–16

divine knowledge for, 50; politics,
23–28; power flowing from, 30;
Speaker's Corner for, 45–46
healing sessions: from Bambara, 29;
ecology of self and, 33; ethics
as therapeutic in, 49–51; in folk
culture, 29, 250n27; freedom
from, 43; group existence from,
30–31; ontological Blackness in,
41; political emancipation for, 40;
racial and gendered identities in,
52; recovery from, 51
hermeneutical extension, 209–10
Herzl, Theodor, 148
Heschel, Susannah, 86
Higashida, Cheryl, 14
Higginbotham, Evelyn Brooks,
107–8, 218
Holocaust, 186
homophobia, 23
Hood, Floyd John, 199
Hooker, Juliet, 241
house Negro, 130, 138–39
Hucks, Tracey, 150, 202, 210–11
human agency, 161
human beings, 153–54, 162–63, 265n16
human dignity, 25, 149; of African
Americans, 103, 106–7; Black
Power seeking, 71; through civil
disobedience, 78; humanistic
nationalism and, 150; Negro
problem and, 26; political action
creating, 153; from voting, 8–9,
246n14
human emancipation, 134
human freedom, 114
human fulfillment, 5
humanism, 33, 223; activism, 114,
144–45; in democracy, 260n9;

ethics of, 120–21, 124, 136–40; M.
King appeal of, 105
humanistic nationalism, 153, 156,
264n12; for African Americans,
75, 157; anti-Black racism response
of, 74–75; Black Power and, 143;
from Carmichael, 221; defining,
148–52; human dignity and, 150;
in human rights activism, 142;
Negroes transformed by, 157;
Negro problem addressed by, 149;
principles of, 155; of SNCC, 57, 61,
76; steps in, 154–55
humanity, 8–9, 58, 237
human rights, 76–77, 97; activism,
197–98; African American's
problem of, 135–36, 139–40;
anti-Black racism violation of,
101, 112; Black women's activism
for, 142; colonialism and activism
of, 176; humanistic nationalism
as activism for, 142; of Malcolm
X, 122, 133; racial injustice and,
121; SNCC activism for, 142–43;
U.S. violations of, 121; Western
countries violations of, 166

identity formation, 224
"I Have a Dream" speech
(King, M.), 86
imperialism: American, 137–38, 198;
Black Power criticizing U.S.,
101–2; ethical subjectivity and,
197; power and U.S., 103; racism
linked to American, 98; religion
and, 198
inalienable rights, 64
infirmary, 44–53
infrastructure, city, 2–3

sensibilities performed by, 109; Vietnam War condemnation from, 80–81, 86–87; *Where Do We Go from Here* by, 68

Ladner, Joyce, 75
language-world, 91
Lasch, Christopher, 168
law enforcement, 68–69
legal political equality, 62
legislation, 65, 68–69
"Let Freedom Ring" speech (Obama), 246n14
"Letter from Birmingham Jail" (King, M.), 203
Levine (Rabbi), 188–89
Lewis, John, 253n5
liberal democracy, 52, 114
liberal egalitarianism, 73
liberal feminist politics, 11
liberalism, 56, 193, 241; anti-Black racism and, 76–77, 93–94, 97, 229–30; of civil rights, 59; racialized, 77, 155, 222
liberal political philosophy, 47
liberal white benevolence, 79
liberal white feminism, 7
liberation: Black Christian theologies for, 40–41; Black movements for, 240; Black people's theology of, 221–27; Black Power struggle for, 41; of Black women, 132–33; God's role in, 205–6; group, 110–11; integration barrier to, 128; of Jews, 173; movement, 182; reflective deliberation and, 161–62; struggle for, 234; theology, 212–14, 221, 227–28
liberty, equality and, 5
Little, Earl, 124
Lomax, Louis E., 110

Long, Charles, 33, 47, 233
Lorde, Audre, 1–2, 194, 242, 246n9; anti-Black racism and, 7; anti-Black society and, 5–6; Black political thought and, 10; day-to-day decisions and, 16; fear and silence impediments to, 12; freedom understanding of, 11–12; human fulfillment from, 5; on political activism, 8; racial and gender hierarchy from, 7; social justice points from, 7–8; theory of difference outlined by, 7, 15; Western individuality and, 3–4; white feminists condemnation by, 9–10
"Love Letter to Black People, A" (Garza), 238

magical beliefs, 210
Malcolm X, 1, 54, 74, 93; as activist-intellectual, 110; African Americans brainwashed and, 140–41; African American's solidarity with, 79, 123; anti-Black racism redefined by, 98; approval of, 256n55; assassination of, 175, 216; ballot and bullet speech of, 111–12; "Black Man's History" speech of, 128; Black nationalism used by, 134, 138; civil rights and, 96, 122, 130; democracy with slavery and segregation, 126–27; gender bias of, 125–26; group liberation, 110–11; human emancipation imagined by, 134; humanistic activism of, 114; humanistic ethics of, 120–21; human rights of, 122, 133; jeremiad motif from, 129; M. King in speeches of, 135–36; liberation barrier and, 128;